When Night Nurse was out in front he kept doing the impossible by standing off his fences, putting together the most enormous leap and accelerating away from the fence as only he could. Then the big ears would work backwards and forwards as he checked on the state of play behind him and snatched a quick breather before again taking off at an unbelievable distance from the next fence.

I left it all to him. I know everyone thought we were finished as Captain John passed us at the last, but I always felt Night Nurse, like the true professional that he was, had saved a little up his sleeve for the final dash to the line...

JONJO O'NEILL

with Tim Richards

Jonjo

An Autobiography

GRAFTON BOOKS

A Division of the Collins Publishing Group

LONDON GLASGOW
TORONTO SYDNEY AUCKLAND

Grafton Books
A Division of the Collins Publishing Group
8 Grafton Street, London W1X 3LA

This revised edition published by Grafton Books 1986

First published in Great Britain by
Stanley Paul & Co. Ltd 1985

ISBN 0–586–06851–1

Printed and bound in Great Britain by
Collins, Glasgow

Set in Times

Contents

Acknowledgements

Jonjo's eldest brother Jerome was dashing to take his family to Sunday mass, but spared a moment to point out the three-foot-high pile of books in the corner of the dining room in his home at Castlelyons, County Cork.

'Help yourself. There could be some useful information in them for you,' said Jerome, bustling his wife Monica, son John and daughter Grace through the front door so they would not be late for church. I was left to start thumbing through the hundreds of pages of cuttings, and quickly realized that if I had prayed for help as I embarked on Jonjo's book the Good Lord could not have answered more positively than by way of Jerome's immaculately kept scrapbooks. Only when I finally came to collate the statistics, which are listed at the back of the book, did I grasp just how golden was that moment when Jerome paused to introduce me to the twelve years he had dedicated to recording the achievements of his brother. The week I spent in deepest southern Ireland with Jerome as my guide was invaluable.

The pint of Guinness his father Tom bought me at the Griffin Bar at Skenakilla crossroads outside Castletownroche (after our 14-mile cycle ride to Jonjo's school and back) was also invaluable! It did not take long for me to see that the O'Neill family and their many friends had put their stamp on the little fellow before dispatching him across the Irish Sea; all of them, down to earth, open and always with that Irish sense of humour.

Jonjo's trainers – Michael Connolly, Gordon Richards, Peter Easterby and Roger Fisher – gave up hours of their busy lives to talk about their jockey. His surgeon, Hugh Barber, priest Father David Murphy, accountant and manager John Lowthian and friend and former jockey David Goulding all helped with colourful tales and details in the life and times of J. J. O'Neill.

The first part of the night spent with Ron Barry and his wife Liz was unforgettable; the second part I can't remember! Luckily, the tape recorder was working and, once the Barry brogue had been deciphered and transcribed by the inexhaustible Ronnie Mutter, there was another story to tell. Ronnie transcribed nearly fifty hours of tapes and also typed the manuscript, meeting even the tightest deadlines asked of her. George Ennor's professional knowledge unearthed many inaccuracies; his thoroughness in checking every fact and willingness to pass constructive comments proved an enormous help. Indefatigable Jack Warner was always on hand to provide his own special brand of enthusiastic assistance when called on at any time of day or night. And without the blessing of the *Daily Mirror* the book would not have been possible.

Jonjo's wife Sheila made Ivy House like a second home. Her warm welcomes and encouragement did much to keep Jonjo and me afloat on those late nights and early mornings of tape recordings and discussions.

By no means least, the courageous Doreen Dobson, who pushed numerous whiskies into my hand before sending me back to my office fortified, and with her writer's motto ringing in my ears: Discipline, Determination and Dedication.

As ever the unsung heroine, my wife Liz, who accepted with enormous understanding the rough end of what must have been six anonymous and lonely months. Whenever the feathers became ruffled she skilfully steered the ship back on an even keel.

T.R.

Photographic acknowledgements
For permission to reproduce copyright photographs in this book, the authors and publishers would like to thank Alec Russell, Eamonn McCabe, Jack Hickes, Gerry Cranham, Rex Coleman, Sporting Pictures, David Hastings, *Cork Examiner* and *Daily Mirror*.

Foreword

The caption above my *Daily Express* column on 19 December 1972 read 'John Joe Future Champ says Tim'.

The previous cold, fog-shrouded afternoon at Catterick had been enlivened, for this observer, by two unconnected events: the course commentator's despairing mid-race remark, 'I can't see any horses but there's a loose jockey by the last flight'; and, despite conditions which caused the last race to be abandoned, the unconcealable verve and talent of the flame-haired twenty-year-old who created the shock of the day when scoring on 20–1 outsider Merkat.

It was the latter's trainer Tim Molony – himself five times champion jockey – who made that prediction, declaring apropos the 5lb claimer: 'He's a sure champion of the future, and not just a fine little rider but a helluva nice lad.'

Tim's forecast was not only swiftly fulfilled but Jonjo has remained the same unassuming self-deprecating personality.

His persistently courageous triumphs over the appalling adversity which is the hallmark of his trade have made him a legend not only in racing but throughout the world of sport.

The Jonjo O'Neill story is an example to all.

PETER O'SULLEVAN

Jonjo
an Autobiography

1

Broken But Not Beaten

The longest journey in Jonjo O'Neill's life started in October 1980 in an ambulance and, for thirteen and a half harrowing months, dragged him through four hospitals, in Wales, England and Switzerland, in search of treatment for his shattered leg. Defeat was out of the question; he believed implicitly that his record-breaking career was faced with only a fleeting hold-up, until, in his rush to return to raceriding, he damaged his leg for a second time, almost beyond repair.

The path he trod with such feeling from the scene of the accident at Bangor racecourse in North Wales finally took him across the Pennines to Wetherby in Yorkshire. *Timeform's Chasers and Hurdlers 1981–82* retains a strong whiff of the euphoria that accompanied Jonjo on his way back to unsaddle that magnificent mare Realt Na Nona after she had helped him to win the long, brave battle back to racing.

'To the racing public at large, the leading jockeys are the heart of racing, its heroes. Anyone requiring evidence of the validity of that remark should have been at Wetherby on December 1st, the day that dual champion jockey O'Neill returned to the saddle after almost fourteen months out of action because of injury. The occasion attracted a record crowd for the fixture and a large contingent of newsmen, photographers and television crews hounded O'Neill like a film star at a premiere; the scenes in the unsaddling enclosure after his success on Realt Na Nona on his third ride of the afternoon were rapturous.'

                                                                    T.R.

I forced my right hand down the bed, but it was like fighting the tide with my strength ebbing away as my whole body, stiff and weak, ached under the strain. Stiff from head to toe. Or was I?

I could just make out that the person sitting on the chair next to my bed was black, a coloured nurse in a blinding white uniform. My mind faltered and wandered between the efforts of trying to penetrate the lower regions of the bed with my hand and of identifying my new neighbour. My fingers at full stretch suddenly registered and started to probe a piece of hard board in the area of my right knee. My heart missed a beat as the haziness returned. They had amputated my right leg. I would never walk again. But perhaps that was the lesser of two evils. At least I would not have to endure the exhausting, mind-wracking pain any more. I knew I could not have stood that for much longer.

I glanced at the nurse and asked, 'Have they cut off my leg? They have. I know they have.'

When she failed to reply I was convinced the desperate deed had been done because my leg had been so rotten they thought I would get along faster without it. The nurse understood very little English and even less of my County Cork accent. Speaking was not made any easier by that unpleasant post-operative sensation of a dry mouth lined with sandpaper.

It seemed an eternity before the nurse stood up, walked to the bottom of the bed and pulled back the bedclothes. She returned to the top of the bed and as her fine, dark hands raised my head I could not believe my eyes. There, staring me in the face, were two sets of toes. I twitched my left foot and the toes returned the signal; then my right and, unbelievably, there was movement. I sank back awash with joy but completely overcome with the effort of working my toes.

I came round two hours later to the sound of a feminine, yet deep, guttural accent as the nurse explained that Professor Allgower had repaired rather than removed my battered right leg and that he was very pleased with the way the operation had gone. The remains of the anaesthetic gripped me and it was all I could do to retain consciousness. I gave up the fight as drowsiness took over and I slept contentedly.

Only hours before I had been telling Professor Martin Allgower, a world authority on plating bones, that if he wished he could amputate my leg. It had tortured me for months and, although my visit to Basle's Kanton Hospital in Switzerland was the result of my own foolhardiness, I would not have objected to the easy way out. Anything to rid myself of the agony, which had gradually weakened me mentally and physically, reducing me to the lowest form of limping jump jockey. Professor Allgower had offered to wake me in the middle of the operation if he thought it necessary and ask if I agreed to having the leg chopped off.

'Oh, hell,' I said. 'I don't want to be brought round to be told. Just get on with it and do whatever is best.'

My endurance was disappearing fast. Even as a child I had never liked entertaining defeat, but now I despaired of ever winning again. In fact, without realizing it, I was galloping towards wholesale surrender. I simply signed the papers and put myself entirely in the very capable hands of Professor Allgower.

The cause of my predicament had come about six months earlier, in December 1980. In the previous October I had shattered my right leg into at least four pieces and cracked the bone like crazy paving in an extraordinary fall from a hurdler called Simbad at Bangor races in North Wales. It was the second time the leg had been broken; the first was at Stockton in 1975. Now, as each day dragged by with increasing frustration as I waited for the leg to heal, a conviction began to build up inside me. By December I firmly believed that the following March, at Cheltenham, two of Britain's best-loved horses, Night Nurse and Sea Pigeon, would reach the pinnacles of their illustrious careers.

When you cannot have something you really want you become all the more desperate for it. Forbidden fruits are always sweetest, so they say. I was unlikely to be fit enough to ride Night Nurse in his preliminary races, but I was sure he would win the Cheltenham Gold Cup and become the first champion hurdler to complete the elusive double of Champion Hurdle and Gold Cup. The more I thought – and my enforced idleness gave me plenty of time for that – the more I pictured Night Nurse soaring over the last fence on his way up the famous stamina-sapping Cheltenham hill to one of the most popular victories in the history of the world's most prestigious steeplechase.

And I would be riding. Of that I had no doubt.

Sea Pigeon was an even greater driving force than Night Nurse. I had won the 1980 Champion Hurdle on him, and his last-gasp finishes had become part of the theatre which enthralled the winter-racing public of the late seventies and early eighties. I honestly could not see what could stop us from winning our second Champion Hurdle.

The bait was laid and, with nothing better to do, I was biting.

Only seconds had ticked by after Sheila had taken little Louise downstairs for breakfast before I threw back the blankets and gently swung both legs over the side of the bed. Across the claret carpet stood the armchair covered with the clothes I had swapped for my blue pyjamas the night before. I estimated it would take me about eight paces to reach the chair. The wind was battering Deep Ghyll, the grey stone house which stood high off the main A6 road between Penrith and Carlisle. The handful of houses around us made up the village of Plumpton, not to be confused with the racecourse of the same name in Sussex. The bedroom window, which overlooked the green but frosty Cumbria fields laid bare by the ravages of winter, withstood a continual buffeting from the strong icy gusts but the low December morning sun streamed onto the bed and brightened the room. I wanted to get up and go and my clothes did not seem that far away.

My crutches were by the bed and that was where they were going to stay for the time being. Lifting myself from the bed and balancing my nine and a half stone on my left leg was no problem. I nervously thrust forward my right leg, supported only by a protective bandage over the nine-inch scar which decorated the misshapen shin. For a split second I transferred my weight to the plated leg as I moved my left leg forward to take the strain again. Would it snap, crumble or just creak as it was asked to perform the task for which God had originally made it and, more recently, Hugh Barber, my long-suffering orthopaedic surgeon, had repaired it?

The movement caused more discomfort than pain and certainly not enough to deter me from trying another half stride. The third time I attempted this newfound short-pace shuffle I straightened up like a ramrod, wincing under the shock of what felt like a razor searing through me. It was all I could do to turn and collapse back on the bed. Simmering towards a fit of temper and frustration, I lay across the bottom half of the bed. As I calmed down my eyes focused on the clothes on the armchair, which now seemed a million miles away. I felt hurt by my failure, though on reflection I was guilty of being overambitious at such an early stage in my quest to ride again. I gave my brow a despairing rub and was surprised to find it spotted with drops of perspiration. For a moment I assumed it was due to the sun, which by now engulfed the whole bed, but then I realized how much my strength had been taxed by this new early-morning exercise. I hauled myself back into bed in time to receive a reviving mug of tea from Sheila, who, fortunately, was unaware of my disastrous first steps towards Cheltenham.

My progress was gradual, but after a week of early-morning bedroom manoeuvres I finally completed the long walk of eight delicate steps to the armchair. I sat comfortably in it and congratulated myself on reaching the first of many objectives. I kidded myself that I was not putting any strain on my leg as walking became easier. When Sheila was not there I would walk round the room, using the chair and the bed as supports whenever necessary, and eventually I achieved the marathon of twenty-five paces. I was beginning to get carried away and float on a cloud which would eventually drop me on the backs of Night Nurse and Sea Pigeon in front of the chanting crowds, whose cheers I could already hear sweeping across the rolling Cotswold Hills from Cheltenham.

My leg had become my life. One morning before Christmas I joined Sheila and Louise in our brightly modernized kitchen and announced, 'I'll flippin' ride in March. I can walk on this leg.'

'Don't be doing too much on it,' Sheila countered cautiously. 'You're not supposed to be putting any weight on it. You know how much Mr Barber has impressed this on you.'

'I haven't been doing too much on it,' I replied.

'Well, how can you walk on it then?' asked Sheila, who had seen straight through me.

I always was a bad liar, but to keep secrets from those close to me I find impossible. I was nothing short of devious on those mornings when I lay waiting for Sheila to leave the bedroom before I started my escapades without crutches, but once I felt I was going well I could not contain myself and had to share the good news with her. But she was under no illusion that I was stupid in trying to accelerate my recovery against doctor's orders. It was only a matter of time before I would be trying to pull the wool over the expert eyes of Hugh Barber, who had already exercised great skill and patience in restoring a number of my limbs to working order.

But I was so caught up in my own little cocoon of a world, which I was convinced was leading to Cheltenham, that I was blinkered to the extent of being selfishly singleminded. And, if I am totally honest, no one mattered a fig during those dark days.

Sheila accepted my inconsiderate actions with a reasoned understanding I did not deserve and yet, perhaps, had always expected of her, because in our two and a half years of marriage she had given me her unflinching support and strength that could only be surpassed by the Almighty. I was taking Sheila for granted in the pigheaded belief that she would not try to interfere.

Hugh Barber has since told me that he believed if he had slowed me down he would have risked destroying me and my motivation. His whole attitude centred on restoring me to full mobility as quickly as possible because my living depended on it. But, blinded by my own impatience, I failed to see that he was in fact trying to push me back into the saddle while at the same time protecting me from further disasters.

Gnawing away incessantly in my mind was a growing concern about my ability to convince first myself and then the owners, the trainers and the fickle public that I could still master those crises which can erupt out of nothing in Cheltenham's rough, tough, drama-packed races. I was involved in my own race against time to prove the point. As the countdown quickened towards February I used to stride up and down stairs with such gusto and confidence that I was beginning to fancy myself walking on water. I knew I was about three weeks ahead of the strict schedule laid down by Hugh Barber, who still insisted I should barely be using the leg. I was flying. That was until I attempted a quiet ride around the local farm lanes.

For someone who had been astride ponies and horses from his earliest recollection the sensation was totally foreign, more like a form of torture than plain discomfort. As I balanced in the saddle, I could have been forgiven for thinking I was sitting on a stone wall, the saddle a sharp-edged rock with jagged corners piercing my tender bottom and weak thighs in the most vulnerable places. After a few days I began to wonder if I would ever make it back to any racecourse – never mind Cheltenham in nine weeks. The bone had knitted exactly where the top of my stirrup iron rubbed against my boot and this pinched and hurt so much I had to pad my boot and ride with my right leg turned out to avoid aggravating the wound.

The style adapted to suit a broken leg screwed together with a six-inch alloy plate became more and more natural as the days progressed. I began to trot and eventually mustered enough confidence to approach a great friend, the late John Dixon, to ask if I could try a canter on one of his horses. John, who trained a handful of horses with considerable success, was a Cumbria farmer, a steward at Carlisle, and a warm character who drew much pleasure from helping others. He agreed reluctantly. I could tell he viewed my rush back to the saddle with guarded enthusiasm.

The January morning mist hung above the desolate aerodrome, shrouding horse and rider but not restricting visibility enough to curtail our plans to canter. Hundreds of white squawking seagulls glided onto the grass ahead of us. Slowly the dank mist lifted; the mass of birds rose skywards to ear-piercing shrills. Visibility improved and two large hangars emerged through the murk at the far end of the airfield, their vast blue doors giving the impression of two enormous eyes watching us. The gulls gone, a quiet descended over White Heather Aerodrome, a peace for which it was not originally designed as a wartime flying centre some five miles from Wigton. The large grass area where John Dixon worked his horses was bordered by the two main runways and smaller tarmac taxiing strips.

My chosen partner was old Skiddaw View, named after the lovely landmark a few miles away in the Lake District, the peaks of which are visible from the White Heather on a clear day. I had won six races on Skiddaw View and he was as relaxed as ever. At fourteen, he must have known every blade of grass on the airfield. I must confess to feeling slightly apprehensive as we prepared to answer the questions that had been nagging at me for twenty-four hours a day ever since I had been loaded on a stretcher and into the ambulance on that black afternoon at Bangor.

Skiddaw View's rubber reins were wet, but I kept a firm grip. My dark blue windcheater was dripping in the damp atmosphere, but my body was glowing within, a warmth generated by eager anticipation.

The horse set off, and as he cantered I concentrated on putting as little weight as possible on my right leg. The breeze on my face was suddenly so familiar that it brought back the years of Alverton, Sea Pigeon, Night Nurse, of Sandown, Newcastle, Ayr – the glory days when excitement banished all thought of injury. The golden memories galloped through my mind, but not for long. Every time Skiddaw View pounded the turf a deep vibration went through my right leg, a new, unnerving sensation which persuaded me to pull him up. We started again and then stopped, fifty or a hundred yards at a time. While accepting that I still had a long way to go, my determination had not been dampened. The worrying vibration in the leg had improved by the time I completed a full circuit and returned to where John Dixon was standing.

'How is it?' he inquired.

'I'm going to give it a try over a couple of furlongs,' I replied.

John didn't utter a word but the expression on his pale, round face summed up his sentiments – 'Don't be such a bloody fool.'

I had not completed the two furlongs when I had to pull up. Something in my leg snapped and the breath rushed out of me. I could hardly breathe. Luckily, once Skiddaw View got the message that I was trying to stop him he slowed to a walk. I was frightened, wondering the extent of the obviously desperate damage I had done. Swamped with pain, I could barely talk, but on returning to John I managed to mutter, 'I shouldn't have tried.'

John was entitled to his reply – 'I told you so, you daft little beggar.'

The unforgettable feeling of the red-hot knife had returned to my leg. I was in agony, but I didn't want John to know. Yet all the time the excruciating pain was weakening me and the effort of trying to prevent the suffering from distorting my face and thereby giving the whole game away was proving too much. But I could tell by his fraught expression that John knew. He knew that I had put the wreckage of my right leg beyond immediate repair.

My attempts at keeping the pain at bay were failing. I managed to announce, 'I'm going for a walk to let him dry off.' The fact that Skiddaw View wasn't even sweating hadn't entered my troubled mind; I wanted to be alone. The dismay, horror and fear which accompanied me on that lonely walk to the far end of the aerodrome shattered me completely.

Skiddaw View loped along underneath me, as safe a conveyance as I could have wished for in the circumstances. We approached a red brick building flanked on the left by the two huge hangars and a copse of pine trees away to the right. The deserted building had seen better days, presumably when the White Heather was playing host to aeroplanes rather than a seasoned steeplechaser and his crippled jockey. Beyond in the distance was a snowcapped mountain nestling in the beautiful Lake District.

I had seen enough and wanted to get home. By now the pain was coming in waves. The intermittence made it more tolerable, but when John greeted me, his countenance covered with concern, I felt myself being overcome with fear. I tried to dismount but my confidence had gone. I was frightened of jumping down on my sound leg in case I jolted the other one. I was convinced I had broken it again. John

Dixon, quick to recognize my plight, helped me off Skiddaw View and into the car.

I was so low that if I had had a gun at home I think I would have shot myself. That morning I had arrived at the White Heather full of hope, only to be driven home a complete wreck.

I didn't break the news to Sheila. I simply told her that my leg was being troublesome and that I ought to go and see Mr Barber. By the afternoon the leg had improved and I reckoned I put on a convincing show as I walked into Mr Barber's consulting rooms in Carlisle.

'Have you tried your leg out on a horse yet?' was his opening shot.

'Yes, I have actually,' I said.

'I knew you had,' smiled Mr Barber.

'It's not very good and I think I'll call it a day,' I conceded.

He took another X-ray and as he held the negative up to the light his kind brown eyes turned to thunder above his bushy muttonchop whiskers, an uncharacteristic look of anger which could easily explode. He was vexed but far too professional to allow his emotions to spill over onto me.

'What in the name of God have you been doing? Have you had a fall or given it a knock?' he asked.

I felt like a naughty schoolboy who had just been found out. 'The other day I got a bit of a twinge,' I admitted sheepishly, and attempted to cover up my overambitious escapade on the aerodrome by saying, 'I was only trotting on the roads.'

Mr Barber obviously did not want to tell me the worst. 'You have not done your leg any good at all,' was all he said.

Little did he know I had realized that even before I had brought Skiddaw View to a standstill. But then Hugh Barber, who so naturally puts his patients at ease, showed his true colours. He immediately brushed my irresponsible actions behind us and stressed that we must work together to ensure the leg made a complete recovery. If I had been in his place I would have felt inclined to wash my hands of the whole business. After all, Mr Barber had done his best for me and, in return, my appreciation of his skills had been to ignore his careful advice and cock up the whole job. He could have taken the view that I had made him look a clown because all his hard work in picking up the pieces of my leg – four not fifteen as appeared in some reports at the time – had failed.

That he should have been so understanding and sympathetic after I had virtually stood up, raised two fingers in defiance and gone my own wrong way bit deeper into me than I at first realized. Imagine how I would have reacted if he had tried to tell me how to ride racehorses. Not long after Mr Barber had brought me to heel and put me back on course for the winner's enclosure I discovered he was taking riding lessons. He used to pull my leg and tell me I ought to be taking evening classes in orthopaedic surgery!

He admitted to me later that he was sympathetic because he seriously believed I might lose the leg. For a few critical days he thought that it might go rotten, become gangrened, and that I would never ride again. In his medical book, I was finished. Thank God he didn't tell me at the time.

Mr Barber explained that I had not given the bone time to knit and that I had been walking on the metalwork, which had become microscopically loosened. He decided to put me back in plaster and sent me home on crutches. I was so depressed by this retrograde step that I wish he had hit me and knocked me spark out to release me from my agony. The leg did not improve and two days later Mr Barber admitted me to hospital and confined me to bed in a full-length plaster from hip to toe. I felt as if I had been thrown back into prison, although the nurses and hospital staff in Carlisle were marvellous. Mr Barber didn't trust me an inch. The drugs he administered helped me forget any idea I had of getting up and walking out. They pinned me to my mattress. After ten days I was discharged on crutches, but I refused to let anyone see me because I did not want people to know I was back to square one.

When I tried to walk again with my stick I still harboured the belief that riding at Cheltenham was a possibility, if only a remote one. Looking back, I must have been crackers.

On that desperate day when I went back to Mr Barber with my career apparently in ruins, he had telephoned Sheila to break the bad news. But he immediately bolstered her by explaining that I had got where I was in life through my will to win and it was this attitude which was responsible for my setback.

My last throw had come on 28 January at the publication of the Grand National weights in London, where I met Fred Street, the England and Arsenal football physiotherapist. At the time my leg was so swollen it would have burst the baggiest pair of trousers. Fred presented me with an amazing hollow inflatable leg which I wrapped round my real one and then blew up, trying to reduce the swelling by pressure.

But Fred spelled it out and pulled no punches. 'If you want to keep this leg of yours, forget about Cheltenham and the rest of the season,' he said gloomily.

If only I had listened to Hugh Barber in the first place.

Handing over the piece of paper to the taxi driver at Basle Airport, I felt utterly helpless. On the paper was written the address of Kantonsspital, which is German for Kanton Hospital. I couldn't understand the signs or the colourful advertising hoardings which decorated the streets, so I sat back and savoured the May sunshine beating down on the distant mountains as the taxi climbed and cornered sharply through the pleasant Swiss city on the twenty-minute drive to the hospital.

This new world brought out a loneliness in me that I had not experienced before, but the knowledge that Huge Barber had sent me here to have the fierce pain relieved proved an overriding comfort.

My morale had degenerated severely. I must have cut a pathetic figure in front of the white-haired professor, and he must have wondered if he was examining the right patient. During those days of May no one could have felt less like a champion jockey. I had given up and allowed myself to sink to the depths. If Professor Allgower were to amputate my leg, I would not object, so long as the pain went with it.

The hospital was spotlessly clean, the atmosphere bright and bristling with efficiency, and the gardens beautiful. I knew I was in the right place.

After the brief preliminaries of checking in and letting the hospital medical staff prod and explore my misshapen frame to confirm that I was still alive, I retired for my first night in a boarding house. The price of a bed in such an exclusive hospital was prohibitive so I thought I'd better rough it for one night.

The next day Professor Allgower and a posse of medics greeted me at the hospital. The professor explained that the state of my leg could be chronic, and that he could not promise to cure it; he might even have to amputate. His English was perfect and his manner most relaxing. I had no hesitation in signing my leg away on the necessary consent forms.

Hugh Barber flew over to see the operation through. His familiar face provided tremendous support at such a critical time, although, if I am honest, deep down inside me I was delighted that the operation was going ahead. My mind had tossed the problem about for too long. Was it gangrene? Was it broken for the third time? Would I be better off without it? Professor Allgower would shortly know the answers.

He removed the plate and eleven screws, cleaned the disfigured bone and then proceeded to chisel fresh bone from the top of my thigh and wrap the pieces round the fracture. In layman's terms, he was grafting fresh bone into the wound. My body had rejected the metal of the original plate and Professor Allgower replaced it with a similar plate made of titanium alloy, which was to be removed by Hugh Barber a year later, after it had fulfilled its function.

The first four days after the operation I spent staring at the white polystyrene tiles on the ceiling as I lay on my back waiting for my strength to return. Soon I was able to appreciate the immaculate gardens from the verandah of my room. I would hobble out and sit there for hours enjoying the clear air and the warmth of the sun.

There is no worse place than hospital when you are getting better. I had so much time to think; boredom set in and then I became enveloped in a deep depression. I couldn't have cared less if I never rode again. My mind became so muddled I even considered ending it all by taking my own life.

Lottie Piller, who lives in Switzerland and, with her husband Peter, owned those well-known long-distance chasers Wagner and Fortina's Express which were trained in County Durham by Arthur Stephenson, probably saved me from such a fearful fate. Armed with baskets of lovely flowers she brought some sanity into those four white walls surrounding me, giving me contact with the only world I knew – racing.

One of Lottie Piller's attractive baskets helped to brighten my days in more senses than one. A nurse who didn't speak English emptied the dead flowers from the basket and brought it back to me. I thought to myself, I don't want that. I can't be seen on the plane home carrying a basket.

'I don't want it,' I tried to explain to the nurse. 'You have it, but I would like an extra boiled egg for breakfast in exchange.'

She seemed to understand, but when breakfast appeared on the tray the following morning there was only one boiled egg. So I rang the bell and when the nurse arrived I said,

'Don't you remember, two eggs for breakfast?'

'Five minootes or three minootes?' came the reply.

I started to laugh, realizing that she was asking me how long I wanted my egg boiled. It was hard work, but I eventually got my two eggs. Unwittingly Lottie Piller had helped me to overcome the language barrier and provided me with a moment of laughter.

Even so, the days seemed endless and I had time to take a detached look at life. As far back as I can remember the world of racing has meant everything to me, but there I was, not in the least worried if I never saw another racecourse. Someone somewhere was trying to tell me that there is more to life than horses, horses and more horses. I asked myself what I had done with my twenty-nine years. I came to the conclusion I had spent every waking minute wondering where the next winner was coming from. Galloping here, there and everywhere in my quest to be more successful than the next man. Sheila and two-year-old Louise had been forced to take a back seat. Flat on my back and on the verge of throwing in the towel, I had got my just desserts for such a self-centred existence.

Suddenly I found myself waking up after being blinkered by racing for nearly thirty years. In so many respects a waste. Much more to life, I decided. Above all, the warmth and love of a young family, to whom I had so often given the cold shoulder. Again and again I chewed it over. Did it really matter if I never rode in another race?

Seven months earlier I had found it impossible to come to terms with the fact that I had broken my leg. The agonies and misery of those months ultimately changed my outlook. There ought to be more pleasure than I had permitted myself on the farm at home with my wife, my daughter and my friends. I genuinely believe that the Almighty was using his way of putting his message across that I must take a pull, steady up and think hard before careering back headlong into the fray.

Although mass was said every day in the hospital chapel and relayed to the patients through headphones, I could not follow the German service. Holy Communion was brought to our bedsides, but sometimes I felt I had prayed so much I had already said my own mass. I am proud to admit my religion was a source of enormous strength and comfort during the greatest crisis of my life.

Ten days after I had set foot on the gleaming floors of the Kantonsspital I was limping out to Lottie Piller's car, bound for the airport. A new man physically and, more important, mentally. But I wasn't allowed to depart without Professor Allgower's stern instructions.

'From now on you must do what Mr Barber tells you,' he insisted with a knowing smile. 'Don't ride until your leg is one hundred per cent strong again. Then give it at least a month to six weeks before you start racing.'

It was three months, September 1981, before I was back in the saddle and I waited until December before I subjected the leg to the rigours of the racecourse.

As I steered that magnificent mare Realt Na Nona into the winners' enclosure on my first day back at Wetherby I wanted to shout out and thank so many people. But I didn't get the chance. Before my feet had touched the ground the press, radio microphones and television cameras had engulfed me.

2

Sea Pigeon

In the summer of 1984 Sea Pigeon, winner of thirty-seven races, including two Champion Hurdles, two Chester Cups and an Ebor Handicap, had a three-hour operation to remove two feet of intestine. Even so, he still had enough guts left to fight through the most critical twenty-four hours of his headline-hogging life. The first signs of illness occurred at Polly Catton's paddocks at Slingsby outside Malton, where Sea Pigeon was enjoying retirement. He appeared to be suffering from abdominal pain. When he did not respond to treatment the vet, Bob Ordidge, decided to open him up. As over 50 per cent of horses do not survive a major abdominal operation, it became a matter of life or death.

On the same day as the operation Sea Pigeon was up on his famous feet which had entertained us so with tantalizing late dashes to the line. He was dazed but alive. Stephen Muldoon, son of Sea Pigeon's owner, Pat Muldoon, spent the first night with him in his box.

Stephen, who won an amateur flat race on Sea Pigeon at Hamilton Park in 1980, says, 'I thought he might die. His heartbeat was racing and he kept walking in half circles in his box, first round to the left and then back round to the right. But then after four or five days he began to perk up.'

Jonjo visited Sea Pigeon during his convalescence and was delighted by his remarkable recovery.

Happily, Sea Pigeon soon returned to the paddocks of Slingsby and according to Stephen, 'You wouldn't know he'd had an operation.'

The vets who saw Sea Pigeon during his latest battle were unanimous. His natural reserves of spirit and fight pulled him through when most horses would have given up.

T.R.

I can put my hand on my heart and say that Sea Pigeon should have won the 1979 Champion Hurdle at Cheltenham.

Looking back, I blame myself. Top jockeys don't need orders, particularly when they know a horse, and I used to pride myself on the almost psychic relationship that existed between us. It was my sixteenth race on Sea Pigeon. Yet, as I gathered the reins in my left hand and thrust back my left leg for Graham Lockerbie, travelling head lad to Peter Easterby, Sea Pigeon's trainer, to lever me into the saddle, Pat Muldoon's last six words, offered more as an afterthought than as strict instructions, reverberated round my head: 'Don't leave it too late, Jonjo.'

Not even the foulest March weather could dampen the expectant buzz of the crowd. But Pat Muldoon was understandably apprehensive after the morning's torrential rain, believing that Sea Pigeon would get stuck in the mud. We all wondered if the heavy going would blunt his blinding speed, and knew what a bonus the bottomless conditions were for Ireland's reigning champion, Monksfield, who loved nothing more than a slugging match up the famous Cheltenham hill.

Pat Muldoon, a large man who always stood out with his full head of white hair, certainly deserved his success with Sea Pigeon if only for his perseverance in trying to buy the horse out of Jeremy Tree's stable at Beckhampton in Wiltshire. Pat, a wine and spirits wholesaler from Armadale in West Lothian, Scotland, had been a great student of the formbook and used to burn the midnight oil trying to unearth possible jumpers to buy. After Sea Pigeon had finished seventh to Morston in the 1973 Derby Pat wrote to Jeremy Tree, who replied that he thought a lot of Sea Pigeon but he was not for sale.

'I had got the impression that while Sea Pigeon may have been slightly nervous, a hard puller and perhaps even ungenuine, he would benefit from being gelded and a change of scenery and sport,' says Pat, who persisted and wrote again to Jeremy Tree, only to be told Sea Pigeon had in fact been gelded with a view to running in the 1974 Cup races. Pat refused to take no for an answer and after a while wrote to Tree for the third time; the letter he received contained the disconcerting news that Sea Pigeon had not recovered from his gelding operation and was in poor condition. In the circumstances Jeremy Tree considered it unfair to sell him.

One day a friend of Pat, John Carey, a small farmer near Jeremy Tree at Marlborough, telephoned to say that he had a nice horse lodging at his place and although it was not in the best of shape he considered him worth buying. It was Sea Pigeon. So Pat contacted Jeremy Tree again and this time was told to make an offer, which he did, and a deal was clinched.

Pat recalls, 'On his first day at Gordon Richards's Sea Pigeon had the fright of his life when he found himself face to face with some cattle. He had never seen cows before and just stood and stared at them in disbelief.'

At the height of his career as an owner Pat had fourteen jumpers, including Canadius, Town Ship and Highway Rambler, who made their mark as talented members of the winter racing scene. After two separate incidents in which Pat's horse started favourite only to be beaten by a stable companion, he moved his string across the Pennines from Gordon Richards at Greystoke in Cumbria to Peter Easterby in North Yorkshire early in 1977.

Now, in 1979, despite the misgivings about the taxing ground, I felt confident Sea Pigeon would take his revenge on Monksfield, who had beaten him by two lengths in the Champion Hurdle the previous year when the Irish champion Frank Berry had deputized for me after I had been knocked out on the first day of the meeting.

Sea Pigeon flew the second last hurdle as we swept down the hill in pursuit of Monksfield, whose forcing tactics had failed to break us. We thundered towards the elbow before the last flight with Muldoon's words still ticking away in the back of my mind; 'Don't leave it too late, Jonjo.'

But they didn't matter. Sea Pigeon was cruising with all his majestic power in reserve. We joined Monksfield on the inside at the elbow and I knew Pigeon would win. The tank was full and I only needed to press the button and Sea Pigeon's instant answer would carry us home. We went into the last flight half a length up on Monksfield and Pigeon appeared to sense our victory run. He pricked his ears as if to say. 'This is it, son. We've got him.'

True to his word, Pigeon put together the perfect final leap, keeping his momentum in full flow. Somehow, Dessie Hughes on Monksfield conjured an even better jump and they landed back level. But I was still confident. Fifty yards after the last Sea Pigeon was poised to leave Monksfield toiling on his favourite battleground, the Cheltenham hill. Then disaster. He went empty on me. Suddenly there was no power and Pigeon spluttered to what seemed a standstill in a stride. Alarmingly, Monksfield had clawed his way back at us. I was helpless but still did the unforgiveable and cracked Sea Pigeon three times with the whip, knowing full well it would make not the slightest difference. Pigeon never went for the whip and to this day I wince with shame when I think how I resorted to hitting him.

We were beaten threequarters of a length and it was not one of my proudest moments.

As Sea Pigeon's lass Monica Jones led us back to the unsaddling enclosure anger took over from disappointment. If only I had been big enough and bold enough to grab the situation by the scruff of the neck, for I knew I had the machinery beneath me, but I lacked the courage to go out on a limb and make best use of it with a daring late thrust on the hill. Not even Monksfield, with his boundless guts, would have had time to hit back. Pat Muldoon was right to express doubts about Sea Pigeon's mechanics working with their customary quick-fire efficiency in the clinging mud. But out there in the heat of the action any jockey worth his salt can size up a changing situation and in a flash alter his tactics. If you like, I shirked it.

Peter Easterby does not agree and lays the blame wholly at Pat Muldoon's door. He has since been outspoken on the matter and to this day is adamant. 'I can guarantee that Sea Pigeon would definitely have won if Pat Muldoon had not come into the parade ring before the race. By going for home too soon, Sea Pigeon gave Monksfield time to fight back at him. Pat knows my view and I am certain it is correct.'

Theories have been put forward that Sea Pigeon did not possess the stamina to win a Champion Hurdle until 1980 when the course was reduced by two hundred yards to exactly two miles, eliminating the first circuit uphill climb past the stands and round the enclosure in the middle of the track. The ex-flat horse, who won at Ascot as a two-year-old and ran well in the Derby before winning two Chester Cups, was all speed. So the argument was valid. I agreed with Peter that he should have won in 1979 over the old distance but for different reasons.

In 1980, when he blew up and still won, his performance, put together after an interrupted preparation, highlighted the brilliance of the horse when he was right – or perhaps, more accurately, half right. Sea Pigeon was at his best when he was 85 or 90 per cent fit. Better underdone than overcooked. When he was 100 per cent and really wound up he suffered from race nerves, sweated up, was too much on his toes and difficult to settle; but later as age crept up on him he began to switch off and go round like an old man. A child could have ridden him at the end of his days.

This was only one of the many incredible facets of a temperamental, classy, highly strung, unpredictable, emotional, deceptive, frustrating, explosive and at times infuriating individual.

Anyone who says that Sea Pigeon was not 100 per cent fit when he won the 1980 Champion Hurdle might with some justification be thought to need certifying, for not only did Sea Pigeon wrest the crown from Monksfield, but he pulverized him by seven lengths. But the truth of the matter is that after a mile, on the far side of the Cheltenham amphitheatre, we met rising ground and Sea Pigeon started to let out the most disturbing gasps and pants. His heaving and wheezing were frightening; but I told myself to leave him alone and let him get on with the race in his own time. Some gravel had got into his foot and made it septic and this cost him vital work in the tense build-up to Cheltenham. Peter Easterby had grave misgivings about getting him ready in time during those worrying February days some three weeks before the Champion, but the Yorkshire horse genius accomplished another miracle and produced Sea Pigeon on the big day. However, as we sped towards the top of the hill, Sea Pigeon's rushed training programme was telling, his lungs fighting for extra oxygen. The last thing he wanted was to be told what to do. So I played at being passenger, watching the rest of the field quicken at the top of the hill. Sea Pigeon appreciated having time to find his second wind; he never once lost his flowing action and kept cantering with the leaders harnessed in his sights. Sea Pigeon was so switched off and relaxed I knew I could wait as long as I wanted. We were a length down on Monksfield going into the last but Sea Pigeon propelled us over and away in one single act of graceful power that swept us shoulder to shoulder with Monksfield and Dessie Hughes. Halfway up the run in I was in front. Sooner than I had planned and the nightmare of the previous year momentarily blacked out my vision of victory. Had I come too soon again? Sea Pigeon answered in characteristic style by accelerating majestically as only he could. That day he oozed class and confidence. There was so much speed under the saddle I had only to change my hands on the reins and Sea Pigeon produced a flash of overdrive I have never exprienced in a jumper.

The following year he had me biting my lip and choking

back the tears of joy and disappointment when I watched him win from the BBC commentary box. At first it was as though Sea Pigeon was rubbing salt into my broken right leg, which I had failed to overcome in my bid to ride him to his second Champion Hurdle triumph. I was hurt and, like a little boy, wanted to cry. But this was a big occasion for Sea Pigeon; why should I spoil it? Join in and enjoy it, I thought. There he was, poetry in motion as John Francome gave him a gem of a ride, saving him until fifty yards from the line and then simply popping his nose in front of Daring Run and winning by a length and a half from Pollardstown, who took second place near the line. Sea Pigeon did not even know he had had a race under John's cool artistry.

Crowds came rushing to grab pole position round the winner's enclosure and share in Sea Pigeon's historic moment. I stood alongside commentator Julian Wilson and stared through welling tears into the monitor. More and more racegoers below us scampered towards the unsaddling pen. But I felt lonely and left out until Julian interrupted my bewildered gaze into the television set and asked me for comments on such a silk smooth performance. Suddenly I was being swept away on the Sea Pigeon wave of euphoria. We had been lucky enough to witness another unforgettable chapter in Cheltenham's history, the script composed by one of the most remarkable characters to grace the Cotswold racing arena.

The atmosphere in the York weighing room was loaded with tension as the minutes ticked towards the 1979 Tote-Ebor Handicap. I knew I must first beat the medical profession before I could throw my leg across Sea Pigeon in the big race.

I was encouraged when I noticed the doctor's dark eyebrows part, replacing his mystified frown with an air of relief as he finally grasped the method behind the madness of the improvised highland fling I was performing for his benefit. The ploy must work, I thought to myself. If I could hop on my broken toes he would surely pass me fit to ride Yorkshire's own hero in front of his home crowd. Only seven days earlier in that eventful August, at Dundalk in Ireland, I had crushed and broken three toes against the running rail.

At first the doctor looked askance, as if it were a psychiatrist and not a medical officer I required. The inquiring expressions of Lester Piggott and Pat Eddery, holding their saddles in the queue for the scales to weigh out before the first race, warmed into knowing smiles. They realized I was making some sort of Irish song and dance to prove a point. After my little hopping routine the doctor flicked his immaculately manicured fingers through my medical book in search of the previous week's entry of the broken – and mighty painful – toes.

I had set my heart on playing the role of battle-scarred jump jockey trying to beat Lester Piggott, Willie Carson and the American Steve Cauthen at their own game. The Ebor in August is one of the flat season's most competitive handicaps, watched by thirty thousand vociferous partisans as well as by millions on television. The challenge was meat and drink. Three smashed toes were no more than a temporary hiccup. Or were they?

The doctor's balding scalp stared up at me while he stooped low over my right foot gently manipulating all five toes. I held my breath and prayed that he would not discover my wicked deception.

'How does it feel?' inquired a Welsh voice from down near the floor. I quickly assured him my toes were fine and he in turn wasted no time in giving me the all clear.

I scuffled as upright as the pain would permit straight into the privacy of the jockeys' changing room. I felt like jumping for joy, but that involved both feet and far too much risk. Instead, I slumped in my place under the peg from which dangled my breeches and the McIntyre tartan and red silks of

Pat Muldoon. Gradually I began to bubble inside at the exciting prospect of starring on one of the most glamorous afternoons of the summer racing programme. It was indeed a day to cherish, having my first flat ride on Sea Pigeon and making my debut on York's historic and beautiful Knavesmire. Suddenly the daydreaming stopped as the next obstacle loomed large. It was the four-hundred-yard walk from the weighing room to the special big-race parade ring out on the course in front of the packed stands.

My great friend and medical mentor Hugh Barber once again had come to my rescue, this time by producing a steel plate to insert from heel to toe in the sole of my riding boot. The plate, which took the pressure off my foot and toes as I pushed down on the stirrup iron, had worked like a dream when I rode out at home, but I quickly discovered that walking on solid steel was even more awkward than stepping out feelingly on three unprotected broken toes. The plate accentuated my limp. As the seventeen jockeys assembled on the weighing-room steps ready to make their way through the crowds to the paddock, I realized that, at five feet five inches, I would tower above many of my tiny fellow flat-race riders. It wasn't often I was conspicuous by my height. I jostled for a position in the middle of the bunch, seeking camouflage among the multicoloured silks, hoping my ungainly gait would pass unnoticed. Relief set in after Graham Lockerbie hoisted me into the saddle taking my weight off the foot. Then anticipation followed during the parade in front of the mass of Yorkshire horselovers, craning forward eager to cast their expert eyes over the runners. I felt a sense of victory, having won my own private battle to compete on Sea Pigeon. Now I was in charge, though very much aware that the razor-sharp cut and thrust of the flat demanded quicksilver reactions and an ever alert eye if we were to grab our opportunities as they opened up before us.

Sea Pigeon was completely shut off in the middle of the

bunching backmarkers and concentrated on galloping through the mud, which at that stage of his career, as a nine-year-old, he still did not relish. Happily, this diverted his mind from his usual tedious habit of trying to pull my arms out and he settled sweetly. Swinging into the home straight we had plenty of ground to make up but couldn't find an opening. So I switched to the outside and as we gradually picked them off one by one I was both surprised and encouraged to see the other jockeys hard at work. The closer Sea Pigeon edged to the leaders the worse they appeared to be going. Pigeon kept pressing forward, on, on, on, and suddenly the winning post was in our sights. We passed the leader Donegal Prince a furlong out and half a furlong later we had it in the bag. The roar from the crowd exploded in our ears and their favourite Sea Pigeon fought through those final muddy yards. But then my confidence ran away with me and, foolishly, I dropped my hands on Sea Pigeon's neck, thinking he could coast home and still win. I should have known better, for he was too wise by half, downed tools and stopped as if I had shot him. Young Philip Robinson cashed in on my clanger and, riding as if his life depended on it, rallied Donegal Prince with a desperate final flourish. We passed the post locked together. But I was certain Sea Pigeon had lasted home. My elation quickly changed to anxiety as Monica Jones dashed out onto the course with a question which brought my head out of the heady clouds with a clap of thunder.

'Have you held on?' she asked, worry written all over her round face.

As if that wasn't enough, Graham Lockerbie appeared alongside with Sea Pigeon's rug under his arm. His red face focused upwards and the Dumfries accent fired a salvo which almost unshipped me.

'Peter Easterby thinks you're beat,' said Graham.

My fingers fidgeted nervously with the reins. I squirmed in

the saddle. My stomach tightened and I felt ill.

'Why did you drop your hands?' Graham asked. 'Have you ever ridden at York? It's a funny old angle, you know.'

Desperately I tried to gather my confidence and parry Graham's barrage. 'Of course I've won,' I said with all the authority I could muster.

Peter Easterby's eyes locked on mine before I dismounted amid the tension of the crowded but subdued unsaddling enclosure. If looks could kill I would have been dead. My heart sank into my boots as defeat stared out from those blue Easterby eyes. I wanted to jump off Sea Pigeon and run for cover, but when my feet touched the soggy turf a sharp reminder knifed upwards from my toes. I could hardly walk, never mind run. Pat Muldoon clearly was not happy, nervously swaying from side to side and picking at his binocular strap. Peter Easterby asked me what I thought but did not give me time to reply before the words I dreaded rang through me.

'You dropped your hands and I'm not so sure you've won,' Peter said bluntly.

Our agony was ended by the announcement that Sea Pigeon had held on. It was the signal for Yorkshire pride to erupt in a wave of delirium which made the famous 'roar of the Irish' at Cheltenham pale into insignificance. Their Sea Pigeon, trained fifteen miles away at Great Habton near Malton, had humped ten stone to a weight-carrying record in the Ebor and, incidentally, had found it easier than his jockey did carting his saddle on the short but painful walk from the winner's enclosure to the weighing room.

The enthusiastic reception of the flat-racing connoisseurs soon had me floating on air, but the stewards quickly brought me down with a bump when they called me in to ask why I dropped my hands. They held me in their stern gaze across the expanse of highly polished table. Then the camera patrol film sent a shudder through me as it highlighted how closely I had courted disaster. I must play this one up, I thought.

'I haven't ridden such a long way for a long time and I got tired,' I smiled.

The icy atmosphere thawed instantly, with Lord Westbury, Lord Zetland and Lord Allendale unable to resist a subdued chuckle. I quickly followed up on a more serious note, pointing out that I thought I had won – which I had – and that it was Sea Pigeon, under his ten stone, who had been tired. The stewards then showed me the photo-finish print which was also too close for comfort.

'Can I keep it?' I asked with a smile, clutching the photo to my chest.

The three North Country landowners immediately res- ponded with smiles but then put me in my place with the warning, 'Don't let it happen again. If you had been beaten you would have been lynched.'

I hobbled out of the stewards' room happy to have escaped a fine – and a mauling from the public – straight into the Welsh doctor who recognized my plight.

'It must be hurting you,' he observed. 'Let me have another look at your foot.'

By now the agony was taking over from the tension and excitement. No longer was there any reason to pretend it was my right foot and I was only too pleased to reveal the real injury to my left foot. When the doctor realized he had been fooled he nearly had a fit. But, quick to see the funny side, he laughed, shook his head and walked away.

The Irish entry in my medical book did not state which foot had been crushed!

God was on my side that day. If the doctor had insisted on inspecting my left foot he would not have let me ride for weeks.

Sea Pigeon's worldwide reputation galloped ahead of him to the shores of America in 1977. We had been invited to take part in the Colonial Cup, but the trip proved something of a disaster for we crashed out during the race. Peter Easterby still chuckles at our misfortune – 'It's the farthest anyone has been for a fall.'

A local trainer, Jonathan Sheppard, son of the former Jockey Club handicapper Dan Sheppard, was kind enough to provide horses for Sea Pigeon to school with before the race. Almost as many race fans as turn out on the big-race day came to watch Sea Pigeon try his hand schooling over American-style fences. In height the green spruce fences stand somewhere between English hurdles and fences, but their appearance is deceptive. It is possible to kick the top off one and survive, as we were soon to discover. The punters must have wondered what they were watching once we started to jump. But their disbelief could not have compared with my horror as the session progressed.

The horse that led us out to our starting point for the schooling session set off at a gallop ahead of us. Incredibly he did not jump, but went outside the fence, just clear of the wing. Predictably Sea Pigeon reverted to his old vice and gave me a hard time: wrenching my arms, he tried to run out and join the leader.

Our first experience of American fences was becoming a bad dream, sure to play havoc with Sea Pigeon's approach to the race. But everyone had been so kind that I felt duty bound to accept what seemed to be a suicidal schooling set-up, although I had visions of the years of patience and hard work that had moulded Sea Pigeon into a super horse being overturned in five minutes of madness.

I could hardly hold him and, to make matters worse, his mind was not on the fast approaching newfangled American fence. His eyes were on the horses galloping alongside the track and my aching muscles told me that he would not be happy until he had joined the leader. He skied the first fence, jumping very big, leaving oceans of daylight between his

tummy and the fence, but frightened himself by landing flat-
footed. The next one he stood off even farther and again
landed deliberately. At the third he took off far too early and
crashed on top of the fence, which disintegrated, brush flying
through the air in all directions. How he didn't break a leg I
shall never know. Sea Pigeon had escaped unscathed but the
drama painted disbelief on the faces of the local jump fans.

'Is this the real Sea Pigeon we've heard so much about?'
they asked.

Peter Easterby called a halt before our confidence was in
the same state as the shattered obstacle. He did not let Sea
Pigeon see another fence for a couple of days and I gave him a
pop twenty-four hours before the race. Happily, he seemed to
have forgotten those first hair-raising jumps.

Overnight rain packed the sandy course even firmer,
providing Sea Pigeon with the fast ground he loves. I have
never approached a jump as fast as we did the third last fence,
which was threequarters of a mile from home. I was talking to
Sea Pigeon, telling him he was tearing into it with
irresponsible gay abandon, and trying to steady him at the
same time, but he didn't listen. He hit the sponge protector at
the bottom of the fence and lost his front legs. Our
momentum was barely checked and we were propelled over
the fence. Somersaulting into a heap, Sea Pigeon jettisoned
me on the solid sand. At the time I thought he was a certainty
as he was travelling with such speed and confidence. But we
still had threequarters of a mile to go and, on reflection, he
never really stayed two and threequarter miles, the distance
of the Colonial Cup.

I lay there on the dusty surface unable to feel my right leg.
No pain, but another dreaded break flashed through my
stunned brain. An anxious Pat Muldoon was quickly on
hand to inspect the casualties of the disaster, but only after he
had seen my fellow countryman Mouse Morris, son of Lord
Killanin, the one-time Olympic chief, who was lying on the

ground at another fence. Pat says, 'Mouse was smiling and told me to get across to Jonjo as quickly as possible because he was dying.'

It turned out that, even though Mouse put on a brave face, his fourth-fence fall from Down First broke his right leg and ended his career. I was much luckier. They ferried me into hospital where I spent the night. The next day I was mighty relieved to be discharged on both legs, if a bit battered and bruised. It transpired that I had clouted a nerve, which had temporarily numbed the leg.

Poor Sea Pigeon was the greater sufferer. Miraculously, he escaped unhurt from our high-speed pile-up, but the exhausting transatlantic trip home took its toll and he returned to Peter Easterby's at Great Habton dehydrated and in a state of shock and depression. He lost condition and looked terrible for weeks afterwards. He had travelled 6000 miles for the first fall of his life and, distressingly, it showed. But the love and affection of his stablegirl Monica Jones was the best tonic for him. Monica took great pride in Sea Pigeon and even used to buy him special rugs. Typical girl, she enjoyed dressing him up and spoiled him with a regular supply of his favourite Polo mints. Sea Pigeon learned that there is no place like home when you are feeling below par.

I well recall those sharp mornings of the mid-seventies above Greystoke Castle in the hilly pinewoods with the weak sun breaking through the trees and illuminating Sea Pigeon's breath as he jigged along the secluded tracks. Ron Barry, Gordon Richards, his son Nicky and I would take it in turns to ride him.

Always cautious Sea Pigeon eyed with suspicion a dead log lying to our right, anxious about what it might conceal. Sure enough, a rabbit, white tail bobbing, darted from behind the log and straight in front of us, interrupting the gentle routine. Sea Pigeon with his nervous side-step ducked away from the disappearing intruder and the weather-beaten log. Then, with no persuasion from me, he returned to an even keel and the well-worn walkway. Sea Pigeon's paradise in those early days was to be miles from anywhere, away from the regimented routine of Gordon Richards's string. Jumping little drains, jogging up hills and walking in the woods. Gordon, who won eight hurdle and one flat race with Sea Pigeon, always sent us on our own way. We had time to think and relax on those bright and dull, damp and dry mornings. The first indelible impressions left on my mind were of a frail, comparatively small horse, such a contrast to the robust jumpers Gordon usually trained.

My great pal and fellow countryman Ron Barry helped me over many obstacles during my career but possibly none more so than all those jumps on Sea Pigeon's back. Ron was strong, but never bullied the horse; he relaxed him, restrained him and helped him forget about the helter-skelter of the track. Sea Pigeon loved jumping for Ron and after racing on the flat, this newfound activity took his mind off the serious competitive world.

When Pat Muldoon moved Sea Pigeon and his other horses to Peter Easterby in 1979, I often wondered if Sea Pigeon was allowed to go out and do his own thing independently of the other Easterby inmates. He was not. One of the first mornings at Great Habton Bob Healy, his lad, thought Sea Pigeon was going to take off with him so he aimed him straight at another horse's backside. Sea Pigeon pulled up and was then content to settle at the back of the string. Mark Birch, Peter Easterby's stable jockey on the flat, and Tim Easterby, Peter's son and assistant, rode him in much of his fast work before each Champion Hurdle.

Peter, who saddled Sea Pigeon to win thirteen jump and fifteen flat races, turned him out for two hours every day in a paddock next to his house. The paddock gate always had to be open before Sea Pigeon was led towards it. Twenty yards from the gate he would take off and no one could hold him. Shamus Donkin, one of Peter Easterby's flat apprentices, was leading a horse to the paddock one day when Sea Pigeon flattened him as he took off to his two hours of freedom. Luckily, Shamus was not seriously injured. Getting away from it all in the paddock and before that on those blissful mornings when we lost ourselves in the Cumbria pinewoods helped to mould Sea Pigeon. Formative times for us both. The flashy, highly strung flat horse was having his outlook changed. The young jockey was storing a knowledge of Sea Pigeon that was to become a bond. Indeed, the beacon of his career.

3

Ireland – Discipline and Danger

The late John O'Brien, Jonjo's teacher at Castletownroche village school, quickly recognized that his tiny pupil was heading for the unacademic world of pitchforks, saddles and horses. The three 'Rs' never did interest Jonjo, who even now takes longer to read up a race than he does to ride in it. While assisting the young O'Neill through his studies, the perceptive O'Brien realized there was more to the bright-eyed boy than his lack of learning suggested and predicted with pinpoint accuracy: 'That smile will get him a long way.'

The smile, which has captivated the racing world, won the hearts of the people of County Cork, and none less than the local bread-van driver, Johnny McCarthy, whom Jonjo helped on his rounds.

Whenever Jonjo is riding on television the large figure of Johnny takes up its place in the armchair opposite the colour set in the small lounge of his house in Banteer, near Mallow. And if his hero happens to win, Johnny cries.

'I am not ashamed to admit it,' says Johnny, eyes welling and an emotional quaver stirring in his Irish voice, 'the tears do run down my cheeks when I watch him winning. It may be difficult for outsiders to understand, but we all loved the little lad. He was like another son to so many of us.'

T.R.

The wind roared round my ears, deafening me to the friendly shrill of the song birds. The chill draught swept up my sleeves on the two-furlong descent down Sledger's Hill; the erect rushes in the bog to the right were the spectators in the stand. Racing past them, head down, legs pumping like high-speed pistons, nothing could catch me. The ivy-clad beech tree at the foot of the hill beckoned. It was my private winning post. One final thrust on the pedals, the handlebars wobbling under the pressure, I sped past the big tree. The loneliness of those solo spins was forgotten as I quietly congratulated myself on winning another race which could have been at The Curragh or Phoenix Park.

The glory of success and the adoring cheers from the crowd dimmed as I swung left past the ornate stonework which supported the iron gates at the start of Lord Doneraile's long drive. As I straightened up, the high grey wall on the right kept me company for the last mile and a half before the enormous beech trees shrouded the final climb into the village. There O'Keefe's garage would welcome you at the start of the drift down into the single street which is Doneraile.

The dread of lessons was nearly enough to make me turn back as I pulled left into school just before the bridge over the river Awbeg. But I knew the reception waiting for me at home if my father realized I had played truant. School was the lesser of two evils. Rain, hail, sleet, snow, fog or wind failed to take the punch out of my pedals as every morning I imagined I was riding to the races. Not to the school I detested.

Dad's terse order – 'You cycle to school every day. If you want to be a jockey you've got to be tough enough to take the knocks' – unbelievably coincided with the start of the Doneraile school bus service. In 1964, when I moved from the local Castletownroche village school to Doneraile, I thought I had been blessed with this new school bus, not realizing it was to be for all the kids except me. The bus stopped outside my father's grocery shop in Castletownroche and delivered the children seven miles away at the Christian Brothers' School in Doneraile. And, to rub salt into my aching legs, I knew it was free. Dad's decision did not make sense to a three-and-a-half-foot, three-and-a-half-stone twelve-year-old. Why waste time and energy pedalling past the Shinnicks' farm, through Dromdeer Woods and round by the impressive white gates at the entrance to Lord Doneraile's estate when you could take it all in from the luxury of a bus seat?

My three brothers before me – Jerome, Dennis and Thomas – had survived the early-morning and early-evening ritual to and from school. But they had no alternative, for there was no bus in their day. Was Dad being bloody-minded in forcing me to maintain their spartan tradition? I thought so at first.

In his heart of hearts Dad, who is a cobbler by trade, would have liked to have been a jockey himself but he never got the chance. One of his brothers went away with plans for an apprenticeship at The Curragh, only to return home, tail between his legs, beaten by the tough life. With his brother's failure in mind, Dad insisted I was too frail and weak to pursue the perilous path to jockeyship and tried to point me in other directions. But he finally accepted that I would not be moved from my goal.

I proposed a deal. 'I'll bike to school on my own every day if I can become a jockey.' He agreed. And I knew that meant every day in term time; I would have had to be at death's door to be let off those fourteen miles on two wheels.

The lesson had been learned from my eldest brother Jerome, six years my senior, who one day found the road close to the river Awbeg in Dromdeer Woods flooded. Along with his pals, he soaked his coat in the water before turning back to cycle the three miles home. He walked into the shop to tell Dad that it was impossible to cycle through the flood, displaying his wet coat to emphasize the appalling conditions. He had not finished explaining before he was pedalling back to Doneraile with Dad's wrath ringing in his ears. Jerome was the only child from Castletownroche that day to shoot the Dromdeer rapids and go to school.

Dad's discipline and singlemindedness in the way he brought us up never wavered. He did what he believed was right for us regardless of the views of others. In our younger days his orders were followed by a clout if we failed to adhere to them; when we reached fifteen or sixteen the rod of iron turned to sound reason and advice and he discussed all manner of matters with us. Despite his stern rule, Dad was warm and emotional to the point of appearing soft, with a grand sense of humour. He hasn't changed.

He was always supported by our hardworking mother, who died in 1977, and it is testament to their devotion that we have remained a very close-knit family. Mum rose before six to cook our breakfasts, which fortified us for the forty-five-minute bike ride to school. She helped run the shop and, I am told, was generous to a fault with the poorer members of the community. She was invariably the last to bed in the early hours after busying herself round the little house, perhaps preparing her special mouthwatering dish of lamb and white sauce.

Even when Dad clamped the boxing gloves on us it was to show us how to fight cleanly and stand up for ourselves. If ever we fell out with each other or had a scrap with another child, Dad would dash upstairs to fetch the boxing gloves, take us into the yard behind the house and make us punch it out until the best man won. I think he got a kick from watching us knock hell out of each other, though we never suffered more than a bloody nose or a raw stinging face.

Dad's warning against the demon drink certainly hit home, for none of us boys or our wives drinks or smokes. He used to stress what folly it is to believe you are a better person with a drink inside you. In excess, drink takes happiness from the home, he told us.

To this day Jerome, Dennis, Thomas and I know we can ask Dad's opinion on any matter or worry that may be playing on our minds. Dad rightly maintains that he is our best friend in times of trouble, but I shall never forget the cold words, 'Don't come to me when drink has got you into trouble.'

I got the message, for I knew that if I could not discuss a problem with Dad it could spell the end of an affinity which had grown up between us during those happy but hard times.

Summer evenings cycling back from school up the long straight overhung by the whitethorn and blackthorn hedges and trees covered with clinging ivy, rabbits playing at the roadside, suddenly the Skenakilla crossroads would halt progress. The Griffin Bar on the far side of this dangerous crossing acted as a reminder that Castletownroche was close by. Mick and Hanna Griffin drew many of their regulars from the village. Farther on, the Shinnicks' grey farmhouse set back behind ornamentally trimmed hedges; at last the water tower standing high on the ridge to the left and overlooking the Awbeg rippling through the glen beneath Castletownroche.

Most children would wend their way after school on a sunny evening to the Castletownroche seaside, the Awbeg – which, folklore has tell, is the cleanest river in Ireland – scattering their towels along the grassy banks down by the Old Mill before splashing into the crystal-clear water. I was often tempted to freewheel down the hill to the bridge by the Old Mill on the road to Ballyhooly to join them, but I knew I must turn right and climb the main street to help with jobs in the shop before starting my homework.

Castletownroche, with a population of around eight hundred, lies midway between Fermoy and Mallow and some twenty miles north of Cork City in Ireland's biggest county – Cork. It takes its name from the Roche family, of Norman extraction, who erected the turreted castle there high above the Awbeg in the thirteenth century. St Mary's Protestant church stands to the east and the Roman Catholic church of the Immaculate Conception, where we worshipped, at the top, west, end of the village. Each front door of the pronounced square houses opens onto the pavement, the scene of much neighbourly gossip and passing pleasantries between housewives leaning on their brooms while resting from their daily chores.

No tea until the jobs have been done: restocking the shelves in the shop with bags of sugar, cartons of eggs, cereals, potatoes; sweeping out the yard behind the house or tending the greyhounds Dad keeps for racing. Even back on the bike to deliver groceries, flat out, crouching in the saddle. Riding another winner, of course.

From the age of six I would disappear into the street in search of the horsedrawn cart belonging to the Hunter brothers, John and David, and their sister Margaret-Rose, who lived a mile out on the Mallow side of the village at the Grove, under the ever watchful eye of the Nagles Mountains which rolled along the horizon to the south. If I found their cart I would scramble into it, pleading with them to take me to their farmyard to play with their donkeys and ponies. My first association with horses.

The Hunters have never let me forget one of my earliest visits when, according to John, I stood only inches above the top of his gumboots. I begged to be thrown up onto the back of their hunter called Tom. The moment I was astride him, my legs at full stretch, he arched his back and threw me to the ground. That was my first fall but I immediately pestered to be lifted straight back again and rode Tom bareback round the field.

My seventh birthday at the Grove is a vague recollection, but again Margaret-Rose is for ever reminding me of the temper I flew into. Seeking refuge from Jack, the Hunters' greedy greyhound, my friends and I laid out a tablecloth on the rocks overlooking a quarry at the far end of a field above the farmyard. With great care we placed my birthday cake, sandwiches and even Easter eggs on the cloth. But we had forgotten the cups and had to dash back to the farm to collect them, only to return to the quarry to find Jack had devoured every morsel – sandwiches, Easter eggs, birthday cake and its seven candles.

Blind with rage, I sprinted the four hundred yards back to

the farm yelling at the top of my voice. Margaret-Rose says she never witnessed such fierce anger in a seven-year-old as when I stamped my feet and expressed my total hatred for Jack. An early glimpse of the O'Neill short fuse.

I remember leaving the low-windowed cottage with its corrugated-iron roof to post old mother Hunter's letters. I rode one of the ponies to Castletownroche post office, my pay of sixpence clenched firmly between my front teeth. Two girls from the village joined me on their bicycles and I couldn't resist showing them how good I was. I'll produce a trick or two, I thought. The pony walked into the village with this whip of a lad standing on its back, turning round and jumping down into the saddle. So easy, I boasted. Until I landed clumsily, crashing my groin against the saddle, and, eyes smarting, swallowed the sixpence. Dad quickly put me on a course of castor oil and religiously maintained a daily search of everything that passed through me but after a week he gave up. That silver sixpence is now in good company inside me with the screws and metal plates which have since been added to strengthen my battered limbs.

There was no escape. The two trucks were on a collision course and evasive action seemed out of the question with nowhere to go apart from the two-foot-high grass bank and bright yellow gorse hedgerow above. A bread van is not designed to leap off the road at a second's notice and the awful truth was we were inextricably hemmed in.

Those few seconds seemed to span a lifetime. Rolling among the prickly gorse bushes would be paradise; instead we were staring death in the face as we charged at forty miles an hour into the solid engine, bonnet and cab of the oncoming van. Behind us rattled rows and rows of empty but heavy wooden bread trays, which would rocket forward on impact, nailing us into the fast-approaching vehicle. The grim prospect was unbearable.

Johnny McCarthy's bulky figure hung heavily over the steering wheel before bursting into life, the large clumsy-looking hands heaving and releasing, heaving and releasing the steering wheel. Johnny was half standing up to balance his hefty frame against the strain of pulling the wheel round to the left. My knuckles were white as I gripped the bar in front of the passenger seat to steady myself. It meant leaning into the collision but I took a crumb of comfort from having a support to hold on to. Johnny was all hands and arms as he wrenched on the black steering wheel and we jolted up, bread trays clattering in all directions in the back. I was sure the van was toppling over, but Johnny, his foot flat on the accelerator, extracted maximum power from her and scythed through the gorse with our clumsy conveyance leaning into the road at a precarious forty-five degrees, miraculously missing the small lorry laden with pigs. A dreadful screeching of metal tore into our eardrums, though it was impossible to pinpoint the damage. Clearly we had not avoided all contact and it transpired that the driver's wing mirror had been ripped off the side of the van. A small price to pay when, only seconds before, total disaster had appeared inevitable. We had escaped death by inches.

The narrow winding lanes of County Cork are not made for racing bread vans but Johnny still accelerated back onto the road and away from that blind bend, the excited pigs and their relieved driver. We had run out of bread at Templemary on the delivery run between Kanturk and Buttevant, and Johnny, in a hurry as always, was returning to the bread depot at Kanturk to reload the van. Settling back over the steering wheel he turned to me, those bold blue-grey eyes and that captivating smile measuring the relief passing through his big body.

'We made it, son,' he shouted above the groaning engine.

The beads of perspiration breaking out in tiny balls across his broad forehead told their own story of how close we had come to ending our great partnership in that bread van.

Before we reached Kanturk I was aware of a new excitement. My whole body was fired by a force it had never experienced before. I found myself waiting to go through those explosive moments all over again. Johnny had made me aware of danger for the first time in my life and I loved it.

Hurtling along the tiny roads, rolling from side to side as Johnny threw the van into its task of taking bread from Keating's bakery in Kanturk to the shops of the surrounding countryside, was a new adventure in the holidays. I was so small I could climb under the shelves in the van and unload the trays for Johnny when he called at Dad's shop. Then I would join him on his rounds, flirting with the exciting uncertainty of every corner.

Johnny was a fast driver and, as I hung on with both hands to the rail across the windscreen in front of the passenger seat, I would pull my feet up onto the bar and balance between my hands. At every bump in the road I soared over Becher's Brook. On landing safely I looked across for the seal of approval from Johnny riding upsides.

'Another good jump,' he shouted with one eye on the fast-approaching bend, the other twinkling encouragement in my direction. 'You'll ride for real round Aintree one day,' he forecast.

As if there were not enough surprises in store as we hurtled round every corner, Johnny took me to be measured in an outfitters in Doneraile. For what, he would not tell me.

We returned a week later and when the tailor produced a pair of jodhpurs for me to try on Johnny said, 'They are payment for the breadman's mate.'

In front of the fitting mirror I cut the dash of a real jockey. I could not contain myself posing there in my first pair of jodhpurs. Johnny says when he saw a couple of tears trickle down my cheek it was all he could do to stop himself from crying.

I am delighted to say that Johnny has transmitted his dash as a driver to the greyhounds he now trains with great success at Banteer, near Mallow.

I emerged from Fermoy Hospital with blurred vision after having my eyes tested. My sight was not as sharp as it should have been for a ten-year-old who had by no means overtaxed his eyes with his school books, although by the time the doctor had finished putting drops in them I could hardly see at all. However, as the medication worked its way round each socket I was able to focus better until my vision was near perfect.

But that was not before Dad and John Hunter arrived home that night to present me with my very own sixteen-month-old pony, who quickly helped me to forget all about my suspect sight. In the morning Dad and John had been to Mallow horse fair, about ten miles from Fermoy. Dad took an instant liking to an unbroken pony, but her owners were asking far too much for her and by six o'clock in the evening they still had not sold her. Dad, never one to give up easily, overheard them arguing about the price with a prospective client and butted in.

'Have you sold her? If not, how much do you want for her?' he asked the owners, who were caught unawares and admitted they were still without a sale. After some fast talking and haggling Dad gave them £27. Plus two bob for luck!

Those £27 I had earned from tips for delivering messages, groceries and running errands and also included my £3 winnings from the Castletownroche donkey race. Every penny had helped to turn golden dreams into the reality of my first pony. I called her Dolly and, after breaking her in, hunted her with the local Duhallows Hunt when she was still only two.

As I weighed only three and a half stone it was no problem for Dolly to lead the pack over stone walls and five-bar gates, filling her postage stamp of a rider with a sense of adventure never experienced before. If the other members of the hunt ever wanted a lead Dolly would not hesitate. She loved showing the way and we had four great years galloping across the Duhallows country, which could not have been a better classroom for a brave young pony and its enthusiastic if inexperienced partner. We complemented each other with similar have-a-go attitudes, a far cry from Neddy, the donkey I could not steer round Castletownroche.

Despite navigational problems, Neddy had carried me to my first riding success, worth £3, a small fortune to an eight-year-old. Neddy, owned by local farmer Bill O'Brien, used to tow his cart laden with milk churns down to the creamery on the banks of the Awbeg at the bottom of Castletownroche. He knew every leisurely pace of the mile route to the creamery and was quite content to follow exactly the same footsteps back with monotonous reliability. So when I got the chance to ride him in the Carnival race, which started and finished at the Castletownroche creamery, I could not wait to show him, and the rows of spectators lining the pavements, who was boss. Neddy could show his paces when he was not anchored by his cart. He flew up the hill under the misapprehension that he was going home, but when I tried to boot him round Donie McHue's corner, sure enough, he refused to deviate from the only street he knew and stood there, feet glued to the tarmac and eyes focused unflinchingly ahead. Only after plenty of persuasive prodding and pushing from the crowd did stubborn Neddy eventually consent to turn and scamper back to the creamery, amazingly still ahead of his rivals.

Dad insisted that I hand over my coveted £3 winnings to Bill O'Brien. I suspect he knew all the time that Bill would not want to deprive me of those crumpled green notes which had been carried home with such pride in my sweaty palm.

My right hand and wrist ached and my writing deteriorated

as yet another slip of paper was surreptitiously pushed onto the desk. I was unable to write fast enough to keep up with the flow of notes gathering at my elbow. The headmaster, my greatest friend on the many occasions when uncertainty hung over the O'Neill career in the classroom of Castletownroche village school, was feeding me information during the Irish exam.

John O'Brien saw the problem. He had a pupil who wasn't interested in learning and yet he still wanted to assist him through another academic crisis. My English and maths were passable for the final exams at Castletownroche, but Irish I never understood for the simple reason that whenever an Irish lesson loomed I asked Mr O'Brien if I could be excused to go and clean the toilets and he invariably granted permission. Now I was paying the penalty, muddling up the answers he so generously passed to me. I was certain I had copied them down wrong.

It took six weeks for the results to come through and I was sweating in the knowledge that Dad was so keen for me to succeed. Eighty per cent was the pass mark. And I got exactly eighty.

4

Ireland – Flight into the Unknown

Michael Connolly, Jonjo's master at The Curragh, sent two champions to England, Killiney, the ill-fated steeplechaser bursting with so much promise, and Jonjo.

Connolly describes his apprentice as 'always the gentleman', but adds, 'I had to put the brakes on him, he was always in such a hurry, trying to run before he could walk. If I had not checked him during those early days his career may not have blossomed the way it did.

'Jonjo did not know what fear was and even now a disregard for his own safety can prove his downfall. Too often he appears to throw caution to the wind. When he won his first steeplechase on Stan Royal at Navan he made three lengths at every fence on a horse that no other jockey was keen to ride.'

By cautiously protecting Jonjo, Connolly believed he was acting in the best interests of his apprentice and preserving his promise for more mature days. But Jonjo, young and inexperienced, could not help wondering if his career was being stifled.

T.R.

To stand accused of killing someone you love suggests a degree of insanity on the part of either the defendant or the person pointing the finger. Michael Connolly, to whom I was apprenticed at The Curragh for three years, believes that I was responsible for the death of Irish Painter, the horse who the year before at Downpatrick had given me my first win over hurdles and whom I now looked after, worshipped and lived for.

Now, Michael is perfectly sane. Furthermore, he is no fool. Yet he reckons I caused the tragedy that overtook Irish Painter when he broke his shoulder in a last fence fall at Naas in 1972. I cried when Michael told me that the way I rode him put him on the floor at the last. Even now I shudder at the suggestion.

I still ride for Michael Connolly when I visit Ireland and I respect his judgement and undeniable ability as a trainer. He has been preparing horses to win races with a regularity that has hoisted him near the top of Irish racing for close on forty years. But I don't think he will object when I say that he can be a hard man at times.

His words bit deep. 'If you had not asked Irish Painter to be so bold at every fence he would not have come down at the last.'

I was young and eager and made plenty of mistakes, but did I really cause the death of a horse who meant so much to me? Perhaps I should not have taken on the trail-blazing leader and instead allowed Irish Painter more time to settle into his fences. On reflection, attack may not have been the best policy. But raw experience was bound to drag me into the pitfalls of raceriding so early in my career.

Michael fits the bill of the old traditional school of trainer, the tough taskmaster who stands no nonsense from the lads – and he is quite right. He maintains he had to put manners on me when I first joined his stable, Westenra, as a sixteen-year-old in 1969. He says I was trying to run before I could walk and he had to apply the brakes. If he had not, he claims, I would have wound up down-country in a small stable surrounded by second-rate horses. I admit I was in a hurry to establish a foothold on the bottom rung of the ladder. I wanted the rides to prove myself. But Michael, in his protective way, kept me on a tight rein.

That January Monday morning after Irish Painter had been killed I dropped into the yard over the back wall from my landlady Mrs Talt's house with the other lads to save the valuable minutes it would take to walk the two hundred yards down the road and through the main entrance to the stables, which are tucked alongside the main Belfast-Cork railway line. If ever we were late there was less chance of Michael Connolly spotting us jumping down onto the barrel below the high wall at the bottom corner of the yard. I hurriedly picked up my kit, together with the usual fistful of carrots to feed Irish Painter, and without thinking went straight to his box, the first in the line across the gravel yard from the Connollys' yellow-painted house. I opened the stable door and only when the stark emptiness hit me did I remember the previous weekend's disaster. I was in such a hurry it had temporarily slipped my mind. Those bare black and white walls, the manger in the corner. Their loneliness hit me like a ton of bricks. I looked down at my handful of carrots and in my moment of sadness allowed them to slip gently onto the concrete in front of the doorway. I dropped my kit beside them and traipsed back, dragging my feet through the grey gravel, to knock on the boss's door.

Fighting back the tears I asked, 'Can I leave on Friday, please?'

Michael recognized my grief and nodded. 'If that's what you want.'

On the Friday I walked through the gates of Westenra onto the busy Kildare Road which was eventually to lead me to England.

Originally I joined Connolly after spending a year at the Mallow stables of Don Reid, a wonderful man to work for. When Don packed up training some of his horses were sent to Westenra and I went with them.

I even left Connolly in the middle of my apprenticeship and worked for the former Newmarket trainer Fergie Sutherland at Killinardrish between Coachford and Macroom in deepest County Cork. Michael Connolly would not release my indentures, preventing me from riding in races for Sutherland. After three months exercising horses, among them Takette, the dam of Jeremy Hindley's high-class flat-racer Muscatite, round the banks of the beautiful Lee Reservoir, I returned to the bustling horse centre at The Curragh and Michael Connolly.

My first winner was Lana on the flat in September 1970 at The Curragh where I deadheated with fellow apprentice Michael Teelin, who was tragically killed in a riding accident the following year. Increasing weight forced me to start thinking about forsaking the flat for a career over jumps. My very first mount in a steeplechase, Stan Royal, won at Navan, after my hurdling baptism on Irish Painter.

My enthusiasm to grab the opportunity of a spare ride on Stan Royal was tempered by his lad when he came to collect the saddle after I had weighed out. In fact he frightened the life out of me.

'Have you seen Stan Royal?' he asked.

'No,' I replied.

'He's 17.2 hands. Real big bugger and pulls like a bloody train,' said the lad.

As I walked into the paddock, I could see for myself that Stan Royal was a powerful chaser. His owner, Mrs Sharrock, shattered what little confidence I had left with the instructions, 'Settle him, he is a hard puller.'

My knees started to knock at the prospect of riding a tearaway in my first steeplechase. But cantering to the start I made sure I had a tight hold of him and, once I knew I was in charge, I let his head loose and rode him on a long rein. We jumped off in the middle of the field as the tapes went up, but as we approached the first fence he was tanking on and I did not know whether to take a pull or give him a kick in the belly. I decided on the more aggressive course of action and Stan Royal jumped the fence brilliantly. Passing the stands for the first time he was running free, so I dropped him in behind the field and to my surprise he settled sweetly. At the last open ditch down the far side he clipped the top and I went shooting up his neck and round his ears before scrambling back into the saddle. There were only two in front of us at the second last fence. One was cantering, the other struggling, and I thought I could be second. Stan Royal jumped the fence brilliantly and, as we bore down on the last fence, the leader was about six lengths in front. I picked up my whip and gave Stan Royal three sharp cracks of encouragement, then gathered him. He measured the fence and took it beautifully. Another couple of belts with the stick and I couldn't believe my eyes.

I muttered, 'Flippin' hell, I'm going to win,' as with each tired stride Stan Royal courageously reduced the leeway. Gradually we wore down our rival to win by four lengths. A spare ride in my first chase. All this, after being frightened out of my living wits by the prerace build-up.

My first chase on a spare ride whose lockjaw antics I had been convinced would sap every ounce of strength from my aching limbs before turning me into a helpless passenger.

A single win in each type of race, one on the flat on Lana, one over hurdles on Irish Painter and one over fences on Stan Royal, is hardly the greatest reference for a new job. But in 1972 it helped me cross the Irish Sea to join Gordon Richards at Greystoke in the Cumbria countryside of northwest England.

I suspect the most influential part of my reference came from Paddy Joe Lombard, Dad's cousin, who farms and breeds racehorses at Ballyhooly just off the road between Castletownroche and Fermoy. After Dad had spoken to Michael Connolly one day at Mallow races about the progress I was not making, he asked Paddy Joe to talk to him. The fine, tall figure of Paddy Joe, instantly recognizable under his big trilby, approached Michael on The Curragh racecourse.

'Michael, Jonjo isn't getting many rides,' said Paddy Joe.

'It's quite a problem,' declared Michael. 'He's getting too heavy and maybe he'd be better going jumping.'

Paddy Joe went to Castletownroche to break the news to

Dad who, having pinned all his hopes on my becoming a flat jockey, was bitterly disappointed. But he understood that the thickening shoulders and lengthening legs influenced my future. If I was to make any sort of life in racing it would have to be among the even tougher breed of National Hunt riders. He instructed Paddy Joe to use his contacts in England and try to find an opening for me over there.

Paddy Joe sold yearlings at the Doncaster Sales run by Ken Oliver, the Scottish jumping trainer. He got in touch with Ken only to be told he was full up with boys, but Ken suggested he try Gordon Richards. Paddy Joe followed up a telephone call to Gordon with a letter stipulating that there was no point in my going to England without the promise of rides. Another dead end, and I knew that Dad would force me to quit racing altogether. But Gordon agreed to take me and provide me with some mounts in public.

I can never leave Westenra without recalling the May morning in 1970 when Killiney, the most exciting jumper to have been dispatched by Michael Connolly across the Irish Sea, won the stamp of approval from the great English trainer Fred Winter. After Killiney had won his bumper race at Punchestown by six lengths Fred arrived at the stables with a view to buying him.

Fred is not easily frightened. But his rugged face was furrowed with an alarm which revealed a rare uneasiness in the former champion jockey.

The high-pitched shriek of the whistle had rudely interrupted the busy but orderly return of Michael Connolly's string from the morning's second training session. Two pigeons had started on one of their daily swoops towards the paddock, but even these local inhabitants took evasive action and, with a flutter of wings, climbed skywards from the deafening noise. In the yard the lads with pitchforks, saddles and buckets bustled in and out of their horses' boxes oblivious of the hideous sound which had become routine at Westenra.

But for Fred Winter, unfamiliar with the surroundings, the piercing blast on the whistle shattered the leisurely echoes of the tuneful birds as he made the acquaintance of the immensely impressive Killiney. Fred and Killiney were in the paddock, which was separated from the main railway line between Belfast and Cork by only a high hedgerow. The whistle heralded the approach of the mid-morning train, immediately followed by a vibrating clatter and roar as ten coaches thundered past at eighty miles an hour only yards from the hedge.

Fred's concern must have been accentuated by a fear of the unknown. The disturbance was unnervingly close at hand on the far side of the hedge but completely out of view, shielded by the bright new growth of spring green leaves. He sat cautiously astride Killiney's massive back waiting for him to rear up, buck, shy, kick or release the power coiled like a spring beneath the saddle into an arm-wrenching gallop. It was the natural reaction. But to Fred's astonishment Killiney confined himself to an inquisitive prick of the ears.

The train and its noise became a distant hush in the southerly direction of Cork and Fred was almost as surprised as when the whistle first broke the silence. He could scarcely believe that Killiney had stood stock still and not moved an eye during the commotion. But the inhabitants of Westenra were adept at turning a deaf ear to such noisy intrusions.

Fred spent half an hour trotting, turning, cantering and receiving the answers he wanted to the questions he put to Killiney. He had come to find out if the big horse lived up to his reputation which had flashed through the training centres of England. Winter, seven times National Hunt training champion, makes it his business to sit on almost every prospective purchase. 'It's amazing what you can learn from half an hour on a horse's back,' stresses the maestro.

I was not much bigger than Killiney's wonderful, intelligent head and, understandably, Michael Connolly would allow me only to walk, trot and occasionally canter on Killiney. Otherwise we may have arrived in Cork before the express.

Predictably, Killiney was to prove one of the most exciting of the many talented chasers to pass through Fred's Lambourn stable, an embryo champion, who was first groomed for stardom at Westenra. In England he won six hurdle races and eight chases, but his meteoric rise to the top was tragically ended by a fatal fall at Ascot less than three years after he had privileged Fred with that first glimpse of his enormous presence and class, to say nothing of his unruffled approach to the most unusual of interlopers in stable routine – the Belfast-Cork express.

Revisiting my roots in Ireland has always proved the warm homecoming I enjoy. Victories and defeats at Leopardstown, Navan, Fairyhouse, Galway, Punchestown, Tralee or Mallow have also meant meeting old friends, acquaintances and the family, whose magnificent support remains as solid and encouraging as it was that winter's day I first left for England in 1972.

But when I returned in the summer of 1982 I didn't see a friend or even a horse ...

The warm, cosy cockpit of the twin-engined Aztec lulled me into a false sense of security. Oblivious of the hazards that lay ahead, I was content to play out the minor part of passenger from the seat alongside the pilot. Until he asked me to take the controls.

'I must have a close look at the map. Here, hold the joystick for a minute,' he instructed, taking my right hand and placing it on the steering column in front of him. He explained how the two main gauges must be kept level, otherwise we would dive into the Irish Sea.

Occasional buffeting and gusting at altitude served as a reminder that I was not flying a jumbo jet to Tralee on the pretty west coast of Ireland. Brief glimpses through the breaks in the cloud confirmed our position. Thousands of feet below, the vast carpet of grey-blue sea neatly bordering miles of dead straight golden sands was fast approaching. The Cumbria coast. Currents in the atmosphere lifted and lowered the light aircraft but she handled smoothly enough. Visibility might have deteriorated marginally since we had taken to the skies without incident from the White Heather Aerodrome near Wigton, the scene in 1981 of my agonizingly abortive attempt to ride again after smashing my leg. This time it was the pilot who was worried, though I couldn't fathom the reason for his concern.

Right hand outstretched, it was a perspiring palm that greeted the joystick. Inside my collar my neck was heating up and giving off beads of sweat to dampen my shirt and remind me – as if I needed it – of the flying nerves I suddenly discovered I possessed.

The seaside passing below waved goodbye to England; the humps, hills and mountains enveloping the serene pockets of water which are the Lake District were behind us and forgotten. Even the ever-present thickening cloud had to be ignored.

The luminous white-on-black gauges were set in my sights and the joystick was firmly balanced to ensure the altimeters remained level. No one had ever told me I would be a pilot. The white-shirted, fair-haired young man on my right wrestled with his maps before eventually pinpointing the route to our first refuelling stop at Douglas in the Isle of Man. Concern covered his countenance on hearing the unwelcome weather reports through his headphones. My confidence increased and my sense of power grew. As I tilted the joystick gingerly to the left then to the right the aircraft dipped slightly one way and then the other. O'Neill Airways were in full flight.

The pilot satisfied himself that he knew where we were flying and in one movement grabbed the joystick in his right hand and waved me to sit back in my seat with the left.

'That's good. We're right on course,' he affirmed with a surprisingly encouraging air. I sincerely hoped we were, for the farther west we flew the worse the visibility became. Fog or low cloud – I wasn't sure which – made for a hazardous approach to Douglas. The forecast for Ireland was so grim the pilot threw in the towel and refused to go any farther.

The weather must not be allowed to win, I thought, annoyed at the pilot's surrender. I had to get to the races for the County Meath trainer Noel Meade, who had made no secret of his fancy for Pinch Hitter, on whom I had won the Galway Hurdle, when he rebooked me to ride him in the £7000 hurdle at Tralee.

The pilot was not happy with the approach to Douglas Airport and the tension in the cockpit reflected his feeling of apprehension as he craned forward trying to catch sight of the runway lights. At last the amber, orange and finally green illuminations alongside the main runway brought relief to both of us and helped guide us to safety.

Spurred on by the prospect of winning the big race on Pinch Hitter, I joined the queue of Manx holidaymakers who were trying to make alternative travel arrangements after their plans had been thrown into confusion by the surrounding fog. That grey day of August 1982 clearly affected their holiday spirits for they were very subdued. But I had no time to contemplate the vagaries of the weather and rang Robert Sangster, Britain's leading racehorse owner and worldwide bloodstock dealer, at the Nunnery, his Isle of Man retreat, to ask if I could borrow his plane and pilot. Robert was not at home, but I succeeded in persuading Air Taxi, a local firm, to have a go.

We took off and, after putting down to clear customs at Shannon Airport, we started the tense search for Tralee's local airstrip at Farranfore, which stands close by the Killarney–Tralee railway line. The new pilot, armed with a positive self-assurance, swept away any apprehensions I might have been harbouring after the nerve-shaking flight to the Isle of Man. But my newfound confidence was soon shattered when he slowed the aircraft and dropped it so that we were almost hopping over telegraph poles as we groped through the haze for a glimpse of those grey parallel strips of metal, the railway line.

'This is how accidents happen,' he said icily.

With those disconcerting words he probed for improved visibility below the long sheet of fog. A winding river appeared and then left us. But no railway line. The pilot persevered with one eye on the map, the other hawkishly peering out of the cockpit for landmarks. Still no railway line. Just thick blobs of unrelenting fog, punctuated by the terrifying intrusion of telegraph poles far too close for comfort. My eyes ached from the strain of staring through the cockpit Perspex. The pilot relieved the clammy tension between us with the curt announcement, 'I'll kill us if I continue this low. I am climbing to safe air above the murk. The railway line is lost in the fog.'

The disappointment of being forced to turn away from the day's centre stage Tralee racecourse gripped my stomach, though by the time we landed at Shannon again to clear customs en route for the Isle of Man any pangs of regret had left me. At Douglas I telephoned the White Heather Aerodrome to ask the original pilot to come and collect me and also rang for the result of the race.

Pinch Hitter had won, with Tommy Carmody deputizing for a fogbound, flight-lagged and by now bemused jockey.

I spat every swear word I could lay tongue to deep into the mouthpiece. Then, tempered by the day's series of setbacks, I viewed this final reverse philosophically. I could still be waiting for a lifeboat in the middle of the Irish Sea. Or worse, be wrapped round the telegraph pole which was relaying this hurtful message.

At nine o'clock in the evening, exactly twelve hours after take-off, we landed back at the White Heather in as bright conditions as we had seen.

I walked through the door at home determined to conceal my day of defeats. Sheila greeted me.

'Did it win?' she asked with almost infectious enthusiasm.

'Yes,' I sighed.

'Oh, marvellous!' replied Sheila.

5

Drought, Depression and
Nearly Back Home

It was a shy, angelic-looking O'Neill who arrived at 13 Park Road, Greystoke, early in 1972. He was nineteen years old. The three-bedroomed semidetached council house was to become Jonjo's home for the next three years. Sheila Lancaster, the landlady responsible for introducing her lodger to English home life, recalls, 'He may have been quiet and shy, but there was a little of the devil behind that lovely smile. One day I had some friends coming so I made a double portion of the chocolate cake which I normally gave the lads. Jonjo, in particular, usually made a pig of himself because it was like the cake his mother used to bake for him at home in Ireland. But when I came to offer the cake to my visitors the tin was empty. Jonjo and Tony Meaney, another of the lads from Ireland, had eaten the lot. I was so annoyed at the time I was on the verge of packing their cases and putting them out on the road. I didn't laugh then, though I can now; they were happy days.

'I have always felt that whatever success came Jonjo's way was fully deserved. He did nothing but work and sleep while he was here. On Sundays when other lads were off you would find him up on Gordon Richards's gallops picking stones.'

T.R.

I threw open the car door, scrambled on to the grass verge and made my first mark on English soil. The sudden sickness which overcame me was the after-effect of the flight from Dublin to Newcastle that February day in 1972, followed by the unsettling undulations of the military road along which Gordon Richards's wife Jean drove me so swiftly en route from Newcastle to Carlisle.

I had never flown before and this was my first visit to England for my new job with Gordon Richards at Greystoke. Nerves were understandably churning around inside me, but they must have received their final telling uneasiness from the rollercoaster which was the military road. It seemed to stretch for as far as the eye could see, rising and sinking so sharply in places that I wondered at times if I were being driven over the edge of the world.

The dry mouth was the warning that I was going to be sick and I quickly called out to Mrs Richards, 'Stop the car.'

Then followed that uncomfortable welling from the stomach before the awful retching motion. I made sure I missed my bright brown shoes which I had polished so thoroughly for my first meeting with my new boss Gordon Richards. It could not have been an edifying sight for Jean behind the driver's wheel and she must have wondered what sort of person she had picked up at Newcastle Airport. An Irish lad who could not ride in a car. I suspect she must have secretly thought, Can he ride a horse!

I climbed back into the passenger seat, presenting a pathetic, white-faced figure to my new trainer's wife, who tried to pull me up by the bootlaces and steer my mind away from car sickness. Close by our emergency stopping point stood Chesters Camp.

'That ancient settlement houses the finest example of Roman baths outside Rome,' said Jean.

Not that I was interested in ancient history, but Jean's easy conversation helped sweep away my embarrassment as we drove across the north of England, with its impressive rolling hills ravaged to bleakness by the freezing temperatures of winter. Jean pushed my temporary state of ill health into the background as she explained how Emperor Hadrian had erected the snakelike fortification which kept popping up away to our right. It was Hadrian's Wall.

The wall punctuated our progress by suddenly appearing and just as quickly disappearing from sight. My mind was continually being distracted from the depths of historic Britain by the dangerous dips in the road, which, according to

Jean, were the cause of many fatal accidents on this narrow highway which scythed its way through Northumberland, linking Newcastle in the east with Carlisle in the west.

On parade in Gordon Richards's stable yard the following raw February morning I felt strange but fully recovered from my journey. I was nothing but impressed. The boxes cosily encircled the entrance to the Richards's flat, and the surrounding Cumbria parkland, hills and fells were a paradise for working and schooling horses. The stables stand above the paddocks of Greystoke Castle, which is owned by the Howard family, who in turn are closely related to the Duke of Norfolk. Variety was the spice of every horse's life at Greystoke. How could they possibly become bored, with the vast expanse of hills, woods and tracks for their daily exercise?

Not long after I arrived the head lad, Ron Lauder, left and I was asked to take over the responsibility of looking after Titus Oates, who only ten months before had won the 1971 Whitbread Gold Cup. Titus Oates provided me with the first leg of a double spanning three days, the memory of which I shall cherish for the rest of my life. I felt I had made it as a fresh-faced nineteen-year-old when I led up Titus Oates for the following month's Cheltenham Gold Cup. I could not believe my luck on my first visit to the Mecca of steeplechasing, being so closely involved with the famous race. Titus Oates's best days had passed him by but he still gave me a memorable experience, although he never struck a blow in the race, which was won by Ireland's Glencaraig Lady, ridden by Frank Berry, whose wife Clare is the daughter of Mrs Talt, my landlady at The Curragh.

Two days after the Gold Cup I went to Uttoxeter, where I rode my first English winner on Katie J, who scrambled home by a desperate short head from Pride of Coulter. I had carved up Richard Evans on Pride of Coulter and paid the penalty. Richard objected and was awarded the race in the steward's room; Katie J was disqualified and placed second.

My immediate fear was wondering how Gordon would react when we got home. Jean, who was with me at Uttoxeter, used all her diplomacy to smooth the way for me and Gordon simply said, 'Oh, you can't do that in England, you know. Just knocking them out of the way like that.'

Our little village of Greystoke did not boast a Catholic church and the only way Tony Meaney, another Irish lad from Kilcullen, near Kildare, and I could get to a Sunday service was by forking out 50p for the six-mile lift to St Catherine's Church in Penrith. Tony and I shared digs in Greystoke and our landlady Sheila Lancaster's father used to drive us to and from church. Tony helped me through many homesick moments but I didn't enjoy our visits to the Boot and Shoe pub in the village, where Tony used to play dominoes with the lads. I could not understand the various English accents, although Tony acted as a great interpreter. I did not drink or smoke and when Tony first mentioned dominoes I wasn't sure if he ate them, collected them or played with them! They were lonely days, and without Tony I don't think I would have lasted long at Greystoke.

I returned to Castletownroche at the end of the season in June with one disqualification from six rides. Gordon left the job open for me but I hesitated, wondering if I would find myself up another dead end as I had done at Michael Connolly's, only this time out of reach of home. Eventually I decided to return to Greystoke in August and my next four rides sealed my future. They all won.

Gordon Richards's Alexandra Parade was my first official winner in England in the Snitterfield Selling Hurdle at Stratford on 23 September 1972. Alexandra Parade, who broke down at the second last flight and then had to survive an objection, clouted the last hurdle so hard he went down on his knees, handing the advantage to the challenging Archook. But Alexandra Parade rallied with such gusto we were four lengths clear of Archook at the line.

Lady Luck smiled sweetly at Stratford, but seven weeks later, in November, at Cheltenham she turned her other cheek and the events of the calamitous afternoon spilled over into the bright lights of my Saturday night out.

The friendly inferno of the dance floor was a welcome if artificial relief. The cacophony of the band, the bustling couples swept me away in the smoky haze of multicoloured lights a million miles from the glare of the earlier unwelcome publicity. Pretty girls, painted and primed for their weekly shindig, and the lads with their pints were more confetti with which to cover the cracks of a bad day.

The Salutation pub at Threlkeld, near Keswick, suddenly became my refuge. Sipping an orange squash I sprawled untidily on the chair and the tension drained from me. The lads' tip-off looked spot on.

'Spend Saturday night at the Salutation and you can't go far wrong. Plenty of lasses there,' they said.

One girl stood out with her short blonde hair, lovely legs and pretty, innocent face, which, from a distance at least, required no heavy make-up for presentation at the Salutation.

I gulped my orange squash, placed the glass on the table and rose to my feet, nervously checking that my blue tie was straight and correct. A dance with the little blonde would raise my spirits high above the day's debacle, which I was convinced had booked my one-way ticket back to Ireland.

Suddenly a thick, piercing finger thrust into my neat tie, met my chest with an unfriendly thud and was followed by a tirade of verbal abuse.

'You jumped off Proud Stone. I know you did because at 20-1 you didn't back him.'

I was confronted by an accusing stranger shoulder to shoulder, eyeball to eyeball. The near empty pint pot clutched to his chest was all that kept us apart.

I needed this inebriated idiot like a lead parachute. Only six hours earlier I had been in tears trudging back to the jockeys' room from the last fence at Cheltenham where I had fallen off Proud Stone in the Mackeson Gold Cup. My inexperienced eagerness had cost us victory in the big race.

My youthful lack of confidence led me to believe that I was doomed never to get another ride in England. I had been shot out of the saddle in full view of the fickle racing world, who were either packed in at Cheltenham or witnessing my disastrous acrobatics on their television screens. My uninvited critic had obviously seen the drama too.

I felt my fists tightening; then I thought better of hitting him. It would only spell more trouble. I wasn't going to attempt to explain the truth for I knew I would be wasting my breath.

'Excuse me, I'm going for a dance,' I said, pushing my way past the unsporting intruder.

To my bitter disappointment the little blonde girl was being whirled round the dance floor. I had missed out for a second time in what had become the saddest, the longest and, I thought, the last day of my English racing life.

Proud Stone was owned by Jimmy McGhie, a farmer and milk retailer from Lochmaben in southwest Scotland. Mr McGhie had won the 1964 Champion Hurdle with Magic Court and liked nothing more than beating the bookmakers into submission.

He had hoped Gordon Richards's stable jockey Ron Barry would be able to ride Proud Stone, but Ron could not do the weight of ten stone. As the Mackeson Gold Cup is one of the most competitive and important early-season races, Mr McGhie was entitled to ask Gordon to engage another top jockey. But Gordon insisted on entrusting me with the pressures of the big occasion and the responsibility for Mr McGhie's cash.

I grabbed the chance with unbridled enthusiasm but first,

before I left Greystoke with Jean Richards, I listened hard to the boss's carefully explained orders. Those forceful blue eyes widened as if to emphasize every word. The thick frankfurter fingers gesticulated to ensure I did not forget the minutest detail.

'Stick Proud Stone in the middle of the field,' said Gordon. 'Bide your time and be sure to wait, wait, wait. Produce him going to the last and you will win.'

To be told I would win the Mackeson against the three-times champion jockey Terry Biddlecombe, Andy Turnell, Bill Smith, John Haine, Philip Blacker and other illustrious names sent my head soaring into the clouds.

Gordon's plan unfolded smoothly: as we bore down on the last fence only Red Candle and Jimmy Fox stood between us and victory. The big time was awaiting me on the other side of the fence. Or so I imagined.

To be absolutely certain of winning I slapped Proud Stone down the shoulder signalling for him to stand off from the fence and produce one big, final, ground-devouring leap. He answered to such purpose and with so much power that he blasted his jockey up and out of the saddle.

Proud Stone cleared the fence fluently enough, but I was left behind in midair before biting the turf. I lay in a heap, totally destroyed, and convinced I would never get another ride in England. I'd be better off catching the boat back to Ireland than returning to Greystoke to face the boss and perhaps even Mr McGhie, whose cash I had lost.

Two St John Ambulance attendants helped me to my feet. My head was almost in the grass it hung so low on the walk back to the jockeys' room. Oblivious of the turned faces and curious eyes of the crowd, I felt the tickle of tears running down my cheeks and was filled with dread at the thought of trying to explain my expensive howler to Gordon. In a matter of strides my wildest dreams had exploded and my whole world collapsed around my ears.

The tactful sympathy of Jean Richards was a bricklike foundation on which I could start to rebuild my shattered confidence.

'You conjured too good a jump out of him at the last after everything had gone so well for you,' Jean said with a warm understanding. 'Proud Stone ran a great race.'

That was one wonderful way of trying to salvage some self-respect out of the wreckage. In my heart, which was still racing with rage, I knew I should have won. And, to make matters even worse, Gordon Richards would agree.

'It's better that I don't come home and see the boss,' I suggested like a coward. 'I'll make my way back to Ireland if you could pack my bags and send them on.'

Jean, never slow to assess a situation, realized that if she did not pick up this pathetic figure and shake off the shackles of defeat and depression, his confidence might never be rekindled.

'I'll speak to Gordon before you see him and all will be well,' said Jean reassuringly on the drive north on the M5 and M6 to Greystoke.

Standing nervously on the steep stone stairs leading to the Richards's flat above the yard I could only faintly hear the exchanges between Gordon and Jean.

'Come on up,' instructed Jean. 'Gordon would like a word with you.'

To my horror Gordon foisted the telephone receiver on me and said, 'Here, Mr McGhie would like to speak to you.'

My hand was shaking until I rested the phone against my ear and offered a feeble 'Hello' into the mouthpiece.

'You tried to be a big name and it didn't come off. But forget it,' growled McGhie's Scottish tones down the line.

I handed the phone back to Gordon and couldn't help overhearing McGhie's voice, 'You told me he was some kid. Well, he may be but he doesn't get my money back for me.'

Gordon put the phone down and I offered my apologetic side of the story. 'You gave me the chance, boss, and I realize I have let you and Mr McGhie down. I'm sorry.'

'Well, I know that. If you had sat still and let Proud Stone jump the last in his own time you would have won,' replied Gordon in a sterner tone of his West Country brogue.

I counted seven newspapers on the Sunday and Monday which carried the dramatic picture of Proud Stone's jockey on his way into orbit above Cheltenham's last fence. The photographers had not seen the like of it before and they made more of my mistake than of Jimmy Fox's triumph on Red Candle. They say all publicity is good publicity and my name was certainly catapulted before the racing world that weekend. Although at the time I firmly believed that my short-lived career in England was over, it turned out that I benefited in the long run from the media exposure.

It was not a swashbuckling O'Neill who was thrown up into the saddle aboard Kirwaugh at Ayr the Monday following the Mackeson fiasco. Indeed, I was desperately looking for a boost to my ailing confidence. Conscious that Kirwaugh was favourite for the first race of the day, I knew I must put it all together this time. Gordon instructed me to bide my time and bring Kirwaugh with a run from the second last hurdle.

All the alarm signals went out when I found myself in front a mile from home. This really was 'Desperation Stakes'. Defeat after disobeying orders would definitely book my ticket back to Ireland.

I must win. Immediately after taking the lead I rode Kirwaugh flat out to the finish, which was an exhausting mile away. Riding with the devil on my tail, I was amazed how Kirwaugh gallantly answered every crucial call. He was so gutsy he won despite me.

I was legless when I jumped down in the winner's enclosure, where Gordon Richards's wry smile said enough to send me shuffling into the weighing room with an enormous sigh of relief.

My luck had changed but my confidence was still in dire

need of bolstering by a series of successes. The trickle became a steady flow and after my first fifty rides had produced twenty-one winners I wound up my second English season, 1972–73, with a total of thirty-eight, which won me the Junior Championship. Gordon's stable jockey Ron Barry was champion with a record-breaking 125 winners.

Twelve months after the Cheltenham fiasco on Proud Stone, a voice came out of the clouds as if it had been sent from heaven. I was leading a novice chaser called Ribbon Hill round the Newcastle parade ring a few minutes after Titus Oates had won the Swift Chase there in November 1973.

I had been successful only twice in the first three and a half months of the 1973–74 season and was worrying where the next winner was coming from. The drought, which followed an early-season broken wrist and collarbone, was responsible for my depression. At twenty-one, I needed to secure a solid future, and leading up racehorses was not my idea of a suitable career. Yet again thoughts of returning to Ireland were playing on my mind.

'Can you ride Clear Cut at Wetherby on Tuesday?' was like music in my ears.

I switched my gaze from the tarmac walkway round the paddock to the far side of Ribbon Hill, where I could see Charlie Hall, the long-established and highly respected trainer from Towton, near Tadcaster in Yorkshire.

'Thank you, sir,' I said, marvelling at the prospect of a mount for the Hall stable. 'I shall have to ask Mr Richards. And if it is all right with him I would very much like to accept.'

Gordon agreed. And four days later I won Wetherby's Castleford Chase on Clear Cut by four lengths from our National Hunt champion trainer to be, Michael Dickinson on Donohill. Clear Cut, a fine big horse with a lovely long neck, used to take a strong hold, and the more you struggled against him the harder he pulled. I wasn't capable of fighting against his headstrong habits and, innocently perching on his back, I suited him.

Clear Cut loved to take his field along, and coming to the last he was still running away in front. He pricked his ears and did not take the slightest notice of the fence. The infectious cheers of the crowd were of more interest. Clear Cut clouted the fence so hard I was shot skywards. By some miracle I landed back safely in the saddle and the big horse's massive stride was barely interrupted.

He marched ceremoniously up the run in to a victory which opened the floodgates for his jockey. From then on the winners began to trickle in: he carried me to victory in the Topham Trophy at the Aintree Grand National meeting in March and by the end of the season in June I had climbed on fifty-one winners.

I often recall that dreary day at Newcastle when the whole course of my career was altered. Without Clear Cut I believe I might have caught the ferry back across the Irish Sea with my tail between my legs.

Clear Cut would often doss in his races and, when you were least expecting it, lapse into the most diabolical blunder. With the Topham Trophy fast approaching, several jockeys said, 'I wouldn't ride Clear Cut over Grand National fences for a fortune.'

I suppose at the time I wasnt fully aware of Clear Cut's idiosyncrasies, but our styles blended. As it transpired, Clear Cut turned in a flowing, faultless round of jumping. They set off so fast he could not reach his customary position at the front so I let him bowl along at his own pace and he was brilliant at every fence. He didn't lose an inch at the giant Chair fence, and I didn't realize we had passed Becher's he took it so smoothly.

I have never enjoyed such an exhilarating ride over the Aintree country. Sadly, it is a course that seems to have turned sour on me – I have failed to complete in eight Grand Nationals.

Clear Cut is now a spritely twenty-year-old and happy as Larry turned out at his owner Bill Hemingway's place at Beckwithshaw near Harrogate.

During the five years between 1972 and 1977 spent at Greystoke, Gordon Richards propped up the ladder and provided the secure rungs for me to climb. He primed the ammunition for me to fire and it was his professionally thought-out training programme which ensured that many of the bullets were on target. The former jockey and boxer from Combe Down, near Bath, gave me the chance I had craved for ever since the days when I played at jockeys, pedalling down Sledger's Hill and through Dromdeer Woods to school.

No jockey, not even Gordon's namesake, Sir Gordon, or Lester Piggott, can go without the horse. Incidentally, to avoid confusion with Sir Gordon, Gordon has added the letter 'W' to his name. It stands for J.C. Waugh, the trainer to whom he was apprenticed in Berkshire during his early riding days. Hence, Gordon W. Richards. It was G.W.'s horses that launched me.

He laid the foundation stone on which I built my career, and I will never forget the impetus he gave to my progress. I am even more aware of his help now as I enter a transitional stage in my life and switch my thoughts to training. The seasons 1975–76, when I rode sixty-four winners, and 1976–77, when I had sixty-five, promoted the Richards–O'Neill combination as a regular winning partnership.

But behind the success pressure was mounting. The roots of my discontent went back to January 1975 when I smashed my right leg for the first time. It was encased in plaster and this restricted my mobility. When I returned to Greystoke my landlady Sheila Lancaster could not accommodate me with a bed downstairs, so I moved into the Richardses' flat above the stable yard.

Having struggled to the top of the steep stone steps, I stayed in the flat, which was furnished with all the conveniences I required – good food, a telephone and an office all on one level. I started to recover my mobility once the plaster was removed, but I did not feel I could return to my digs. I felt I would be insulting the Richardses by rejecting the comforts they had laid on. The situation was awkward and gradually became fraught. I was very comfortable, but possibly too available. I answered the telephone, assisted in the office, and generally helped Gordon and Jean as, indeed, they had helped me.

I chauffeured Gordon to and from the races and, on occasions, he would stay behind after a meeting and have a drink with his owners to discuss the horses. As a result my spare time in the evenings was rarely my own and I was finding it difficult to pursue my various interests and meet my friends, including Sheila, my future wife. I first met her in 1973 when she used to stay with her aunt, Gwen Smith, two doors down from my digs in Park Road. Our romance started that summer when Sheila, who worked in a hairdressing salon in Carlisle, used to cut my hair.

Gordon probably did not realize it, but I felt that in a way he was dominating me and restricting my lifestyle. I could see the pressures building up in him. His outlet was to blow a gasket and lose his temper, either with someone in the yard or with me in the flat. I wasn't strong enough to take it and occasionally would let fly back. Once I threw the car keys at him, jumped in the back of the car and left him to drive us home.

And yet, underneath Gordon's fiery exterior, there is a soft-natured person. He is like a horse: the more you play with him and humour him the easier he is to handle. If I had had the confidence of Ron Barry, who was a great foil to

Gordon, I would probably still be stable jockey at Greystoke now.

To leave Gordon would either be the best or the worst thing I could do. I was not sure which, but I felt I had to make the break. If I had stayed with him I would probably have partnered his two Grand National winners, Lucius and Hallo Dandy; on the other hand I would not have ridden a record 149 winners in a season.

It was a drastic decision that took a mighty amount of heartsearching. I sought the views and opinions of many, many friends. I spent evenings with Ron Barry and his wife Liz at their attractive house overlooking Ullswater in the Lake District, driving them barmy with the never ending question: 'What shall I do?'

I addressed the same question to John Lowthian, my accountant and business manager, in his office in Carlisle, where we sat for several hours well into the night shortly before I announced my decision. We kicked around all the possibilities, explored every avenue and angle, trying to foresee the outcome if I stayed or if I moved on.

Ginger McCain, trainer of Aintree's greatest hero, the triple Grand National winner Red Rum, and his wife Beryl at their house in Southport provided two more shoulders for me to cry on. My Roman Catholic priest, Father David Murphy, was a wonderful rock, to whom I could reveal my innermost feelings. But the mental anguish became unbearable as I turned the problem over and over in my mind. At times I wondered if I was not better at enduring physical rather than mental pain.

At the end of the day the Barrys, the McCains and John Lowthian agreed that if I left Gordon I would have to settle for around half my regular haul of winners which we reckoned would work out at about thirty. In the circumstances, I would be happy with that, and in any case, if I was going it alone, I would have little option, I thought.

I returned to Castletownroche in the summer of 1977 with the troubles of the world resting on my shoulders. I still did not know what to do. I asked Mum. I asked Jerome. I asked Dennis. I asked Tom. I sought help from the Almighty. All the time I knew the final decision had to come from my own muddled mind.

And yet it was probably Dad's simple appraisal that suddenly slotted the previous weeks of mental agonizing into perspective.

'If you are not happy you won't do a good job,' he said. Really that was the last word, for once I had digested Dad's view I was in no doubt – I was leaving Gordon Richards.

With Dad's words uppermost in my mind, I returned from my holidays in Ireland, called on Gordon's mother at Combe Down in Somerset, and then travelled north to Greystoke.

I braced myself, walked into Gordon's office and announced, 'I want to broaden my career and experience. I want to leave.'

Gordon, visibly shocked, asked me to go away and think seriously about my decision. I told him I had tormented myself with the problem and had made up my mind.

I left Gordon's office with a spring in my step, relieved of the burden which had weighed so heavily. My confidence was bolstered. I was my own person again.

6

The Season

Jonjo's newfound independence helped launch him on his record-breaking season in 1977–78 in which he rode 149 winners.

Peter Easterby, three times National Hunt champion trainer and the mainstay behind Jonjo's record run, supplying nearly a third of his haul, picks out two of his horses – Netherton and Major Thompson – on whom he believes O'Neill excelled that winter.

'Netherton at Newcastle in January is one horse that definitely should not have won,' recalls Peter. 'He blew up twice in the race, but Jonjo still drove him over the last two flights as only he can. It was at a time when the horses and the whole yard were in full swing and the jockey was in top form. I know Jonjo gave him a very hard race, but Netherton was a very tough horse.'

Jonjo won two hurdles on Major Thompson that season and, according to Peter, 'Major Thompson was a difficult ride simply because he was not honest; a villain of a horse, who hadn't a heart as big as a pea. But Jonjo was brilliant on him and got on so well with him that Major Thompson didn't even know he was racing.'

Peter moves on two seasons to Grand National eve 1980 to find Jonjo's greatest race, the Kennedy Asphalt Hurdle, which he won on Starfen by a neck from Hill of Slane. Jonjo called on all his and Starfen's resources without resorting to the whip.

Peter recalls, 'It was very bad ground at Aintree and the whole field, including Starfen, was stone cold. If Jonjo had gone for his whip he would never have won and he knew that. So he sat tight, rode him with hands and heels, held him together and just won. If he had panicked or flapped at all he would have been beaten. By holding Starfen together and asking him for one final effort right at the death he just lasted home. No one else would have won on him.

'Jonjo is the strongest jockey I have ever seen. Fred Winter never rode for me so I don't know as much about him as I do about Jonjo, but he certainly could not have been any better than Jonjo.'

Peter trained Majetta Crescent, on whom Jonjo won his 126th race of the season at Perth in 1978, beating Ron Barry's five-year-old record. In its essay on Majetta Crescent, *Timeform's Chasers and Hurdlers 1977–78* highlights O'Neill's gritty will to win.

'O'Neill is the most reliable of jockeys riding over the sticks today; we cannot recall seeing him lose a race which he ought to have won during the season. He is also, by some way, the most masterful finisher in the game; his driving power on the flat is phenomenal. His overwhelming determination to get to the line first at all costs seemed at times to inspire his mounts to do the impossible for him in a tight finish; time and again he won races that lesser riders would have lost. Make no mistake, any horse that O'Neill partners gets the best of riding. If he keeps clear of injury he should have a long reign as champion.'

T.R.

The Monday of the last week of the 1977–78 season was producing pressures unique to me and, indeed, never before experienced in the history of National Hunt racing. The burning question was: Would I ride 150 winners by Saturday?

I was confident I would reach this landmark as I stood in the tiny wooden stewards' room at Hexham racecourse in Northumberland. Three hours before my appearance in front of the stewards, Toughie had won the first race to provide me with number 148, and while punters eagerly waited outside for the outcome of my objection in the last race, I was certain I would be awarded the 149th. My mount, the odds-on Shirello, owned by the North Country steward Alan Mactaggart, had finished second, beaten by one and a half lengths by Even Cooler, ridden by the wisecracking Dennis Atkins.

After I had presented my case for the objection, Dennis quickly stepped in with a telling observation. From behind his ruggedly misshapen face, bashed and bent in a series of crashing falls, he snorted, 'It's all lies. And I must point out that Jonjo is desperate to ride 150 winners this season, while this is only my nineteenth, less than one sixth of Jonjo's total.'

For a moment Dennis's plea sounded valid and looked like

winning the sympathy of the stewards, so I again stressed that he had bumped me and virtually turned Shirello round approaching the last fence, checking our momentum and costing us many more lengths than the one and a half by which he had beaten us.

'It's all lies,' repeated Dennis, who could not contain himself any longer. His dented and distorted nose started to wrinkle, betraying the first signs that the whole Atkins act was a charade. He began to shake and then broke into a gushing roar of infectious laughter, which quickly enveloped me, and we rocked to and fro in front of the stewards. They must have thought we were standing there as some kind of joke, and not for the serious business of trying to elicit a fair result from them. If we weren't careful we would both be stood down for insubordination, I thought.

Dennis's saving grace was the fact that the incident had taken place between the last two fences, partly out of sight of the stands, and there was no camera patrol film for the stewards to study. I make no bones about the rights and wrongs of the affair, in which Dennis was entirely in the wrong and I should have been awarded the race. The stewards overruled my objection; they only had my word that Dennis had drifted out towards the middle of the track and, suddenly realizing he had left a gap for me, had brought Even Cooler back to block my run. Not only did he carve me up but he gave me such a heavy bump that Shirello was turned sideways and left facing in the opposite direction.

It was a miracle that the horse remained on his feet; Dennis should have been suspended for months for reckless riding. He admits that he would not have beaten me had he not come across and given Shirello the 'treatment'.

Out there on the course in the thick of the steamy action no quarter is given and only the toughest survive. Dennis broke the Rules of Racing but was not reprimanded or disqualified because, in illegally plotting my downfall, he chose a part of the race which was out of view of the stewards. Then, during the final act in front of the stewards, rather than introducing tension and nastiness into the inquiry, he brought laughter and frivolity, which softened the blow that helped to prevent me from reaching the magic 150 winners. The night of my champion jockey's party at the Scotch Corner Hotel in North Yorkshire a few weeks later, Dennis was laid up with an injury, but he still telephoned to tell me how useless I was not to have made it 150!

Helpless was how I felt watching another chance to reach that magical figure pass me by as I had a bird's eye view of Pleasure Seeker, whom I should have ridden, winning the first race at Market Rasen's night meeting on the following Saturday, the final day of that epic season. Earlier that afternoon at Stratford I had managed number 149 on Lothian Brig, owned and trained at Ponteland in Northumberland by John Alder, whose chaser Tant Pis and hurdler Low Pastures put him on the racing map before his delightful daughter Valerie did so well on Bush Guide, the horse he gave her for her twenty-first birthday.

I had agreed to share a plane from Coventry to Market Rasen with amateur riders John Docker and Tim Thomson Jones, whose father later made such a successful switch from training a mixed string to concentrating on flat horses at Newmarket. Tim rode in the 4.50 race, which was a three-and-a-quarter mile chase, and consequently we did not leave the course until about quarter past five, only an hour and a quarter before Pleasure Seeker's race at Market Rasen. John Docker's wife drove us to Coventry Airport about twenty miles away but the heavy Saturday traffic snarled us up and as we tried to sit patiently in the weekend procession of cars I wondered quietly to myself whether we would be able to keep to our tight schedule. We dashed from the car to the twin-engined aircraft waiting on the tarmac at Coventry Airport and within minutes were speeding above the Midlands. On the descent to the strip in the middle of Market Rasen racecourse my heart sank. The runners for the first race were parading in the paddock and I knew we would not be allowed to land while the horses were walking round. I have never experienced a better view of a race, circling the course as the little objects below chased each other round the tight track, but we were flying at too great an altitude to be able to pick out the colours. Two horses raced to the line clear of the rest of the field and I joked, 'That's Pleasure Seeker winning.'

John Docker and Tim Thomson Jones agreed and started to pull my leg. 'You've blown your 150, Jonjo.'

Not until we walked from the middle of the little Lincolnshire course through the enclosure to the weighing room did I realize the true meaning of the maxim 'Many a true word spoken in jest.' I was crestfallen when it registered that Pleasure Seeker, with my near neighbour Phil Mangan deputizing, would have given me my century and a half if I had not arrived late. At the time it did not really matter, for I thought that Three Musketeers, my mount in the fourth race, would win. I held Three Musketeers up for a late run and was still brimming with confidence when we swept into the lead approaching the last flight, but he clouted it hard and was too tired to answer my final despairing lunges and the late rally of Any Second ridden, would you believe, by Phil Mangan. It was a night Phil, who was once apprenticed to Sir Gordon Richards, still recalls with justifiable pride from the far side of the beer pumps at the String of Horses, his pub, which is about five miles from our farm at Skelton Wood End.

Dennis Atkins, who also retired to a life of pulling pints at the Plough and Harrow at Gaulford, near Malvern in Worcestershire, still gets a great kick out of reminding me, with that wicked twinkle in his eye, how he cost me my 150 by knocking me sideways at Hexham. But, in fairness, he was also responsible for setting the seal on the greatest day of my racing life, Wednesday, 19 April, at Perth – or, rather, it was the untimely intervention of the driver of a dark green Volvo saloon car.

Dennis had stayed overnight in Perth for the second day of the meeting and was taking the Scottish air on a walk round the streets of the town with his fellow jockey David Munro. As Dennis sauntered across one of the main roads he did not notice a green Volvo bearing down on him. He had to break into a run to avoid being picked up on the bonnet. As the wide protruding bumper missed his legs by inches Dennis jumped and only half landed on the kerb, losing his footing on the edge and going down awkwardly on his left ankle. He was in desperate pain, unable to put his foot to the ground and was convinced he had broken it. David Munro secured a lift to Perth's Bridge of Erne Hospital where Dennis underwent X-rays, which did not reveal a fracture, but he was discharged with a heavily strapped ankle and later limped onto the racecourse on crutches. Of course, he had to give up his booked rides, and Bill Atkinson, the Carlisle trainer of Dennis's last-race mount, Tiger Feet, asked me to step in as it was the one event open to me for which I had no booking.

The day before, after winning on Father Delaney at Perth and taking my season's total to 124, within a winner of Ron Barry's five-year-old record of 125, I had telephoned Sheila, to whom I had become engaged on my twenty-sixth birthday, the previous Thursday, to tell her that I doubted that I would ride another winner at the meeting. I knew Peter Easterby planned to run Father Delaney again the next day if he showed no ill effects from his victory, but I had looked through the runners and, frankly, believed there was one to beat each of my four mounts. I relayed this message to Sheila, told her I did not have a ride in the last and would be able to make an early getaway so as to be back in reasonable time after racing.

Perth is Scotland at its most serene, putting man at peace with himself. The racecourse lies four miles to the north of the town, in Scone Park in the grounds of Scone Palace, owned by the Earl of Mansfield. The River Tay, famous for its salmon fishing, flows past the racecourse at the far end of the track by the two-mile start. That Wednesday, under a warm Scottish sun and a cloudless blue sky, Perth racecourse was at its most appealing. A friendly crowd added to the easygoing atmosphere which sent the fourteen jockeys filing out for the first race in more of a holiday mood than a fighting spirit. It was an unlikely setting for two and a half hours of history-making drama.

For me it was an inestimable asset to be able to embark on the day that was to become the most memorable in my racing life without a care in the world. I had completely written off, if only for the afternoon, the chance of equalling or passing Ron Barry's record.

Besciamella, trained in East Lothian by Wilf Crawford, was my mount in the first race, Division One of the Breadalbane Novices Hurdle. She started 7–2 third favourite and, in my book, had no chance of toppling the favourite, Tempting Times, trained by Tony Dickinson and ridden by his son Michael. How wrong could I be? Besciamella belted the last hurdle with her front legs and still won by seven lengths, with Tempting Times only fourth.

Our victory nudged the temperature of the sleepy jockeys' room up a degree or two as the valets beavered away and the other jockeys became more intense. Or was it just me? The lads would not allow me to forget that Ron Barry and I were the only two jockeys in the world to have ridden 125 winners in a single season. There was a slight tightening of the tummy muscles and fluttering of butterflies as I pulled on the black and white colours of Jimmy Jack, the owner of Majetta Crescent.

My mount in the Charles Campbell Memorial Handicap Hurdle would not have been in the line-up if his trainer, Peter Easterby, had had his way. So the prospect of his rider sweeping into the history books was a remote one. To this day Peter tells the tale that he only sent Majetta Crescent to Perth because his owner, Jimmy Jack, lived nearby. Majetta Crescent had been suffering from a blood disorder, but Jimmy Jack had been keen for his horse to run at his local meeting. As the Perth meeting approached Majetta Crescent started to carry more condition and looked better but a blood test showed that the red and white corpuscles were not matching up correctly. Peter wanted to save Majetta Crescent for a later engagement but felt that he could not keep on trying the owner's patience with the news that his hurdler was still not ready to run. After being prescribed every vitamin imaginable Majetta Crescent began to bloom again and Peter decided to risk sending him to Scotland. Even with so much uncertainty surrounding his wellbeing, Majetta Crescent started 13–8 favourite and I broke Ron Barry's record on a horse, who, at the time, could only be described as an invalid. The happy ending was typical of my association with Peter Easterby that season when we won numerous races with the odds apparently stacked against us. Peter, who provided forty-five of my 149, admits that we were successful with some animals who had no right to win.

Perth, with its small timber weighing-room block, holds warm memories, partly because racing is never held there in deepest winter owing to the inaccessibility of Britain's most northerly course when the Scottish snow blizzards are in full cry. But also thanks to the local Perthshire lairds, dressed in kilts and carrying their crooks, who provide a unique racecourse atmosphere – an air of *joie de vivre* cloaked with Scottish respectability. It is extremely unlikely that the outstretched acres of Scone Park have ever attracted such a posse of pressmen, photographers and television camera crews in a single day.

Majetta Crescent's walk from the course to the number-one spot was lined with jumping enthusiasts, who, to a man and woman, heaped congratulations on us. The cameras clicked and as we neared the winner's enclosure two separate television crews ran on each side of us, bumping into onlookers while they filmed the winner of the 3.15 at Perth for the national news on BBC and ITV. I dismounted and, as Graham Lockerbie fastened the rug under Majetta Crescent's proud neck, microphones were stuffed under my nose. But there was no time to conduct interviews; the priority was to weigh in. This I did, but the moment I handed my saddle over to my valet, Peter Saint, Ron Barry descended on me in one merry mass of euphoria. The big fellow grabbed my hand and shook it, wrapped a congratulatory arm round my shoulder, hauled me to the weighing-room door, hoisted me onto his shoulders and carried me aloft out into the full glare of the cameras to be greeted by the hundreds of Scottish throats roaring appreciation. Celebrations were cut short by the call for me to weigh out in time to ride Crofton Hall in the fourth race, the Killin Handicap Chase, for my great friend the Cumbria farmer John Dixon. Top weight of 12 st 7 lb and the presence in the field of Tommy Stack's mount Wylam Boy would prove Crofton Hall's undoing, I thought, even though Tony Dickinson's Old Sid was likely to start a well-backed favourite. I was wrong again. Crofton Hall was left to coast home ten lengths clear of Wylam Boy after Old Sid had crashed out in the lead four fences from the finish.

Father Delaney started slightly odds on for the Crieff Novices Chase, although I must confess to being worried about how much his race the previous day had sapped his strength. My concern was unfounded, for he won almost as easily as he had twenty-four hours earlier. The chief danger, French Pin, and his jockey David Goulding parted company when delivering a menacing challenge at the third last fence.

Besciamella, Majetta Crescent, Crofton Hall and Father Delaney, my first four-timer, hoisted me onto a pedestal from which I could look down on racing with a heady confidence I have never experienced before or since. I find distasteful success that changes a person so that he or she suddenly believes that his achievements put him above his colleagues and out of reach of those who helped shove him towards the top during the early formative days. Without wishing to put too fine a point on it, people, however clever, successful, foolish or uneducated, are too precious to be treated with contempt. Even the most unsavoury character will have a good side to his or her personality, even if it may not at first be apparent. Always give people the benefit of the doubt before writing them off, and never allow a few winners, goals, runs or records to force a wedge between yourself and the crowd. After all, God created us all and it is up to each of us to make the most of our different lives. Having pontificated about the pitfalls of believing your own rave reviews, I must come clean and admit that for a few unreal moments those four winners and breaking Ron's record put a crown on my head and made me feel king of the world.

Trotting round the Hunters' fields on their ponies in Castletownroche, roaring along the lanes of County Cork in Johnny McCarthy's bread van, jumping ditches on my pony Dolly with the Duhallows Hunt, pedalling flat out down Sledger's Hill on my way to Doneraile school, or just wrestling with my homework under the ever watchful eye of Mum and Dad above the shop in Castletownroche, I was spurred on by my boyhood dream of becoming a top jockey. And here I was, dazed by the realization that the rungs of the ladder had run out.

Peter Saint gave me the kick I needed to bring me back to the floorboards of the Perth jockeys' room.

'It's not all over, Jonjo,' he said. 'Remember, you are riding Tiger Feet in the last.'

I had completely forgotten about my late booking and Dennis Atkins's close shave with the big green Volvo in Perth. The cloud suddenly enveloped me and I thought, Why the hell should I ruin a perfect day by ending it with my only loser? I became annoyed at the prospect of struggling round Perth racecourse on Tiger Feet when I could be speeding back to Sheila. Tiger Feet's form was not strong enough to suggest she would win and I went out onto the course with the experienced and discouraging opinion of Dennis Atkins ringing in my ears: 'She is not very good.' But I hadn't forgotten the cries of the boys in the jockeys' room as I walked out through the door – 'Go on, Jonjo, whatever you ride will win.'

Their sentiments rang rather hollow when I realized that the favourite Pennington, trained by Ken Oliver just outside Hawick in Roxburghshire, had boasted winning form at Kelso and Sedgefield and was strongly fancied to make it three in a row. But in my favour was my own recent form, which meant my confidence was sky high. Somehow – and don't ask me how – Tiger Feet and I hit it off: we threw down our challenge to Pennington, the leader, over the last hurdle and on the flat Tiger Feet asserted her authority to win by three lengths at 7–1.

It was some sort of miracle, the way I came by the ride through Dennis's unfortunate accident, and managed to crown the climax of my career with five winners from five races.

On the drive home to Braithwaite Hall, the farm managed by Sheila's parents, Stan and Audrey Mounsey, at Ivegill, where I had moved in to my own room and makeshift office, I was still riding on a cloud of elation. Sheila greeted me with my favourite cup of tea and then, as all too often happened, the telephone took over, interrupting what little chance we had of looking back together on the happiest day of my life. It started to ring again before seven the next morning, leaving Sheila and me with no time to digest and grasp in any detail the wonderful events of the previous hours. The phone continued to ring throughout the morning until I left for

Ludlow races in Shropshire, where Ginger McCain, whose Red Rum had sadly gone lame on the eve of the National three weeks earlier, laid on a 10–1 winner – Pewter Spear – for me, making my total 130.

The racing circus continued at Uttoxeter, Hexham and all points north, south, east and west, allowing no time to stand still and reflect. It wasn't until June, after the curtain had finally fallen on the season, that Sheila and I were married. We spent our honeymoon in Jersey, and it was only when we visited my family in Castletownroche that we began to appreciate the magnitude of 149 winners, and the achievement of breaking Ron Barry's record and riding five winners all in a single day.

The people back home in Ireland left us in no doubt about the depth of their pride and how they had been rooting for me when I approached and eventually passed the 100-winner milestone on Sweet Millie. They had ticked off every winner as I crept towards and finally just failed to reach 150. Friends and family recalled with hearty pats on the back and firm handshakes the very first day of the season at Market Rasen where I rode a double – Border River for Clifford Watts, the Yorkshire haulage millionaire, and Night Adventure for Ginger McCain. That had been the winning start I so badly needed after the public announcement that I was splitting with Gordon Richards.

Then on Monday, 7 November, the day jumping moved centre stage, I couldn't believe my luck. Forty-eight hours after the flat season had ended I booted home Birdland for Peter Easterby at Wolverhampton to reach the personal milestone of thirty winners that I had set myself when I decided to leave Gordon Richards. By proving the doubters wrong, I had erased any lingering worries about the wisdom of that desperately difficult decision. In that golden, wet and wintry November I had twenty-four winners in eighteen racing days.

Sheila told the rest of the family how, on 5 December, she had taken the day off work from her hairdressing salon in Carlisle to drive me on the two-hour journey from Ivegill to Peter Easterby's in time for me to ride out with the first lot at about eight o'clock in the morning. We left Skelton at half past five and arrived at Great Habton in time for a cup of Marjorie Easterby's welcoming tea. I had not been to Peter's many times before and was anxious to do the right thing, so I leaped out of the car as Sheila applied the handbrake and dashed into the kitchen to discuss work plans with Peter. We finished our tea and wandered through to the stable yard, and before I had time to consider Sheila I was mounted and heading with the string towards the gallops. We returned to the house an hour and a half later and I couldn't understand why Sheila was not in the Easterby's spacious kitchen with Marjorie, whose warmth and inquiring friendliness makes everyone, even the remotest stranger, feel at home in her company. I walked out to the car parked beneath the ash trees alongside the high wall by the entrance to the Easterby's garden to find Sheila sound asleep in the driver's seat. I opened the door and asked, 'Why didn't you come in?'

'I nodded off,' she replied apologetically.

Peter greeted Sheila in the kitchen. 'Did Jonjo bar you from the house, then? I wouldn't have done that to the dog. How could he leave you in the car for two hours on a cold morning like this?'

Sheila caught up with some breakfast and realized how much of Marjorie Easterby's hospitality she had missed. Then she drove us to Southwell, where my first-race winner David Tudor, for the Newmarket trainer David Ringer, was my number fifty. I also won on Harry's Fizzale, trained not far away in Lincolnshire by Basil Richmond, and Nellie's Lad, whose Malton trainer Jock Skilling had been one of the most accomplished work riders in the north of England.

My father and brother Thomas related stories of how

customers would call at the family grocer's shop for a packet of sugar or biscuits and spend half an hour discussing my winners and prospects of becoming champion jockey or breaking the record. I wasn't sure if I was good or bad for business in the family shop. In Castletownroche they had clearly monitored my every move.

I was surprised and flattered by how much detail of the dramas of the season they had digested. They asked me about my luckiest winner – Alverton in a two-horse race at Teeside in January when the bookmakers refused to bet on the result because they considered Alverton already past the post. He was, I suppose – apart from the fact that he completely misjudged the seventh fence, sprawled on his belly and tossed me out of the saddle. Colin Hawkins on our only rival Kruganko, trained by Neville Crump, was so close on our tail that we brought him down. Fortunately, I had clung on to the reins, which took a couple of minutes to untangle from around Alverton's ears. Colin had also kept a firm grip on his reins but I managed to remount before he did and by the time he had struggled back into the saddle we were a fence clear. Alverton came home unchallenged. I was mighty relieved to have averted total disaster and at least salvaged the race from the wreckage of the seventh-fence fiasco, but poor Colin received the rough end of Neville Crump's tongue.

'Only two f— runners, and you put Kruganko so close up Jonjo's arse that you couldn't avoid him,' blasted Neville, whose tirade was justified, for there is very seldom an excuse for being brought down in a two-horse race. After all, Kruganko's only chance of beating Alverton was if we failed to complete the course.

My eldest brother Jerome inquired about one of the foulest afternoons of the season at Doncaster in January when I had the pleasure to be introduced to the dual champion hurdler Night Nurse in the William Hill Yorkshire Hurdle. On Boxing Day at Kempton he had crashed out, giving his regular rider

Paddy Broderick dreadful concussion, which eventually finished his career, and I was asked to partner Night Nurse for the first time. Before the race Peter Easterby walked the last half mile of the Doncaster hurdle course with his head lad Keith Stone. They discovered that the ground along the stand rails was less poached than the rest of the track and if Night Nurse hugged that rail it would mean that our principal rival Bird's Nest would be on our left with no rail to keep him straight. Bird's Nest had this frustrating problem of veering under pressure and, sure enough, when he challenged and looked to be travelling better than Night Nurse he hung to the left, causing his jockey Andy Turnell to concentrate on keeping him straight rather than throwing every ounce into the frantic finish. They momentarily wrested the lead from us as we rose at the last flight, but Night Nurse's courage and the better ground made the difference by a heartstopping head.

I was asked several times while we were in Ireland if the high spot of the season had been reaching 100 winners in record time on Sweet Millie in a selling hurdle at Haydock on 8 February, five weeks ahead of Fred Winter's fastest hundred, which the great man had achieved a quarter of a century earlier. Of course, to have clocked up the fastest ton underlined just how smoothly the well-oiled wheels were running, but it is unfair to compare my season with Fred's in 1953. The unpredictable weather and injuries are dominant factors, however confidently you are riding, to say nothing of the run of each individual race.

I still treasure the lovely cigarette case presented to me by the chairman of Haydock, the late Tommy Whittle, who commented, 'I have read so much about you approaching your fastest century that I was beginning to think you were a cricketer, not a jockey!' At the time a lot of play was made of the fact that I had received an inscribed cigarette case and had never smoked a cigarette in my life. Well, it sits on the sideboard in the lounge with a ready supply for any visitors wishing to smoke.

People also reminded me of the quote from Sweet Millie's trainer Charlie Dingwall that she was 'quite the worst horse' I had ridden all season. She may have been a selling plater and I certainly had to pick her off the floor at the last hurdle before driving her to the line, but she could not have been better named.

Everyone at home admitted that the Scottish Champion Hurdle at Ayr in April had cast a dark cloud across Ireland with the highly rated but ill-fated Golden Cygnet, trained in County Tipperary by Eddie O'Grady, falling at the last on his way to certain victory. Golden Cygnet had been heralded as a future champion hurdler, but sadly had to be put down following the injuries he sustained in that Ayr crash. However, Ireland's loss was my gain for I managed to manoeuvre Sea Pigeon round the bodies of Golden Cygnet and his jockey Niall Madden to snatch Scotland's championship from under the nose of Night Nurse.

The people of Castletownroche had obviously spent many laborious hours preparing a celebration carnival in our honour, erecting loudspeakers, making colourful floats and perfecting the band. The procession started at the creamery at the bottom of the hill by the River Awbeg. Mary Warlow, with whom I had spent many happy hours out in the hunting field with the 'Dashing Duhallows' Hunt, had produced her beautiful two-seater gig, brightly coloured yellow and pulled by her excitable twenty-year-old piebald pony Sunshine, to transport me through the streets. We were instructed to follow the float carrying Sheila and my brothers Jerome, Dennis and Thomas. I climbed in alongside Mary and quickly realized that we were confronted with one of the toughest rides of the year. Castletownroche hill is so steep and the procession was moving so slowly that poor Sunshine was having his work cut out to tow us and the gig uphill at snail's pace. Mary and I leaned forwards, trying to ease the burden for the little black and white pony. As we crawled along Mary had us both dreaming of my early days hunting with the Duhallows. I used to wear a soft black velvet cap held together by a black velvet bow above the peak. She and her mother Sheila, a great supporter of the local pony club, horrified by my lack of head protection during my first excursion with the Duhallows, took me back to their farm at Ballymagooly, four miles from Castletownroche, and presented me with a proper riding hat, which I took with me in a plastic bag when I first went to England.

Mary is now married to Wiltshire farmer Robert Wilson and lives at Froxfield, near Hungerford, managed to keep Sunshine remarkably restrained until seconds after I had alighted. As I was walking from the gig towards the village school where I was to make my dreaded speech from a dais which had been set up specially for the occasion, a horrendous crack suddenly bellowed out over the loud-speakers, almost sending the assembled mass rushing for cover. Sunshine took fright, reared up, leaped into the air with the gig and crashed down on a parked lorry, ending up with the shafts of the gig across his back. Mary, who is a fine horsewoman, quickly had the nerve-wracking situation under control and trotted Sunshine quietly back along the lanes to Ballymagooly. As we had toiled up towards the church at the top of the village I had been telling Mary how dangerous I had found camel racing, a sport to which I had recently been introduced at Malton Show in Yorkshire, where I had been competing against fellow jockeys Colin Tinkler and Alan Brown. For a few precarious seconds Mary's seat in the gig had been fraught with many more hazards than the awkward camel's hump.

During our stay in Ireland it gradually dawned on me how the arduous winter and spring had sapped the last ounces of strength and energy from my body. Only when you begin to unwind do the tension and tiredness find a way out of your muscles and mind, often leaving behind a trembling wreck. I never quite reached that extreme state, but Peter Easterby, whose keen eye and observant manner have played such a big part in hoisting him to the top of the training pile, remarked that I had lost all the colour in my face. The usual brightness and bounce were missing and Peter told me he had never before seen a man so utterly drained and exhausted, both mentally and physically. He reckoned that even by the start of the following season, after two months off, I had not fully recovered. Indeed, only when I was totally immobilized after breaking my right arm at Kelso in October 1978 did I have to put my feet up and take a complete rest. That was possibly one of the luckiest breaks I've had, for it provided me with the opportunity to catch up on lost sleep and recharge my batteries. I even found myself snatching forty winks in the armchair in the lounge of our new house at Plumpton. At the height of the season I would wake up in a muck sweat and wander round my bedroom in the middle of the night, or lie awake wrestling with the various phone calls I knew I must make at dawn, then suddenly remember one that I had forgotten about the previous evening. Keeping all the trainers informed about my commitments and therefore my availability was of prime importance, for a freelance jockey must try to keep all his contacts sweet so that none of his sources of mounts dries up.

I was not retained by Peter Easterby but we had a tacit agreement that if I was offered a better ride than one of his horses I should accept it. Peter reasoned that if there was an animal with stronger claims than his he could find an alternative race. In this way we worked for each other. I could climb aboard the possible winner of the race and he could save his horse for a more suitable engagement, thus giving me the chance of another winner. All part of an understanding that boosted my confidence sky high.

Sea Pigeon, Night Nurse and Alverton were a far cry from

the three yearlings Peter had bought for 380 guineas at the Newmarket Sales in 1951. He cycled the five miles from his father's solid, square stone house, where he still lives, at Great Habton to the late Billy Dutton's stables in Malton where he caught a lift in the Dutton horsebox to Newmarket. His purchases averaged 126 guineas and, satisfied with his day's work, Peter hitch-hiked home in a furniture van, which dropped him at the Bramham crossroads where the A1 joins the Tadcaster-Leeds road. He thumbed another lift to Tadcaster where he caught a bus to York and then another bus to Malton to pick up his bicycle and pedal the final five miles home. His first job on his return was to sell the three yearlings to prospective owners and this he had done within twenty-four hours of his return.

Peter always maintains with Yorkshire pride that his father lived off his wits, which may be partly true, although he also farmed some 25 acres from the Dutch-style house with its overhanging slate roof and symmetrical windows flanked by dark blue shutters. Peter now farms thousands of Yorkshire acres, and his brother Mick, who trains twelve miles away at Sheriff Hutton, also farms on a large scale. Their successful horsedealing enabled them to take the training world by storm and led them into real estate.

Peter Easterby could read me better than any other trainer I know. It was uncanny the way he could tell what I was going to do on a horse; I suppose we shared similar ideas and theories about horses and this meant we were always working together rather than pulling against each other.

He is renowned for being a man of very few words but what he says invariably carries a lot of weight. He agrees that we won races we should not have won that season simply because our confidence in each other ran so strong. He did not give me a single order before I went out and rode those forty-five winners for him in the 1977–78 campaign. Some days in the paddock before a race he would discuss his latest crop of corn or a new tractor he had just bought, but that's not to say he did not send me out onto the course armed with all the necessary information about my mount if I didn't already know it. He maintains, 'When you're out there I can't tell you that the gap is about to shut in your face or that it won't even open for you. You're on your own and I cannot help you.'

Even when the best-laid plans had misfired Peter would never lose his composure. In fact, I cannot recall an instance when he has allowed himself to become worked up over a beaten horse, even the most fancied. It was comforting to know that he meant what he said. 'If the race conspires against you and there is no chance of winning, don't worry because there will be another day.'

Pulse Rate, in the Night Nurse colours of Reg Spencer, started 5–2 on for his debut over hurdles at Teesside in the New Year of 1980, but after he had been badly blocked off at a hurdle down the far side I was not hard on him. Peter greeted me with a sympathetic 'Gee, you were unlucky' and said no more. I had allowed Pulse Rate to recover from the nasty experience in his own time and we came home in a manner designed to restore any lost confidence. Sure enough, Pulse Rate won his next race at Catterick; sympathetic rather than strong handling had paid dividends.

Peter certainly had me fooled, and, I suspect, plenty of punters too, when I partnered No Bombs in his first race over hurdles at Sedgefield in October 1978, just three days before I smashed my right arm at Kelso. No Bombs, a classy handicapper on the flat, had won for me at Newcastle and Hamilton, and was entitled to start even-money favourite even though he had no form over hurdles. But as the race progressed I began to doubt I was riding No Bombs for he ran through every hurdle – I would have finished closer if I had gone round on my own. Remarks passed to me on the racecourse afterwards suggested that several 'informed' people had put their cash on No Bombs. But, according to Peter, they ignored him the next time he ran, at Teesside at the end of the month, with Alan Brown claiming his 4-lb riding allowance on him. No Bombs won by three lengths at 11–2. Peter recalls that he was a funny horse, who needed to know what hurdling was about before he put his act together. The Sedgefield experience started him off right because Peter did not wind him up completely for his first run. After his Teesside triumph No Bombs went from strength to strength.

7

Alverton

In the summer of 1973 Peter Easterby was looking for an owner for a three-year-old called Alverton. He approached Paddy Brudenell Bruce, who at the time was managing the racing interests of the late Stanhope Joel. Paddy agreed to pay £1500 for Alverton with the contingency that if he won a race he would give another £1500. Paddy and his wife Dana, daughter of Stanhope Joel, watched the family's new purchase win over hurdles at Newcastle and Wetherby to become ante post favourite for the Triumph Hurdle at Cheltenham the following spring. But then disaster struck. Alverton broke down and missed the next season. But this tough, brave and remarkably versatile horse returned to scale the heights. He was then owned by the Snailwell Stud, which belongs to the Brudenell Bruces and Stanhope Joel's other daughter, Solna Jones. Alverton became a fairytale character for his owners by repaying his purchase price many, many times over with eleven flat-race victories and another eleven over jumps.

T.R.

The March skies above Cheltenham were heavy with the threat of more rain, or perhaps even snow, and the turf underfoot was soggy after the previous night's downpour. But the bitter elements of Cheltenham Gold Cup morning, 1979, had not deterred the gathering of racing purists, wrapped against the cutting wind in their waterproofs, windcheaters, caps and trilbies. They had come in enthusiastic anticipation to watch the final workouts of the potential stars on this last day of the glittering National Hunt Festival.

At dawn on Gold Cup day Cheltenham's exercise area in the middle of the course below the steep and protective slopes of the beautiful Cotswolds is the traditional hatching ground for the build-up to the big race. It is here that the buzz and chat are gathered by eager racecourse gossips, who inevitably try to turn their tips into hard cash later in the afternoon.

Standing up in my stirrup irons, I allowed Alverton to ease to a trot after cantering two and a half furlongs with Peter Easterby's other Gold Cup candidate Night Nurse.

'Do you think you've picked the right one?' asked Jack Warrell from the back of Night Nurse. The question was funnelled into my ear through icy gusts of wind.

'Yes, I think he will win,' I replied with confidence.

Jack had looked after Alverton for six years and in 1978 took over Night Nurse from Keith Stone, who had left Peter Easterby to set up as a successful trainer in Malton. Before Keith embarked on his new career he used to come close to blows with Jack as they argued the relative merits of their respective heroes Alverton and Night Nurse over a pint of beer. Now Jack found himself in the enviable position of 'doing' two runners in the Gold Cup.

He decided to lead up Night Nurse, the mount of Graham Thorner, leaving Kevin Hodgson, who is now successfully riding for Peter Easterby on the flat, to look after Alverton. After the race, to both lads' eternal credit, Kevin offered to let Jack lead Alverton into the winner's enclosure. But Jack declined.

'No. It was my choice,' he said. 'You enjoy your share of the glory, Kevin.'

I learned later that my answer to Jack's question when we were pulling up after early-morning work prompted him to go shuffling into the big-race betting ring and have £10 on Alverton at 6-1. By opting to lead up Night Nurse, who tired quickly after clouting the thirteenth fence, Jack gave himself two bites of the Gold Cup cherry.

The Irish horse Tied Cottage looked as if he had set up an unassailable lead, maintaining a relentless gallop at least twenty lengths ahead of the field at the top of the hill. The fierce snow blizzard may have restricted visibility from the packed stands but the big flakes were incidental as I peered through my goggles trying to assess how well Tied Cottage and his evergreen jockey Tommy Carberry were going.

They were not coming back to us, for sure. After jumping the fourth last we started the long run down the hill and I shouted across to Phil Blacker on Royal Mail, 'We'd better get after him or we'll never catch him.'

The chase started in earnest. But as soon as we began to cut back the leeway Tied Cottage appeared to raise his tempo and increase the yawning gap.

Three fences out Alverton's power proved too much for Royal Mail and we drew away from him in pursuit of Tied Cottage. Approaching the second last I pulled Alverton to the right in search of better ground. By now we were closing and I made sure we were not in Tied Cottage's tracks in case he fell. If anything happens and he brings me down I'll look a right clown, I thought. Alverton was tired and trying to hang in behind Tied Cottage. We were still a couple of lengths down on him at the second last.

Tied Cottage held his slight lead as both horses and both riders tried to throw off the cloak of tiredness and draw on new energies for one last telling leap before the final hill. I knew Alverton was exhausted and I suspected Tied Cottage's tearaway tactics must have drained his resources, too.

The confidence Alverton transmitted to me won the day. No more honest horse ever ran in the Gold Cup. My wish was his command. Wherever you wanted him to be in a race he would go. If you met a fence wrong he would measure the obstacle, balance himself and take off at the correct stride. He could weigh up the job himself. Alverton knew exactly what every situation demanded, and this professional touch rubbed off on his rider.

We were facing a crisis. Defeat was staring us in our drained faces, unless Alverton could produce a big leap and land running. He was too tired to gather himself if a sloppy jump checked his momentum. It would stop him in his tracks.

Not satisfied with simply standing back and putting together an extra long one, Alverton took off a stride before I expected and stretched himself to the limit. I thought he was sure to land on top of the fence but he reached out as only he could and his front legs cleared it, the reliable undercarriage touched down as ever and we pounded on up the hill.

I was surprised by the doggedness and sheer power of Alverton's attack on the fence when he must have been nearly unconscious on his feet. Tied Cottage was literally floored by it. As Alverton caught up with him in mid air Tied Cottage spotted him out of the corner of his eye and lost concentration for a split second. His limbs had exerted every ounce of their strength catapulting him over the previous twenty-one fences at a good gallop considering the tacky ground. To correct his faulty landing was too much and Tied Cottage knuckled over. For him the battle was lost.

For Alverton came the medals of victory, carved out of bravery at a time when lesser horses would have taken the easy option and given up the chase. But Alverton was an expert at beating the odds. He broke down twice and still won eleven races on the flat as well as eleven over jumps, including the Arkle Trophy at Cheltenham and the Greenall Whitley Chase at Haydock Park only twelve days before the Gold Cup. His legs were as hard as iron and his tendons of matching toughness. They had to be to withstand so many battles.

As I entered the winner's enclosure I could sense the Yorkshire pride about to burst out from behind the placid exterior of Peter Easterby. Years of canny horse care had brought Alverton back from the brink of the knacker's yard to the pinnacle of steeplechasing.

Sixteen days later at Liverpool I found myself stumbling out of an official's car, numb from the neck up, and shoving Alverton's bridle in the direction of Jack Warrell. The chunky little stable lad stuck out a hand to take it, his face quickly turning a ghostly ashen colour. Without thinking, I had passed on my grief with the bridle.

Jack Warrell was standing at Aintree's metal gate through which the horses enter and leave the course, and next to him was the Scot, Graham Lockerbie, Peter Easterby's ruddy-complexioned, ever ready, travelling head lad. They were anxiously on the lookout for my Grand National mount, expecting him to appear riderless at any moment. As he had been Alverton's adoring lad for six years, Jack was the most natural person to whom to give his bridle.

I was unaware that Jack did not yet know of Alverton's death at Becher's Brook second time round on his way to what seemed certain victory in Rubstic's 1979 Grand National. The white-faced chestnut had been an integral part of Jack's life for six colourful years and yet there I was unwittingly thrusting forward this last tearful reminder of the horse he loved. During those painfully long minutes it had taken me to return from the crowded disaster area of Becher's Brook to the quieter haven of the jockeys' room my mind was a blank. I did not think; indeed, I could not think. And it was only later, after Jack had jogged my memory, that I could recall my thoughtless deed.

I can now understand why he felt like throttling me as I walked off, totally oblivious of the hurt I had inflicted, leaving him clutching the bridle, which was still stained by the sweat, blood and thunder of the world's greatest race. Jack registered his deeply felt grief by whipping the air with Alverton's reins before starting to walk back to the racecourse stables, but he could not keep his emotions from bubbling over and was forced to take refuge behind some large sheets of metal leaning against a shed. He knelt on the ground and cried like a baby.

To this day he unashamedly admits that he broke down. The gritty resolve of this Yorkshire lad had been shattered by the horrors of the afternoon. He eventually made his way to Peter Easterby's horsebox which had brought Alverton on the last fateful journey across the Pennines from Great Habton. There he sat in solitude for half an hour before he felt able to face the razzamatazz of Aintree's Grand National atmosphere.

The following day Jack was full of remorse. He recalls, 'My immediate reaction was wanting to strangle Jonjo for the thoughtless way in which he handed me Alverton's bridle without saying a word. That was the first inkling I had that Alverton was dead. Of course, I now accept it was in the heat of the moment and twenty-four hours later I regretted it, for Jonjo was equally upset and in no state to think straight either.'

In truth the shock of Alverton's death at Becher's left me in a daze which hung over me for a couple of hours.

Alverton was so intelligent he would quickly weigh up the tiniest details of a race and adapt himself accordingly. Fence by fence he was loving the new experience over the Aintree country, pricking his ears, putting himself right. Through the reins he transmitted a joy and exhilaration I have never found before or since in the Grand National.

My best ride in the National became my worst in the space of twenty uncertain strides. What happened remains a mystery. Alverton changed legs crossing the path twenty yards before Becher's. That was the first distress signal I received, although at the time it did not register as red for danger because it was routine for Alverton to lead with one of his battle-scarred legs and then the other almost as a matter of convenience.

The world's most famous steeplechase jump loomed larger with each hesitant stride and its individual sprigs of spruce were easily visible as we thundered ever closer. But still Alverton had not put himself right.

'Come on, mister. Come on,' I yelled at him with a

deepening desperation. 'You'll be in a muddle if you don't gather yourself and measure the fence.'

I had never corrected his approach to a jump before. Why start now? He always met the fence in his own time if you left him alone. So I did.

But Alverton failed to leave the ground. He galloped straight into the bottom of Becher's, his momentum hurling him over the fence and brook, and was dead on impact. At the time I thought he had broken his neck, but he died instantly, probably from a heart attack.

He lay alongside the brook, into which Captain Becher made his celebrated splash, with the shadow of the big fence covering his prone body like a caring cloak. I picked myself from the turf and walked back to witness those final quivering death throes. Then I knew the sickening truth. Alverton was dead.

The only mistake he made was hitting the twentieth fence – two before he crashed out – and he was galloping so sweetly I was up with the leaders earlier than planned. I cannot believe that he would not have beaten Rubstic.

I received the predictable postbag of vindictive letters pointing accusing fingers and stressing how greedy and selfish I had been in killing Alverton only sixteen days after his glorious and richly rewarded victory in the Cheltenham Gold Cup, worth £30,293 to the winner. In racing the know-alls who crow with the benefit of hindsight are always ready to dance on your grave. There was no greater admirer of Alverton's steely determination than his jockey. I mourned his passing with as much sorrow as his owners, Mrs Dana Brudenell-Bruce and Mrs Solna Jones, his trainer Peter Easterby, his breeder, the Northallerton bookmaker Bill Pratt, and his devoted lad Jack Warrell.

Mrs Brudenell-Bruce and Mrs Jones thought long and hard before giving Peter Easterby the go-ahead to run at Aintree. While enjoying the Grand National as a spectacle they admitted that they were hesitant when it came to running one of their own horses after watching Frenchman's Cove, owned by their father, Mr Stanhope Joel, knocked over and robbed of a winning chance in Kilmore's year, 1962. But Mrs Brudenell-Bruce finally left the decision with Peter Easterby, who, after all, was her trainer and professional racing adviser.

Peter was absolutely right to run Alverton, who had never been better in his life. It was as if the Cheltenham triumph had put him right for Aintree. If there is such a thing as a handicap certainty in the Grand National then Alverton was one, with only 10st 13lb. A year later he would have been allotted top weight. Any trainer in his right mind with a class horse like Alverton in top form would have made the same decision.

Sadly, Peter's fighting policy blew up in his face and ended in tragedy. But the fantastic feeling Alverton gave me with his arm-wrenching enthusiasm at every fence left me utterly convinced that he died doing what he loved most – jumping.

8

Ron Barry

Fulke Walwyn, the Queen Mother's trainer and revered as a living legend among his own profession, was very keen for the northern-based Irish jockey Ron Barry to move south and ride as first jockey to his Lambourn stable after he had won the 1973 Cheltenham Gold Cup for him on The Dikler.

'He was strong and beautiful horseman,' recalls Fulke, who has been training since 1939. 'All horses went so well for him, particularly The Dikler, who could be such a hard puller.

'I was always very fond of Ron and we got on well together. I asked him to join me as first jockey, but he had just become engaged and wanted to stay in the North.'

T.R.

Ron Barry's medical book would make an ideal item for the National Racing Museum at Newmarket provided it is displayed open at the page showing the entry made by the Uttoxeter racecourse doctor on Friday, 16 March 1973. The ten words written in red ink – 'Off colour. Pulse 90. Headache. Should be all right tomorrow' – conceal one hell of a story and I know Ron is a good enough friend not to object to my repeating it. On the contrary, I suspect he will chuckle quietly to himself as I relate an almost unbelievable episode in the colourful and extremely tough life of a man who successfully combined riding at the top of his profession with a fun-loving attitude which endeared him to everyone inside and outside the jockeys' room.

Twenty-four hours before seeking the help of the Uttoxeter doctor, Ron had ridden the race of his record-breaking life to win the Cheltenham Gold Cup on The Dikler, snatching victory in a dramatic finish by a short head from the odds-on favourite Pendil, partnered by Richard Pitman, who is now a popular BBC television commentator. The biggest moment of Ron's career could hardly be allowed to pass without the necessary celebrations and Ron was always the man to take the bottle by the neck and make sure his many friends around him shared his enjoyment. If, like me, you do not drink, you still could not have resisted joining Big Ron in the leg-pulling and laughter, even if you were stone cold sober.

Ron crawled out of bed in his Cheltenham hotel the morning after, realizing that he must refuel with champagne if he was to manage the drive to Uttoxeter where he had four rides. So he drank a glass of champagne, believing it to be the hair of the dog, and was flying again. The short journey through the Midlands went well until he and his fiancée Liz Young reached Birmingham where the champagne apparently evaporated from Ron's system, leaving him feeling like death again. But he persevered to the racecourse where he struggled into his colours and breeches in readiness for the first race. As he walked into the paddock, he was greeted by the guv'nor Gordon Richards, who trained his mount Pneuma.

Gordon took one look at Ron and said, 'Ronnie boy, are you all right? You don't look too good.'

'I've never felt better,' replied Ron, desperately trying to kid himself that he was no more than one degree below par.

'I'm pleased to hear that,' said Gordon. 'We have backed Pneuma and gone for a real touch on him. Are you sure you're OK?'

'Not so good,' Ron conceded. 'But there's nothing we can do about it now.'

Gordon instructed Ron to go out in front and try to make all the running. That way he would keep out of trouble. Ron obeyed his orders to the letter and as they reached the first flight he kicked Pneuma in the belly, causing him to lurch forward and lose his rhythm, very nearly dislodging Ron. After that Ron patted Pneuma on the neck and said, 'Son you are on your own, but please look after me!'

They led all the way to win by two and a half lengths at 9–1. Ron managed to dismount, carry his saddle to the scales, where he was relieved to sit down again, and take a rest, until the room started to spin round. Waiting for the clerk of the scales to give him the all clear, Ron tried desperately to take a firm grip on the precarious situation and prevent himself from falling off the scales and almost certainly being disqualified.

'Would I be able to see the doctor, please, sir? I'm not feeling very well and think it may be a touch of flu,' said Ron.

The doctor appeared and inquired, 'What's wrong, Ron?'

Ron owned up. 'If you want to know the truth, doctor, I have got alcoholic poisoning and I am dying. I won the Gold Cup yesterday, had a monumental party last night and a glass of champagne this morning. I am going very badly and cannot possibly ride the rest of my mounts today.'

The doctor's worried look betrayed his understandable ignorance of how to handle a jockey suffering from alcoholic poisoning. 'Oh Ron,' he said, 'I can't possibly put that in your medical book.'

To be fair, it was the only time Ron rode under the influence and, of course, if he had lost the race there is no way I could have told the tale. But, to my mind, it reflects the side of Ron Barry which made him a legend in the jockeys' room. The public figure of Ron out there in the thick of the action was the other side everyone knew and the reason that he is acknowledged to be the great horseman he undoubtedly is.

About ten days before the Gold Cup Ron broke his collarbone in a fall at Kelso and from then he was worried how he would ride The Dikler to the start. I remember him telling me that if The Dikler took a strong hold after the pre-race parade instead of going quietly to the start, he would probably end up being run away with. He would not be able to restrain him because of the pain of his broken collarbone. His wife Liz has never let him forget how during every one of those ten days he nagged her while he tried to devise a plan which would enable him to anchor The Dikler on the way to the start. Nursing his broken collarbone, Ron won the Panama Cigar Final at Chepstow on Dark Sultan the Saturday before the Gold Cup.

As it turned out, The Dikler arrived at the Gold Cup start with Ron very much in control and once the tapes went up Ron settled him behind his front-running stable companion Charlie Potheen and Clever Scot. Because his collarbone did not allow him to fight against The Dikler, Ron believes that big horse switched himself off and went to sleep and they both enjoyed a quiet, uneventful first circuit. That was Ron's modest explanation, but anyone lucky enough to witness the epic finish with Pendil will know that neither jockey nor horse was ever anywhere near having forty winks.

As if to emphasize that he was making more of a fuss about his collarbone than was necessary, Ron went out and finished second on Reignon, beaten by a head by Current Romance in the County Hurdle, only thirty-five minutes after the Gold Cup. He appeared to have no chance at the second last but conjured a characteristic Ron Barry flourish out of Reignon, only to be denied by inches.

After the glory of the Gold Cup Ron was entitled to sample a glass or two of his much-loved tonic, champagne. He provided the lads in the jockeys' room with a case and finally emerged to go to the Cellar, a haven reserved exclusively for jockeys and their closest friends under the Cheltenham grandstand. The Cellar, which disappeared in the Cheltenham rebuilding programme in the late seventies, was the storeroom where the Cheltenham caterers kept their supplies. No one enjoyed perching on a champagne case and joining in the knees-up there more than Ron. After a short singsong Ron and Liz left the party to meet friends for dinner at the Queen's Hotel in the centre of Cheltenham. As Ron walked through the hotel entrance an admiring racegoer handed him a glass of champagne and he attempted to sit on a bar stool which was not there. He hit the ground, throwing his champagne everywhere. Once it became clear Ron was in no fit state to eat his dinner, Liz took him to his room so he could sleep off the celebrations. Ron lurched into the wall of the corridor on his way to his room, banging his broken collarbone and the excruciating pain almost sobered him up. Liz recalls how she eventually laid him in the bed with his hands crossed over his heart as if he was ready to die, but how he quickly burst back into life again when he announced that he was going to be sick. Ron's plight may have been self-induced but, to be fair, he had been wasting hard and sweating to lose weight for some light rides the next day at Uttoxeter and no one, not even Ron Barry, can drink on an empty stomach. Before finally sinking into a deep sleep Ron spat out his words of regret: 'If I've got to feel like this I wish I'd never won the bloody Gold Cup.'

'Don't be so silly,' Liz admonished him. 'Tomorrow you will feel fine and you will still have won the Gold Cup.'

The next day's events proved Liz's predictions only half true. But Ron's dizzy spell was only a temporary hiccup in his record-breaking season which wound up with him riding 125 winners and breaking Josh Gifford's five-year record by three winners.

Ron Barry's life was one big laugh. That first morning when I was riding out at Greystoke as a raw, new lad from Ireland he approached me and said, 'How are you getting along in those shoes?'

Mystified, I asked, 'What shoes?'

'The ones you're wearing. You never used to wear any in Ireland!' he said.

When he introduced me to people at the races – and some of them were influential owners, stewards and racecourse officials – Ron used to tell them quite seriously that wearing shoes was a new experience for me.

'What a job I've had getting Jonjo used to these shoes,' he would say. 'When I met him off the boat I had to walk him up and down the quayside – left, right; left, right; left, right.'

For a second his listeners would believe him.

There can have been few more dedicated stable jockeys and it seemed to be Big Ron's prerogative to take the mickey out of everyone in the yard, including Gordon, whom he would rub up the wrong way and then humour in the space of minutes. One bitterly cold morning, when most of us were concentrating on keeping the unfriendly elements at bay, Ron couldn't resist having a go. As Gordon and he, leading the string, pulled up at the gate, Ron dismounted and opened it. He turned to Gordon and said with touch of sarcasm, 'It's a good job there are no young lads about, boss.'

Predictably, Gordon swung round in the saddle and ripped into the nearest young lad, roughly tearing him off a strip. They reached the next gate, which Ron duly opened. 'Where's the young lad now, boss?' he asked.

There followed an instant replay of the previous tirade from Gordon. Fortunately, the lads realized that Ron was putting him up to it.

Ron would often drop someone in the cart so as to gee up Gordon, and in their different ways both parties accepted that he was stirring things and no one came to any harm. Gordon swallowed the bait another morning when Ron told how his powerful Audi could not keep up with the stable's driver, Martin Todhunter, as he steered the massive Gordon Richards Super Eight horsebox over the twisty A66 across Bowes Moor between Penrith and Scotch Corner.

'Boss, what's the speed limit on horseboxes?' asked Ron, affecting an air of innocence. 'Our box must have been doing over seventy miles an hour yesterday and I couldn't keep up with it!'

Martin Todhunter good naturedly accepted Gordon's abuse, knowing that Ron had mixed it for him.

If I had ridden a winner the day before and was looking forward to several fancied mounts that afternoon, Ron would say, 'Jonjo got run away with on that winner yesterday, boss. Do you think he will be strong enough to handle those three this afternoon?'

Ron's playful half hour helped defuse Gordon when pressures were building up and he was becoming agitated. At the same time he involved the lads in the crossfire and chitchat and we all knew it was a bit sharp. I believe everyone in the stable benefited and Ron helped to create an atmosphere of camaraderie and to mould team spirit.

On a more serious note, Ron was not afraid to keep any of us in check and tell us what we were doing wrong. It was at his suggestion that Tony Meaney and I swapped rides one morning when I was on Golden Fort and Tony on Sedge Warbler. Neither of us felt we got the best out of our rides and Ron suggested to Gordon that both the horses and the jockeys might be better off with a change. Gordon agreed to the plan, which resulted in Tony winning on Golden Fort and my being successful on Sedge Warbler.

When we talk over old times Ron insists that, in his view, my greatest moment was my first English win on Katie J, who was subsequently disqualified, at Uttoxeter and that event had the greatest influence on my career. For, Ron maintains, the sweet and sour taste of success followed by instant disappointment changed me. Apparently, I had been too keen in trying to secure rides in races early in my career. He saw me becoming more and more keyed up and tense, it showed in my riding work and even when I was away from the horses. I was unaware of this trait, but Ron's opinion supports Michael Connolly's early criticism of me that I was always wanting to run before I could walk. Ron insists Katie J's victory and disqualification was the making of me, but I suspect Ron played a bigger part in that side of my life than the mare did. Ron taught me to swim, introduced me to numerous respected racecourse personalities and, particularly during his record-breaking season of 1972–73, stuck me in for plenty of rides and winners he could not accept because of the heavy demand for his services. Ask him, and he will tell you what a help I was to him. He would tell trainers, 'Jonjo will ride it for you, he will do exactly what you want.' But, to put the matter in perspective, Ron did far more for me than I could ever do for him. Perhaps I released him from the hook on occasions when he was tangled up with too many engagements in one race, but in off-loading some of those commitments onto me he was advancing my career.

I would lay 1000–1 against anyone naming Ron's favourite horse. It isn't Grand Canyon, his Colonial Cup winner of 1976 and 1978, nor his Cheltenham Gold Cup ally The Dikler, on whom he also won the 1974 Whitbread Gold Cup, nor his other Whitbread winners Titus Oates and Charlie Potheen. Playlord, Ron's Scottish Grand National and Great Yorkshire Chase winner, has a special place in his heart. Irish Fashion gave him his victory in the highly competitive Schweppes Gold Trophy Hurdle and, for me, Ron's greatest ride was in defeat on Easby Abbey when he nearly pinched the 1973 Champion Hurdle from Comedy of Errors with as bold a piece of forceful riding as I have ever seen at Cheltenham. But it is none of these. It is Sheil, on whom he won a £240 novice hurdle at Warwick on Guy Fawkes Day in 1971 and then an equally insignificant £170 hurdle at Teesside. Two years later they scrambled home in a £240 Carlisle novice chase and won a £647 Ayr chase in which Sheil's only rival finished lame. That was the sum total of their success together on the racecourse. Neville Crump, one of the greatest and most enthusiastic trainers of steeplechasers ever to grace the National Hunt scene, bought Sheil for 14,500 guineas out of Bruce Hobbs's Newmarket stable and later sold him and he was sent to be trained by Gordon.

Those lads who were in the stable at the time still recall the crisp, Cumbria-fresh autumn morning when Gordon introduced Ron to Sheil and said, 'Ronnie boy, get on this fellow and take him out, but I must warn you he won't leave the yard.'

The concrete surface was slippery under the wet, icy conditions and Sheil kept whipping round and refusing to go towards the stable exit which led to the gallops, so Ron gave him a crack with his whip. It had little effect. Ron hit him several times and Sheil began to lose his footing, went down on his front legs and nearly fell. Ron, the true horseman, persevered as only he could in that tough yet persuasive way which eventually showed Sheil who was boss. Sheil condescended to leave the yard from that day on. Ron looks back on that icy morning with a feeling of great achievement because thereafter he and Sheil almost became a circus act. Ron used to go into Sheil's box and let him take sweets out of his mouth; if Ron asked him to Sheil would go down on one knee before taking a sweet; he would shake hands by offering Ron a front foot; Ron used to ask him to leave his box; and on his command Sheil would roll, or even lie flat out with Ron still on his back. They struck up this relationship because Ron knew exactly how far he could go to bring the best out of Sheil that first morning. When Ron was away racing, Sheil was not exercised because there was no one who could persuade him to leave the yard. On the rare occasions when Sheil was tempted to go beyond the secure sanctuary of the stable yard, he would invariably drop his lad on the gallops and canter off, leaving his rider searching for his pride and a lift home.

Periodically, Gordon would send Ron off on Sheil, accompanied by Liz on another horse and her labrador Honey. There is a wood alongside the track which leads back to the stables and as Honey used to dash through the undergrowth, chasing after rabbits and squirrels, the loud crack of breaking sticks would interrupt the quiet of the morning. Sheil used the noise of the snapping wood as an excuse to drop Ron on the ground. The first time this happened Ron laughed, gave Sheil a pat on the neck and told him what a good fellow he was before remounting him. Honey cracked another twig, Sheil stuck his toe in, dropped his shoulder and Ron found himself on the ground again. The third time Honey trod on a rotten twig Sheil did exactly the same and stood waiting for Ron to remount. This he did, but he lost his temper and inflicted some sharp cracks down Sheil's flank with his whip before turning the air blue with a stream of swear words directed first at Honey, who was told never to go near the wood again, then at Liz, who should never have allowed Honey to have come with them, and finally at Sheil, who had succeeded in depositing Britain's top jockey in a helpless heap on the Cumbria terrain. Again Ron's natural instinct with horses told him exactly how far he could go in scolding Sheil to assert his own authority without causing the horse such a fright that he would never cooperate again. They still enoyed their circus act together after that funny and extremely frustrating morning out with Honey.

I am sure Ron will agree that we both learned more from Gordon on the car journeys with him and his late wife Jean to and from the races than at any other time. Hours spent enclosed together in a car cultivate understanding and friendship, and Gordon always made a point of discussing the day's runners and our outside mounts with us on the way to each race meeting. His perception and theories provided food for thought, and then he would go over riding plans with us and ask Ron and then me for our views; thus we pooled our knowledge and information. Listening to Gordon and Ron sounding off with their deep understanding of the horses left an indelible mark on me. The car became my classroom. Gordon always used to say if you did what he told you and you were beaten he would shoulder the blame. On the journeys home Gordon rollocked us if we had lost a race after disobeying orders, even if we had won and not done as he had instructed. That was a good thing because he made sure we learned from our mistakes. Gordon is the first to admit he was hard on both Ron and me, and that we had our differences. Ron broke his seventeen years at Greystoke with a year's freelancing and for one season was retained by Ken Oliver after a difference of opinion with Gordon, but went back to finish his remarkable career in the shadows of the Cumbria castle.

Sitting at home with a gin and tonic and staring into the bright log fire at Roehead Cottage overlooking Ullswater in the Lake District, Ron decided to pull down the curtain on a quarter of a century of raceriding – five years with Tom Shaw in Ireland before joining Wilf Crawford in Scotland and then moving on to Gordon Richards – the night before he was due to partner the appropriately named Final Argument at Ayr on 31 October 1983. Ron suddenly felt win, lose or draw, he would hang up his saddle. The ending came in fairytale fashion – Liz greeted him in the winner's enclosure in floods of tears and, after Ron had weighed in for the last time, Neville Crump's stable jockey Colin Hawkins and I carried him out shoulder high into the cheering Scottish crowds. It was not final, for how could anything about Ron Barry be final. The stories about Big Ron, from Raheen, County Limerick, are legion. He became the first jockey to be awarded a testimonial, and between appearing at all the Ron Barry functions, which were organized by amateur rider Peter Greenall, he was busy developing his business building looseboxes at Penrith. Behind the hard-living, fun-loving tough exterior is a soft centre, a heart that pumped Ron over thousands of fences and hurdles – 824 times ahead of the field – and still found time to stretch out and help many less fortunate than himself.

On one occasion Ron's fast talking at Southwell in 1972 landed me in front of the stewards and cost me £25. He was on Sir Guy Cunard's staying chaser Bountiful Charles and my partner was Katie J. Over the last mile it was tit for tat between us and as we turned into the straight I led Ron by a couple of lengths.

'You're going to run away with it,' I heard him shout. 'You'll win. You're going awfully well.'

As I glanced back I could see Ron kicking and shoving, throwing out distress signals, and this immediately made me think I was sure to win. Jumping the second last Ron shouted, 'Go on, go on. You'll win now – there's nothing going well behind you.'

Ron was drawing closer and closer but he still called out, 'You're on the winner, Jonjo. Keep going.'

Galloping to the final fence Ron was almost level and he shouted 'How are you going now?'

'I'm struggling,' I called.

'Go on, kick on. There's nothing coming up behind you,' was Ron's cry.

We jumped the last and Ron looked across at me with a broad grin and said, 'Thanks very much for the lead, Jonjo. I'll take over now.'

He won, and I was so mad I forgot to weigh in. The stewards fined me £25 for my lapse of memory and Katie J was once again disqualified.

On another occasion Ron's immortal words, 'Don't worry, if you're in trouble give us a shout,' were just what I wanted to hear as I walked Hidden Value round at the start of the John Eustace Smith Trophy at Newcastle in 1977. Ron was on Forest King, who had made a name for himself leading pony trekkers through the Cumbria fells before a highly successful campaign of steeplechasing. Hidden Value was a fierce puller and I knew Ron was likely to make the running on Forest King, so I asked him to ensure a good gallop so that my fellow would not run away with me and exhaust us both before we had even reached halfway in the three-mile chase. Ron, true to his word, set off in front, but by the time we reached the second fence I could feel Hidden Value taking control and as we took off he flew. I shouted, 'Ron, Ron, Ron, he's gone with me. I can't hold him.'

Ron moved across and as Hidden Value went to go past him Ron grabbed his bridle, gave it a hefty yank and pulled me back about four lengths. There we settled until, a couple of fences later, Hidden Value started to go again. Again I shouted, 'Ron, Ron, Ron, I'm in trouble again.'

Ron repeated his move by coming across as Hidden Value roared alongside, caught hold of his bridle and pulled him back so I could settle him again. After jumping the two fences galloping away from the stands, Hidden Value once more got the better of me, and my distress signal of 'Ron, Ron, Ron' was enough to alert the big fellow and he did his rescue act for a third time. Hidden Value scrambled over the next fence, making a bad mistake as a result of losing his rhythm, which was not altogether surprising.

This forced us back and I thought I had finally anchored him. Down the far side he started to jump with tremendous enthusiasm and accuracy, gaining a couple of lengths at each fence. He was gradually closing the gap on Forest King, who was still in front. Once Hidden Value saw a bit of daylight he grabbed the bit between his teeth and I was a mere passenger for the fourth time. I shouted, 'Ron, Ron, Ron,' but this time there was not the usual response.

Instead, Ron replied, 'I'm f— fed up with all this Ron, Ron, Ron.'

And with that he gave Hidden Value a couple of hefty cracks round the backside with his whip. We rocketed ten lengths clear only to blow up before we reached the home straight, leaving Ron and Forest King to go on to the victory they so richly deserved.

9

Religion – The Original Pick-Me-Up

Father David Murphy, who was Jonjo's parish priest at Penrith before he moved on to Whitehaven, is still his mentor in times of strife and problems. He highlights a passage from Psalm 1 in the Jerusalem Bible as an example of Jonjo.

> He is like a tree that is planted
> by water streams
> yielding its fruit in season,
> its leaves never fading;
> success attends all he does,
> it is nothing like this with the wicked,
> nothing like this

Father Murphy explains: 'Jonjo is like the tree that keeps returning to water when he needs refreshing. In other words, when he has a problem or injury he draws the necessary strength from God to help him through the crisis.'

T.R.

I do not know how anyone can grow up without any religion at all. Such a sweeping statement will provoke controversy and may be misconstrued, making me seem to be a smug Bible-puncher. I am aware that there are thousands – no, millions – of people in the world today who do not call on religion for strength and support. Of course, there are millions who do. I was lucky to be brought up through my childhood with the Church as the foundation of life.

Far be it from me to preach to anyone; I have no intention of telling other people how they should conduct their lives in modern society, which seems to change so fast we hardly have time to blink. But my Catholic faith has helped me to claw my way out of numerous holes and without it I have no doubt at all that I would not have survived long as a jockey.

I do not believe it is possible to marry success with happiness without the help of an outside source and, for me, that assistance and support has come from the Church. During my record-breaking season and, indeed, whenever I feel the world is closing in on me and everything becoming too much, I simply cut myself off from the outside by going into a church and sitting quietly alone. I do not necessarily pray on these occasions, but sit in complete peace and let my mind unwind and clear itself of all the prevailing problems. I genuinely believe that I can then think much straighter. It does no one any harm to take a few minutes out of the day to go and sit in a church, whether you are religious or not. It is a process that can help you see problems through new eyes and at times gives you a refreshed outlook on life. In a way, by sitting and meditating in church you are clearing your mind and almost making a confession. You may think to yourself, Why did I have that fall? and you suddenly become aware of a recent instance when you poached a ride from someone else or let a trainer down at the last minute by taking another mount when he had expected you to partner his horse in the same race. Everyone has to have something to hide behind; somewhere to seek solace. I find this relief from God and the Church.

My Church upbringing became a way of life and, to be honest, I suppose I took it for granted at times. But once I left home and moved to England I had the good fortune to find Father David Murphy, who was the parish priest at St Catherine's in Penrith, where I still take my family. As a shy nineteen-year-old in a foreign land for the first time, I was looking for comfort, although I did not realize it then. I was wrapped up in my new job with Gordon Richards and felt very much at home in my digs in Park Road, Greystoke, with my landlady Sheila Lancaster, who looked after me with an attentive warmth, helping me overcome my homesickness.

But, at that stage of my life I was naturally not sure what lay ahead and whether I had made the right move. There was a tension inside me after taking the plunge and leaving my family and roots so far behind.

Father Murphy invited me to his house one day after mass and then I discovered that he came from Charleville in County Cork. We shared a common background. We used to split a bottle of lemonade and he would recall the days during the 1940s when he represented County Cork at hurling and Gaelic football. He used to be a six handicap golfer and I still remember the story he told me after mass when we were chatting about our different experiences at Castletownroche and Charleville.

A local doctor, who I believe is still alive in Charleville, was playing a round of golf at the local course. As he was preparing to play his ball onto the green, a sixteen-stone farmer's son walked across the fairway. The farmer's son, unconcerned that the doctor was desperately trying to concentrate on hitting the ball straight, announced, 'Doctor, I haven't been feeling very well of late.'

The doctor put his hand in his pocket and pulled out a dirty handkerchief, wisps of straw, car keys and finally some pills which were yellow with age. He handed the pills to the farmer's son, who asked, 'What do I do with these?'

The doctor replied, 'You take two tonight and if you are still alive in the morning two more!'

Father Murphy assures me that this is a true story and I can already hear the cries from the English, 'It could only happen in Ireland.'

If only the officers of the Racecourse Security Services, the Jockey Club's police force, could have heard me the night I went over to Whitehaven to open the newly built St Benedict's Social Club, which adjoins the church and Father Murphy's house on the vast Mirehouse housing estate. Father Murphy introduced me to hundreds of parishioners who were racing enthusiasts and punters and inevitably extracted a couple of tips from me for the next day. Incredibly one of them won, but several punters whom I did not manage to speak to complained to Father Murphy that they had missed out on a winner. Was I guilty of breaking the Jockey Club's controversial rule, which states that jockeys are forbidden to tip horses? Certainly it was for no monetary gain and it was done with the best will in the world, but I suppose, strictly speaking, I was very close to crossing the thin line which separates the lawful suggestion that someone may back a certain horse from the unlawful tipping to a jockey's regular punter.

A great bond of friendship grew between us and I always felt – and still do – that I could take Father David completely into my confidence. Sunday afternoons were one of the few occasions when Sheila and I could take time out together and go for a drive in the car and, wherever we were, I would stop off and nip into evening mass, leaving Sheila sitting alone in the car outside. After a while Sheila felt she might as well come inside and join me and, after considerable help and discussion with Father Murphy, she was eventually converted from the Church of England to the Catholic faith.

When we started having an increasing number of people to stay Sheila was concerned about being able to entertain them as it was a side of life which was completely new to her, having come from a quiet farming family in Cumbria. She discussed her fears with Father Murphy, whose sympathetic hearing helped give her the necessary confidence to cope with the great variety of people we had to stay. Now, I can hardly believe that she was ever worried by the problem, for she seems to be in her element with other people, even when she is trying to look after Louise, Gill and Tom at the same time.

Father visited me in Carlisle Hospital just after I had broken my right leg for the second time, in 1980. I know he was not wanting to preach to me, but to try and bring me a

crumb of comfort at a time when I thought there was nothing
left in my world. He explained that even in such critical
situations God is to be found and that nothing totally
destructive can happen to us. He quoted the case of the
Spanish army officer Ignatius of Loyola, who had a
marvellous career ahead of him and moved in the highest
circles but at the Battle of Pamplona in 1521 had his right leg
shattered by a cannon ball and was forced to lie flat on his
back for many months. During the long, weary and painful
healing process his whole career changed in the light of his
experience. Time hung heavily on his hands and, as novels
were in short supply in those days, he read the Life of Christ
and the Saints. He swapped horses, so to speak, exchanging
his romantic and chivalrous approach to life for a life devoted
completely to God. He founded the Jesuits, a strict order of
the Roman Catholic Church. Father Murphy recalled that
Ignatius of Loyola used to get involved in brawls during his
army days, but that nursing his broken leg gave him time to
think and take stock of his life. Father Murphy was quick to
stress that he was not expecting me to take on some new
religious order, he was simply trying to convey to me that
there was no situation outside God's design on us and that
this particular crisis would serve to give me more time to
think about my life, as it had done for Ignatius of Loyola.

I was lucky to have Sheila to help me through such a long
and often depressing process, as well as our baby Louise,
whose visits were a source of great pleasure and a wonderful
distraction from the routine of hospital life.

Father Murphy had sown the seed of the lasting message
that life is not confined simply to trying to ride winners;
before that anyone monitoring my daily habits would have
been aware of my blinkered existence. Gradually it dawned
on me that a great chunk of life was passing me by as I
concentrated on jockeyship rather than enjoying myself with
the family. I was awakened to the fact that I was constantly

feuding inside myself, striving to marry a successful career with a happy family life. Having totally ignored such matters during the first two or three years of marriage, I am now deeply conscious of how I split myself between the job and the home, although it is difficult being made the way I am – a person of perpetual motion, unable to sit still for long.

It is a very natural fault to allow the world to go by without appreciating the many material belongings we use from day to day. I am as guilty as the next man of taking too much for granted.

I sometimes ask myself what have I done to deserve the depressing series of injuries during my career. Why does it happen? I wonder. Perhaps to make me appreciate the good things in life of which I am lucky enough to have more than my share.

When there was a real possibility of my losing my right leg I must have bored Father Murphy silly seeking his reassurance that I would one day recover my confidence on two legs and in the saddle. Even when I was having a bad run with my riding I could consult him and talk through my trials and tribulations in the knowledge that our conversations would go no further.

The only recollection I have of Louise's early days is that I barely saw her during her first year. I was present at her birth on 8 August 1979, which coincided with the start of another long season, and so I did not play a major role with nappies and feeding bottles. In fact, I had never experienced children before, having been the youngest member of our family of four boys. So I was bemused to find myself in charge of a tiny baby girl, although, it goes without saying, I was a very proud father.

I had bought Deep Ghyll, our first home, at Plumpton the winter before we got married and it was while we were entertaining a few friends there that I was shocked to find out what a thoroughly neglecting father I had been. Sheila's mother Audrey greeted Louise and said, 'How's Daddy, then?' and Louise turned and ran straight to Audrey's husband Stan, believing he was her father. As Stan quite naturally picked her up and held her in his arms I felt a knife turn in my guts. I didn't say a word, but thought to myself that small children are totally uninhibited and don't tell lies. During that first year Louise had seen more of my parents-in-law than of me, but what a way to let me know. After the initial hurt, I tried to learn from the painful lesson and made a conscious effort to spend more time with her. Splashing around together during her early-evening bath became a ritual for us on the occasions when I was not away racing. Now, of course, Gill and Tom are also part of the bath routine and I often wonder if Louise went across to Stan during that party at Deep Ghyll for a very special reason.

Gill was born in Penrith on 20 June 1982, the day I was due back from riding Gaye Chance, who had finished third in the French Champion Hurdle at Auteuil in Paris. I telephoned from Manchester Airport but couldn't put the money in the box, though I heard Sheila answer the phone before the pips started and was happy to learn that she had not been admitted to Penrith Maternity Hospital. I enjoyed a relaxed journey home, which by then was Ivy House, a 45-acre farm at Skelton Wood End near Skelton, only a quarter of an hour's drive from our original house at Plumpton. On arrival I found Stan sitting alone in the lounge and he greeted me with the news that Audrey had taken Sheila into hospital. I made myself a cup of tea and only as an afterthought telephoned the hospital to see how she was doing as I thought the birth was still some time away. The sister said, 'You'd better hurry up or you'll miss it.'

My cup of tea was left to go cold as I sped through the night, reaching the hospital in the nick of time to witness Gill's debut. Tom was far more considerate and arrived on 20

April 1984, which was Good Friday – one of the few days in the year when there is no racing. Tom is already known as the Head Lad in the family. Having been given such a nickname he will probably grow up with not the remotest interest in racing. Who knows?

10

Night Nurse

Suggest to Peter Easterby that Jonjo was not as effective on Night Nurse as his fellow Irishman Paddy Broderick, who won the 1976 and 1977 Champion Hurdles on him, and you almost stir the great trainer's Yorkshire blood with a touch of anger. While admitting that Broderick and Night Nurse were brilliant together, Peter highlights the 1982 Bradstone Mandarin Handicap Chase at Newbury. He says, 'No one could have ridden a better race on Night Nurse than Jonjo did that day. People who say his shorter legs and crouching style were not as effective as the longer-legged, more upright Broderick are talking rubbish.'

Night Nurse's owner Reg Spencer always recognized Broderick as the number one jockey for his horse after they had forged their golden partnership over hurdles in the seventies. But Reg says, 'I have always admired Jonjo's loyalty. He elected to stick with Sea Pigeon in the 1978 Champion Hurdle, even though he had the chance to ride Night Nurse, who was favourite.'

Reg adds, 'He also passed up the tempting offer from Michael Dickinson to partner the 1982 King George VI winner Wayward Lad to stand by Night Nurse in what turned out to be his last race.'

T.R.

Michael Dickinson's phone call just before Christmas 1982 caused me enough heart-searching to last a lifetime. But then Night Nurse, who himself suffered from a heart murmur, had provided me with enough memories and thrills in our eighteen races together to last a lifetime. Michael, who grabbed winter racing by the jugular and squeezed enough big prize money out of the sport to make him champion trainer three times on the trot in the early eighties, telephoned me to ask me to ride Wayward Lad in the King George VI Chase at Kempton on Boxing Day. Michael's Silver Buck, winner of the 1982 Tote Cheltenham

Weighing out . . . checking my weight on the trial scales in the jockeys' changing room

Victory smile – unsaddling Alverton after the 1979 Cheltenham Gold Cup

Ron Barry – a tough face masks one of the warmest blokes you could meet

Alverton and Tied Cottage (far side) plunge through the snowflakes over the last fence of the Cheltenham Gold Cup. Tied Cottage crumpled on landing, leaving the way clear for an exhausting victory

Smiles of relief – silver-haired Pat Muldoon and Peter Easterby share our moment of triumph after Sea Pigeon's nail-biting Ebor Handicap triumph at York in 1979

The chips are down – Sea Pigeon (centre) challenges Monksfield on his way to win the 1980 Champion Hurdle at Cheltenham

Ouch! Badsworth Boy bangs his head and catapults Robert Earnshaw into orbit at the final fence at Aintree's Sunratings Chase in 1982. I am in pursuit on Little Bay . . .

. . . I can't avoid the pile-up . . .

. . . and we did our best to step over Badsworth Boy's tummy and through his legs . . .

. . . to victory. The circus act enabled Little Bay to forget about racing and before he realised it his brilliance had won him the race

John Francome and Brown Chamberlin chase Burrough Hill Lad (Phil Tuck) away from the last in the 1984 Cheltenham Gold Cup. John couldn't catch them but had ridden one of his greatest races

Night Nurse chests the final fence but still feels like Concorde as we hurtle to victory in the 1982 Pennine Chase at Doncaster

Dawn Run gives me that never-say-die feeling as she leads Desert Orchid on her way to victory in the 1984 Champion Hurdle at Cheltenham

All smiles – even Dawn Run has a laugh as we enter the winner's enclosure

Castletownroche celebrates: (left to right) brothers Dennis, Jerome and Thomas stand behind Monica (Jerome's wife), my father Tom, and Sheila holding Jerome's son John, on the float at the Castletownroche Carnival after my record-breaking season in 1978

Baby Tom gets in on the family act with Sheila, Louise and Gill

Gold Cup, was hot favourite to complete a hat trick of victories in the King George, but Wayward Lad was strongly fancied too.

Night Nurse was the nigger in the woodpile, though I hasten to admit I could hardly choose a more unkind description of a horse who made the experience of jumping every fence as exhilarating as riding a winner. Realistically, I knew Night Nurse had no chance of beating Wayward Lad, who, at seven, was being hailed as the rising star among chasers. But I had never shared so many breathtaking jumps with another chaser; Night Nurse invariably brought off the impossible with incredible leaps few other steeplechasers have the courage to contemplate. I was in a quandary.

I tossed the dilemma over in my mind early in the morning and last thing at night, and sometimes as I lay awake in the middle of the night. I wanted to ride Wayward Lad but could not bring myself to desert Night Nurse. My head said Wayward Lad; my heart Night Nurse.

The King George is the climax of the heavy racing programme over Christmas and it runs second to the Tote Cheltenham Gold Cup in terms of prestige. The £24,000 prize was another tempting incentive; Wayward Lad could win it, but I doubted whether Night Nurse, at eleven years and battle-scarred after numerous spirited races, had retained enough sparkle to beat his juniors.

I consulted many friends but all the time knew that the final decision rested on my shoulders. In the end it became no contest. I owed it to Night Nurse, his owner Reg Spencer, an estate agent from York, and the indomitable Peter Easterby. In the event Wayward Lad, who was finally ridden by John Francome, carried the day in an epic finish with Fifty Dollars More, trained by Michael Dickinson's big rival Fred Winter, and his stable companion, the favourite Silver Buck. Wayward Lad's win was to become the middle leg of a unique hat trick for the remarkable Michael Dickinson, who had saddled Silver Buck to take the 1980 King George. In 1983 Wayward Lad again won the race, which had been frozen off in 1981. Incredibly, Michael's father Tony Dickinson had won the two previous runnings of the King George with Silver Buck and Gay Spartan.

Poor Night Nurse trailed home fifth, over fifty lengths behind Wayward Lad, and I surprised myself by feeling no regret when I walked him back to be unsaddled knowing that I could have ridden the winner. Five days later Reg Spencer and Peter Easterby announced Night Nurse's retirement; I would certainly have been hit by a pang of regret on hearing the end of the great horse's career if I had abandoned him in what turned out to be his last race, even though he provided me with only a long-range rear view of Wayward Lad and John Francome. His reign had been long and glorious and to have been part of it was an honour. I did not ride him as well as Paddy Broderick. No one did. I may not have shared in his greatest moments – his two Champion Hurdles and his lion-hearted second to his stable companion Little Owl in the 1982 Cheltenham Gold Cup – but I savoured the aspirations of all young jump jockeys when I partnered him over fences. It was like the power of Concorde on take off as he flicked you over each jump.

Night Nurse's slight heart irregularity created problems for Peter Easterby when he tried to sell the horse. Peter tried eight prospective owners before veteran Midlands business-man Edgar Rudkin, who was nearly blind, finally agreed to purchase him, but as soon as he realized Peter intended to send him jumping Mr Rudkin wanted to opt out because he could not bear for his horse to be subjected to the hazards of hurdling. Reg Spencer was with a party of friends at Ripon night meeting in June 1974 when he was taken with this fine three-year-old walking round the paddock before the last race.

Reg recalls, 'I thought to myself, By, that fellow will make a cracking hurdler. I liked him so much I told my friends to have a few bob on him and most of us secured 20–1 for our cash before his odds shrank to 9–1. Mark Birch led all the way on Night Nurse and of course my pals were suitably impressed. I bought him after that and while I thought he might win a hurdle race or two I never dreamed he would reach such heights as champion hurdler twice, not even after I had watched his first win over hurdles at Market Rasen less than a couple of months after that memorable evening at Ripon. I telephoned Peter after Paddy Broderick had made virtually all the running on Night Nurse to say how I had never seen a horse get away from his hurdles with such speed. Peter won his first Champion Hurdle with Saucy Kit seven years before Night Nurse's Market Rasen debut, and I must have got carried away when I told Peter that Night Nurse was, to my biased eye, the best I had seen since Saucy Kit. Little did I know how accurately I had assessed him – even if more by luck than judgement!'

Paddy and Night Nurse went on to win five of their seven races that season, including a six-length victory at Cheltenham in September – a foretaste of the historic events that lay ahead on the Gloucestershire course.

Night Nurse suited Paddy, and the silver-eyed, fast-talking lad from Rathowen, County Westmeath, complemented the many attributes of the big horse. Paddy had the best of Night Nurse's years during his early hurdling career. Brod, as he was affectionately known in the jockeys' room, was a brilliant horseman and his long legs curled round Night Nurse's large frame in a way that mine could not. If I gave Night Nurse a kick in the belly it was like a fly touching him. When Paddy gave him a prod with his heels Night Nurse knew all about it. I had to ride with a shorter stirrup leather than Paddy did. The bigger the horse the more I have to pull up my stirrups to stay with my mount and keep him balanced. To ride as effectively as Paddy, I had to shorten my leathers, sit up, balance and relax Night Nurse. I always tried to understand the horse and I had some fantastic rounds on him, but Paddy was the ideal jockey for him. He maintains that Night Nurse's second Champion Hurdle triumph in 1977 was the climax of their partnership.

'Night Nurse did not like the bottomless ground but was still brave enough to outclass those fine hurdlers Monksfield, Dramatist and Sea Pigeon.'

It was Paddy's dream to win a Cheltenham Gold Cup on the horse that made his life and he could not stop telling us all how one day he would. There was never the slightest doubt in Paddy's mind, but sadly his hopes shattered in a split-second miscalculation at Kempton on Boxing Day 1977.

Paddy, who describes Night Nurse as 'the machine of my career', looks back to that gloomy December day. 'I asked Night Nurse for a long one, but he caught the top of the hurdle and turned a somersault. As a result of the fall I suffered from concussion, was dazed, unbalanced and felt like a drunken man. I got bad headaches and after a series of deep X-rays of my head I was told by the doctors that another knock would turn me into a cabbage.'

Ten years earlier Paddy had lain unconscious for a fortnight after a terrible spill from Dashing White Sargeant at Uttoxeter. But he had courageously picked himself off the floor, gathered his career together and forged the golden partnership with Night Nurse. He now lives in County Durham with his wife Nan and their daughter Alyson, who provides him with enormous pleasure as she rides with considerable success in local gymkhanas and shows.

During Paddy's battered career he rode nearly five hundred winners; in addition to the 1976 and 1977 Champion Hurdles, he won two Welsh Champion Hurdles, one Scottish and the Irish Sweeps Hurdle on Night Nurse. It was sad that Night Nurse, who had put the glorious touches to his life in the saddle, should be responsible for the fall that finished

Paddy. But Paddy did what we have all tried, and asked for the impossible going into the last hurdle. It was just not there, but that's the chance we are paid to try and calculate. If it had come off Paddy would have returned to cries of 'Wasn't Brod brilliant?'

He battled bravely to try and team up with Night Nurse a month later in the William Hill Yorkshire Hurdle at Doncaster, but Paddy's loss was my gain and it was on that wet, wintry January afternoon that I rode Night Nurse for the first time. Had Night Nurse realized that his greatest pal had lost the fight after their calamitous Kempton exit? I almost felt that he knew how hard Brod had been trying to climb back into the saddle and when he failed to renew their famous partnership Night Nurse said to himself, 'If Brod can't win, then I will.' Night Nurse called on all his inimitable courage to get us home. We turned into the home straight in the lead ahead of our two rivals – Bird's Nest and Decent Fellow – and I did not think Night Nurse was travelling particularly sweetly. As I glanced back to take stock of the state of play behind me I could see Bird's Nest and Decent Fellow travelling ominously well so I asked Night Nurse to quicken up and go for home. At the second last flight Bird's Nest was absolutely cruising, ready to canter all over us whenever his jockey Andy Turnell pressed the button. But the more I rode Night Nurse the lower he got, the more he stretched like a greyhound going flat out, and he flew over the last, kept galloping and refused to allow Bird's Nest to nail home any real advantage, though he led momentarily at the last. The race proved a real eye-opener for me as Bird's Nest looked like taking us at will all the way up the straight, and yet there was no way Night Nurse was going to let him.

There was no shortage of courage in the amazing mixture of speed, stamina, brilliant jumping and the will to win that fuelled his tank. You would be thinking about preparing to take off and all of a sudden he would be off. He would take the obstacle in his stride, not rising very high, just zipping over it at tremendous speed. Then in a flash it all happened. He landed, switched on an extra engine which accelerated him away from the hurdle the instant he touched down, and you were powered back into the saddle. That was where he won his races, by leaving even the fastest hurdlers toiling as he roared away, his hurdles disappearing behind him in a mass of flying hooves and earth. If ever he wanted to take off with you there was no answer – you'd had it, though happily he never took advantage of me. He was a kind horse, until you visited him in his box where he seemed to take exception to any intruders and in a miserable way put his ears back and greeted you with a nasty nip if you were not on your guard. In that respect he had little personality about him, though when you were on his broad back he was like a tame lion, a kindly fighter. At home with the string he would not go in front but stopped, spooked, ducked and dived, and yet in a race he wanted to be out in front all the time.

Just over four years after our initiation we returned to Doncaster in 1982 to take on Midnight Court, the 1978 Cheltenham Gold Cup winner, in the three-runner Pennine Chase. Night Nurse was impressive that day and, as if to show off, gave the crowd standing round the last fence an exhibition of taking off a mile too soon, just breasting and parting the top of the fence, but was still able to gallop away for a twelve-length victory over Midnight Court. In my mind there was no doubt that Peter Easterby had him spot on for the Tote Cheltenham Gold Cup twenty days later.

My confidence was sky high until I asked Night Nurse to take up his starting position. Peter Easterby believed that Night Nurse would be more effective on the new strip of ground by the inside rails. It was not as squelchy as the rest of the course which was heavy and in parts extremely sticky. I persuaded Night Nurse to start against the rails but he did not like being enclosed on the inside and started to sulk. With hindsight it is easy to see that he would not enjoy being squeezed by the other horses and would have raced far more happily if I had allowed him plenty of room and daylight. I eventually pulled him up approaching the second last fence, by which time Silver Buck and Robert Earnshaw had made it a memorable one, two for Michael Dickinson by beating stable companion Bregawn, ridden by Graham Bradley. That was a bitter disappointment because I knew exactly what Night Nurse could have done.

During his first season chasing in the spring of 1979, six months after he had unshipped me at the fourth fence in his first chase, for which he started 2-1 on, at Market Rasen the previous September, we were reunited at Liverpool on the eve of Alverton's fatal Grand National. Two miles round the Mildmay course trading jumps with Fulke Walwyn's exciting prospect Dramatist was as testing an experience of competing in the cut and thrust of a steeplechase as you could wish for. It was tit for tat down the far side, and three fences from home Bill Smith, who now works for the International Racing Bureau as a racing guide for the Maktoum family from Dubai, pinched a slight lead on Dramatist, but Night Nurse's jumping was not only faultless but also effortlessly packed with more power than you find in most top-class chasers. He regained the lead approaching the last fence and quickly put ten lengths between us and Dramatist by the line. Night Nurse rounded off his first season's chasing by winning the London and Northern Group Future Champions Novices Chase at Ayr on Scottish Grand National day, leaving me in no doubt that he possessed the chasing capabilities to achieve what no horse had done before – add the Cheltenham Gold Cup to his victories in the Champion Hurdle. Sadly, that dream never quite materialized, although Alan Brown booted him to within a length and a half of historic glory when he was beaten by Little Owl in 1981.

Alan, a Geordie from Blakelaw, Newcastle, rides for the

Easterby stable and enjoyed some glittering moments on Night Nurse, including their 1979 triumph in Ascot's Buchanan Whisky Gold Cup. He is adamant that Night Nurse would have won the 1981 Tote Cheltenham Gold Cup had he not gone lame turning for home. Night Nurse kept hanging to the right because of his lameness and Alan insists that his temporary leg injury cost him the glory. However, he recalls, 'I felt afterwards that Night Nurse had won, because he received a far greater reception from the crowd than Little Owl. They really loved him in the South and I have never heard such cheers for a horse who finished second as when Night Nurse was beaten by Tragus in the Freshfields Holidays Handicap Chase at Sandown six weeks before his courageous encounter with Little Owl at Cheltenham.'

Alan maintains modestly that Night Nurse would have beaten Silver Buck in the 1980 King George VI Chase at Kempton had he not 'fallen off' at the last. I hasten to add that Alan uses the words 'fallen off' when he recalls that day at Kempton, but in fact Night Nurse made a monumental blunder when challenging Silver Buck and gave him little chance of keeping the partnership intact.

A month after Night Nurse and I had had our calamitous introduction to fences at Market Rasen in September 1978, I broke my right arm at Kelso and Ian Watkinson took over on the big horse. He proceeded to win five chases on him, one at Wetherby, two at Newcastle – where Ian also won the Fighting Fifth Hurdle on Sea Pigeon half an hour before his third victory on Night Nurse – and one each at Ascot and Wolverhampton, before they teamed against Silver Buck in Haydock's postponed Embassy Premier Chase Final, which was one of the most nerve-tingling spectacles of my career. I watched in awe from the stands, and the way Night Nurse and Silver Buck attacked each other fence by fence over the last mile and a half conjured memories of the titanic struggle between Grundy and Bustino in Ascot's 1975 King George VI and Queen Elizabeth Stakes, which became billed as the Race of the Century. Tommy Carmody on Silver Buck did not let Ian out of his sights on the first circuit; then Silver Buck took over the lead at the awkward downhill first fence on the far side, but Ian kept Night Nurse in close touch as they tried to stretch each other over the last seven fences. Ian recalls that probably the greatest thrill he experienced on Night Nurse was jumping the last ditch down the far side. 'I was half a length down on Silver Buck. Both horses stood a mile off the fence and for a second you wondered if they would reach it, never mind clear it. They both jumped it perfectly, landed galloping and continued the epic struggle.

'Going round on Night Nurse was like sitting in an armchair, he was such a comfortable ride. Perhaps not the brilliance and sheer speed of Sea Pigeon, but he managed to keep up a relentless gallop and jump like a bird. Turning into the straight at Haydock I thought I'd win. But Night Nurse had not run for nearly ten weeks, while Silver Buck had had a recent run at Windsor, though he had been brought down there. This told against Night Nurse and, while I was accused by Peter Easterby and others of hitting him too often and too hard as we both gathered our last ounces of energy up the straight for a final cut at Silver Buck, I can assure everyone that I did not strike Night Nurse with as much venom as they all thought. Going to the last fence I thought we would get back at Silver Buck, but halfway up the run in I knew he was beaten.'

The pace was breakneck, their jumping impeccable and they were both in there slugging it out as they rose at the last fence. Night Nurse was legless on the run in; so was Silver Buck, but he managed to summon enough strength to claw his way home two and a half lengths ahead of his never-say-die rival.

Exactly seven days after his momentous ride on Night Nurse Ian's career was ended at Towcester where his mount

Regal Choice, trained by former jockey John Haine, cartwheeled and landed on top of him. Several onlookers feared the worst and thought Ian was dead as he lay motionless on the turf. He was unconscious for seventeen hours and in a semiconscious daze for six weeks while his brain recovered from bad bruising.

Ian, a Newmarket lad, is the son of a Royal Navy engineer and he was all set to follow in his father's footsteps and pursue engineering at Anglesey College until he turned up one day at a point-to-point at Cottenham near Cambridge at the age of fifteen.

He says, 'I watched a horse rear up before the race and come down on his rider, smashing his leg. During the pandemonium that followed I went up and tapped the shoulder of Maurice Bailey, the Newmarket personality who was leading the horse away, and said, "I'll ride it next time for you." That was at the Moulton point-to-point, where I pulled him up. But I raced round for long enough to find out what I wanted to know – that my heart was set on a career in the saddle.'

Ian who was in the same class at Newmarket Grammar School as Bill O'Gorman, the successful local trainer, remembers when they were both up in front of the headmaster at the same time. He recollects, 'We both got the cane together, though I'm not sure what we had done wrong. The headmaster gave us alternate strokes across the backside!'

Ian rode about 200 winners before that fateful day at Towcester. He says, 'I was staying with Bob Champion, who was in the bath when John Haine rang up to ask him to ride Regal Choice. I answered the phone and Bob shouted from the bathroom that he was not going to Towcester and so John asked me to take over on Regal Choice. You never know what's round the corner.'

After training 112 winners in two seasons at Cootamundra,

three hundred miles southwest of Sydney in New South Wales, Australia, Ian pulled out of racing. 'I found the magnet of raceriding was still too much of a pull. That's all I really wanted to do, so I thought it best to make a break from racing,' said Ian, who nowadays subjects his thirteen-stone frame to a daily run to 'clear my nose', which he broke five times.

During a bad patch in his riding career Ian turned his hand to odd-job man and jack-of-all-trades at the Eden Hall Hotel near Penrith and he is now putting that experience to good use in Australia, where he is assisting a friend who has invested £850,000 in the Leg Trap Hotel at West Lakes, Adelaide.

The Embassy was the first of seven encounters between Night Nurse and Silver Buck, who was a year younger. Night Nurse came off best only once, in the 1981 Tote Cheltenham Gold Cup, when he finished second to Little Owl. Silver Buck was ten lengths behind in third place. But I always felt that Night Nurse should have taken revenge for his Haydock defeat in their next clash there in the 1979 Edward Hanmer Memorial Chase, which was to become a benefit for Silver Buck, who won it four years on the trot.

This time I was on Night Nurse, with Tommy Carmody again on Silver Buck. Tommy set a slow pace for the first mile until our only other rival, John Francome on Border Incident, took over and then Night Nurse went on a mile from home. After jumping the second last, victory was in sight but was cruelly wrenched from our clutches when disaster struck. As we galloped to the final fence I felt Night Nurse's surge of power evaporate under me; he changed legs before jumping the fence, but when we touched down the punch had left his normally powerful stride and, courageously though he battled, he reluctantly gave way to Silver Buck, who won by a length and a half. Night Nurse had not broken down but pulled up lame and the heat in this leg was warning enough for Peter Easterby to rest him for a year.

Arguments as to the relative merits of Night Nurse and Silver Buck will never be resolved. The Dickinson camp will not hear of Night Nurse being lauded as superior to Silver Buck, particularly with the score at six to one in Silver Buck's favour. Night Nurse should have beaten him that November afternoon at Haydock in 1979, but, having said that, they were two great horses. Silver Buck was lazy inasmuch as he would win by only as much as he wanted and seldom as easily as his enormous talent allowed; but the Easterby stable always used to insist that in top form Night Nurse would beat him. Silver Buck's thirty steeplechasing victories included two King George VI Chases and a Cheltenham Gold Cup. He holds the record for prize money won by a National Hunt star, but before he embarked on his chasing career he did not win two Champion Hurdles as Night Nurse did. They were two superstars of the winter game and their spinetingling encounters will be discussed and debated by their fans long into the night for many years to come.

It was with great sadness in September 1984 that the racing world heard of Silver Buck's sudden death at the Harewood stables of Monica and Tony Dickinson, who had only recently taken the reins back from their son Michael, now seeking new challenges as a flat trainer in Wiltshire. On a happier note, Night Nurse is still enjoying his retirement in Peter Easterby's paddocks at Great Habton and occasionally can be seen carrying his trainer, son Tim or Dudley Taylor, stud groom at Peter's Easthorpe Hall Stud, across North Yorkshire for a day's hunting with the Sinnington.

I had a great ally in Night Nurse when I was trying to piece my career together again after breaking my right leg the second time. Only a month after my comeback win on Realt Na Nona at Wetherby in December 1981 the artic weather closed in and hit racing very hard, but Newbury managed to stage its New Year meeting, the feature of which was the

Bradstone Mandarin Handicap Chase. It was a wonderful opportunity for Night Nurse and me to show the racing world in the South and on television that we were no back numbers.

It was the first time I had ridden him in public for over two years, the last being that unhappy day in 1979 at Haydock when he pulled up so feelingly behind Silver Buck. Emotions ran high through the enthusiastic and adoring Newbury crowd as Night Nurse went ping, ping, ping, ping, ping at full speed and with perfect precision over the five fences down the far side of the second circuit. At the cross fence before the straight and five from home he landed running, whereas the threatening challenge of Dave Goulding on Captain John was checked by a mistake. The Mandarin may have been won and lost there, for Captain John fought his way back and actually led Night Nurse at the last fence. When Night Nurse was out in front he kept doing the impossible by standing off his fences, putting together the most enormous leap and accelerating away from the fence as only he could. Then the big ears would work backwards and forwards as he checked on the state of play behind him and snatched a quick breather before again taking off at an unbelievable distance from the next fence.

I left it all to him. I know everyone thought we were finished as Captain John passed us at the last, but I always felt Night Nurse, like the true professional that he was, had saved a little up his sleeve for the final dash to the line. I only had to ride him out with hands and heels for a two-and-a-half-length victory from Captain John. It was the most understanding of the eighteen races we had together. Night Nurse's brilliance and guts transmitted all the confidence I needed and produced a performance as near perfection as I shall ever experience.

The knowledgeable Newbury crowd was quick to salute Night Nurse's flawless jumping and courageous fightback from the last. We returned with their roar in our ears and for a moment I thought we must have won the Cheltenham Gold Cup. They knew they had witnessed a steeplechasing exhibition to behold. That bleak January afternoon Night Nurse gave me the greatest thrill I have ever had on a horse.

In nine seasons jumping Night Nurse won thirty-two of his sixty-four races, amassing over £132,000 in first-prize money. He may or may not have been as good a chaser as Silver Buck but there is no doubt in my mind that, after Arkle and Red Rum, he was the most popular jumper in my lifetime.

11

The Wrong Breaks

No one has been closer to Jonjo during his spells in hospital, in plaster or on crutches, than Hugh Barber, consultant orthopaedic surgeon at Carlisle's Cumberland Infirmary. He knows the full details of Jonjo's injuries and the suffering they have caused him.

Barber says, 'I would not like to give the idea that Jonjo does not feel pain. If he breaks a leg it hurts; it's got to. Most people feel pain to pretty much the same extent, but there are big personality differences. Some enjoy ill health and others steel themselves against the pain.

'They say: "Right, this is going to hurt but, nevertheless, I'm going to do this, do that and carry on as normally as possible." Jonjo regards a break as a nuisance, but a necessary part of the way he earns his living. He has to get over it as fast as possible and knows that the less he dwells on it the better he will be. Not many people are as clear-cut about it as Jonjo – he just gets up and goes.

'I have never seen him cry with pain, though you know he is in pain and he will tell you so. Some men make a terrible fuss about the pain they are feeling, but never Jonjo. He wants to be riding again yesterday, like most well-motivated sportsmen. It's what they are missing today that matters; any hold-up is bloody.'

Barber is adamant. 'No one else would have continued as a jockey after the suffering and discomfort Jonjo went through with his broken leg the second time. I don't know what motivates him; it's not money, greed or fame. He says he would do it all for nothing and I believe he would.'

At times when there appears to be no light at the end of the tunnel depression can set in and one inevitably explores every avenue in search of relief. That's not to say Hugh Barber has ever failed him. On the contrary, wherever the accident, whatever the injury, Jonjo always insists on returning to Carlisle and the Barber mending skills.

But there was a time when Jonjo tried new remedies in the bleak winter of 1981 as he found himself losing the agonizing battle to return to the saddle.

T.R.

The Land Rover slowed on the narrowing approach to the steep humpback bridge, the wipers working furiously to sweep the large flakes from the windscreen. Visibility was restricted through the biting blizzard and the drifting snow on both sides of the bridge reduced the roadway to a hazardous single lane. The driver was faced with the unenviable task of maintaining enough revs to power the four-wheel-drive vehicle up the incline but to retain enough control to be able to stop on the slippery surface if a car suddenly appeared over the brow of the bridge from the opposite direction. For a second there was a suggestion that the wheels would lose their grip, start spinning and we would land in Hermitage Water, as Stan Mounsey, my father-in-law, played on the steering wheel, desperately trying to keep the snowladen bonnet pointing forwards.

We dropped sharply from the hump bridge; Stan flicked the indicator to turn right and John Dixon's directions came back to me: 'Over the bridge, turn right and Mrs Scott's place is the first on the right.' John had recommended this nightmare journey after witnessing the agonies of my abortive comeback canter on his horse Skiddaw View in those dark days of January 1981. Unknown to us at the time, the steel plate in my right leg had moved under the stress of trying to ride again.

'Mrs Scott will bring you relief,' John had predicted.

Stan gingerly turned the Land Rover across the road and up the right-hand fork. Even through the heavy snowfall the sign was discernible: exactly 18 miles south of Hawick and 24 from Jedburgh in Scotland's bleak Border country of Roxburghshire. We crawled a few more yards along the Jedburgh road. In disbelief, I searched beyond the first house on the right for Mrs Scott's but the only other visible building was a solid grey church twenty yards further on from an almost derelict building which crouched beneath beautiful virgin-white trees, its roof laden with snow.

I peered long and hard at the house and asked for reassurance. 'Is that really Mrs Scott's?'

By repeating his movement with the right indicator Stan had already answered the question. As he prepared to drive into the snowfilled gateway he nodded. 'Yes, but don't be put off by the appearance. You will be a changed man on the way home.'

Encouragement, and plenty of it, was what I needed for the final shove over the threshold of what was rapidly appearing to be a rundown house. The windows at the back looked as though they had not been opened for years, and as for cleaning – well, that was obviously a dirty word around here. How could this house belong to a lady whose reputation stretched far and wide in the world of healing?

Our thirty mile drive through Arctic conditions from Carlisle to the sleepy village of Newcastleton was looking more and more like a bad mistake. Not only had we been doubtful finishers from the moment we set out from Deep Ghyll at Plumpton, besieged with snow high above the A6, but I harboured even graver doubts as we walked through the front door, stepping over a basin and a bowl in the cluttered hall. On entering the treatment room a dank stale odour pierced our nostrils. A two-bar electric fire glowed in the hearth, old magazines were stacked on the table in the window and the brown varnished piano sported a photo of a grateful patient, a rugby player about to score the winning try at the Gala seven-a-side tournament. If he could get off Mrs Scott's couch to run in the vital points for his side I was sure the frail grey-haired lady who appeared at the door could help restore my weakened, aching limbs to full strength.

'Mr Jonjo O'Neill?' inquired Mrs Scott in a quiet Scottish accent as she entered the room, thrusting out her right hand. The firm handshake belied first impressions, suggesting there was more to this elderly lady than her stooping frame would have you believe.

The couch was quite simply a bedstead and mattress concealed by a colourful duvet. It stood across the room against the wall which was covered with a heavily flowered wallpaper and supported a vast mirror and its gilt frame. I stretched out on the duvet, aware of the warmth thrown out by the electric fire, and noticed how the snow-bowed tree overhanging the window darkened the room, but not enough to disguise Mrs Scott's obvious dislike for housework. My eye was caught by small photos of John Dixon and his horses Skiddaw View and The Last Light. John was another satisfied client.

I lay on my tummy and Mrs Scott placed a cloth on my shoulders and started to massage them with her two middle fingers.

'No, Mrs Scott, it's my right leg not my shoulder that's giving me trouble,' I said. But Mrs Scott continued, explaining that she would massage me from my neck down my back and then work onto my legs. She explained how she was breaking up tiny lumps of blood and helping to improve my circulation. I soon became completely relaxed and fell asleep, to be awakened by a different and odd remedy. Mrs Scott was wrapping brown pieces of what appeared to be bark round my right leg and applying an oily potion. I was intrigued and pulled myself onto my elbows so I could see exactly what was going on.

She secured the brown bark close against my swollen leg with a bandage. 'This is slippery elm bark,' she said. 'Keep it on for three days and then come back and see me.'

Stan's predictions had been right. I did feel relieved and toned up on the return journey, though at that stage I wasn't sure if it was just in the mind. But over the next three days I became convinced that Mrs Scott's massage had helped me rediscover some of my lost energy. The leg was certainly more bearable. There must be magic in those ageing fingers.

Jessie Scott – or plain Mrs Scott as she is known

throughout the locality, where anyone with a bad back, an ache or pain seems to swear by her – qualified in massage and electrotherapy at Edinburgh. She then followed this up by pursuing the study of connective tissue technique, which, she maintains, by the use of her hands increases the chances of finding out exactly where the trouble is rooted. Mrs Scott explained that, although I was very fit, I had strained ligaments and muscles in my arms, shoulders, back and legs as a result of my falls, and my energy was being drained.

Some medics have laughed at me when I have told them about Mrs Scott's treatment. But her remedies have worked for me, I even took Gill to see her when she suffered from bad bouts of colic as a baby, and Mrs Scott succeeded in relieving her. However, she has not yet persuaded me to take a dip in Liddel Water and Hermitage Water, the two rivers which meet behind her house. She encourages some patients to float twenty yards on their backs, then wade back up Hermitage Water and walk to the house through her 'jungle' where she keeps her bees. Mrs Scott insists that the floating and treading water, the paddling and the walk back make an ideal therapeutic circuit.

Almost exactly a year after my unforgettable introduction to Mrs Scott I found myself driving back across the rolling slopes of Roxburghshire knowing it was my final throw before the 1982 Cheltenham Festival. And, if I was to believe the misinformed press and the growing rumours in racing, the dice were heavily loaded against me. Indeed the talk was that I would never see another racecourse from the back of a horse. Finished – not just for the fast approaching National Hunt Festival, but for good.

I was clutching at straws after being flattened and completely laid out by the most unpleasant bout of flu I can recall. I had been sent home from Haydock at the beginning of March, three months after my comeback in December 1981, suffering from flu. The simple remedy was a couple of days in bed and then I should have bounced back. But I could not have been farther from the mark. My condition deteriorated to such a low ebb that I simply wanted to curl up and die; and it turned out that plenty of people in the racing world had given me up for dead – or thought that I would certainly miss Cheltenham and perhaps even retire. Apparently, my body resistance was low as a result of the infection I had contracted in my broken leg the previous year and any illness or bug was still inclined to exploit my weakest part – the leg itself.

A reporter telephoned to ask if the rumour that I had had my right leg amputated was true. I left him in no doubt, telling him that the next time I saw him I would kick him with my left foot and then even harder with the right so that he would never forget it. But the situation reached crisis point when I learned I had been replaced on a horse for which I had been firmly booked in the Triumph Hurdle at Cheltenham. Peter Easterby told me afterwards that his phone had been red hot with calls from owners and trainers asking the same question: 'Is Jonjo's leg hanging off?'

Could Mrs Scott come to the rescue again? I was sure I would make it back in time for Cheltenham, despite the after-effects of flu leaving behind the usual underpowered body. My recovery had not been assisted by the persistence of the knockers, who had reduced the O'Neill confidence to such an all-time low that a shy kitten could have bluffed its way past me.

Four trips to Mrs Scott picked me up and ensured that I arrived at Cheltenham, even if only to show the racing world that I had two legs on which I could walk and ride! But I was not content with simply arriving at Cheltenham and going through the motions. I had a point to prove. My great ally Realt Na Nona could be relied on and carried me into second place behind John Francome on Brown Chamberlin in the Sun Alliance Chase, and then Path of Peace brought my wildest dreams to life by edging home in a threeway photo with Prince of Bermuda and Roadway in the County Hurdle. He enabled me to win the Ritz Club Charity Trophy, which is awarded to the top jockey at the Festival meeting. I am not sure who was most surprised – me or those know-alls who had been ready to dance on my grave.

When a reporter greeted me with, 'Jonjo, how do you feel now?' it took all my self-control not to reply, 'Jonjo? Jonjo? I thought he was finished.'

I met Hugh Barber on the recommendation of Ron Barry for the first time in 1978, courtesy of Red Well, a handicap hurdler trained in North Yorkshire by Mick Naughton. Red Well gave me a soft fall at the first hurdle in the back straight at Kelso. He threw me off the track and I was lying on my back in the field alongside the course enjoying the sunshine when a straggler jumped the hurdle, veered badly on landing and trod on my right arm. One minute I'd been lying peacefully under the Scottish skies gathering my thoughts and preparing to trudge back to the weighing room; the next writhing in agony and en route for Peebles Hospital. My arm was put in a cumbersome plaster from wrist to armpit, but it had been set wrongly and the aggravation and pain which accompanied the bad union of the bones drove me to Hugh Barber at Carlisle's Cumberland Infirmary. Hugh, in his late thirties, did not hesitate from behind his great bushes of muttonchop whiskers. 'I think there is a good case for putting a steel plate on that fracture, keeping your arm mobile and preserving as much muscle as possible. By the time the fracture is united you will have an arm that will work and you will be able to get straight back into raceriding. You see, the problem with keeping your arm in plaster is that all the muscles around it become weak and wasted.'

A man after my own heart, I thought. We were on the same wavelength. He was interested in my retaining maximum fitness during the mending period so that I could climb back on a horse in the minimum of time. The orthopaedic surgeon then quoted an article published in a medical journal by Dick Francis, the celebrated author of racing thrillers and former jockey to the Queen Mother. Dick Francis's plea, which Hugh Barber often refers to, is that sportsmen should be treated differently from other people because they want more than the average patient. They are prepared to put up with infinitely more discomfort than the average person and hence can be cured that much quicker.

Mr Barber says quite openly, 'You know that one day you are probably going to be arthritic and perhaps a bit lame. But yours is not a life in which you can think in terms of fifty years ahead. If we can agree on that sort of philosophy, then I can get you going sooner rather than later.'

At that comparatively early stage of my long list of injuries I did not appreciate the impact Hugh's thinking would have on my career.

Much to the annoyance of the sister in charge of the casualty ward at Wrexham Hospital I discharged myself the day I broke my right leg at Bangor. Not, I hasten to add, because they would not have done an admirable job on the leg, but because I was always happiest when I knew Hugh Barber was sticking me together again.

The Bangor fall from Simbad was a freak accident which was to become the biggest single hiccup in my career. Simbad caught the top of the hurdle, slipped, sprawled on the grass and skidded along on his belly for twenty yards or so. I was still on him and only when he started to roll over did I step off him, just like jumping off a bike. I pulled my right leg up and over and as it stuck out I pushed it in between the hind legs of another horse. It is virtually impossible to put the handle of a brush in between the hind legs of a horse when he is going at full gallop, but somehow I managed to poke my leg there.

I saw what happened. The horse's legs scissored mine in a cutting action. I heard a horrid crack. Felt excruciating pain as I lay on the Welsh turf nursing the lower part of my leg, which was like a bag of gravel. Lots of broken bones.

The first time I broke my right leg, at Teesside in 1975, I was out of action for six months, compared with the thirteen months after Bangor. But I had to endure more pain from the Teesside accident on Night Affair. A horse ran out in front of me, causing Night Affair to crash through the wooden wing of the hurdle. He wrapped my right leg round the wooden pole at the end of the wing and as I slid down to the ground I could see the bone below the knee sticking out through my riding boot. It was like an enormous nail protruding from my boot and, after staring at it for a second, I leaned forward, grabbed the bone and straightened the leg.

After those initial seconds the pain took over, roaring through my whole body. Every nerve was stretched to breaking point. I wanted to haul myself to my feet and run away to take my mind off the agony. But all I could do was lie and wait, tearing at the Teesside turf with my fingers. The ambulance came, and on the drive to the ambulance room on the racecourse every bump scythed through my body. It felt as though we were crossing a ploughed field. The journey seemed never ending.

At last, in the ambulance room I was given an injection but it took an age to overcome and ease the pain. I was admitted to the North Tees General Hospital where I was under Mr Ellis, who plastered my leg from ankle to hip. Blood seeped through the plaster but I was allowed back to Greystoke after a couple of weeks. By this time I had moved in with Gordon and Jean Richards in their flat above the stables.

They looked after me very well; Jean Richards set up a bed for me in the sitting room so that I could watch television. But when I went to bed I could not sleep because of the savage pain that started to build up behind my knee. Jean would say,

'Come on, it's all in the mind, try and go to sleep.' She suffered from a bad heart and would give me some of her heart pills to help me sleep. I would lie there, changing position as the pain crept up on me. But whichever side I rested on the pain kept coming and I would start crying. I tried not to shout out and be a nuisance, but I could not help myself. Finally I gave up the struggle and would lie there roaring at the top of my voice. Then I would be embarrassed, thinking how soft I must be. In the end, Jean had to ring Mr Ellis, who told her to bring me back to Teesside.

I was beginning to think the pain was affecting me mentally, for once I had returned to normal after an attack I could not remember what had happened. For this reason I did not want to go back to Mr Ellis because if I did not have the pain when I was with him I would have difficulty describing it and he would probably think I was making it up.

We were just leaving the M6 and heading towards Scotch Corner when I felt an attack building up; so I squeezed my leg at the top of the plaster and that eased it a bit. I tried not to let Jean see that I was in pain and turned to look out of the passenger window, which was enough to alert her.

'Are you all right?' she asked.

I nodded.

By the time we reached Temple Sowerby about five miles farther on I was roaring my head off. 'There is no way you are all right,' Jean said.

She pulled off the road into the King's Arms in Temple Sowerby, where she made me drink a cup of tea and take some painkillers. As we approached Scotch Corner the pain came in waves but shortly after Scotch Corner I felt fine, popped up as bright as a button and said to Jean, 'You can turn round now, I am much better. If I get to hospital I won't know what to tell them.'

Jean was adamant. 'I've come all this way and put up with

your roaring and I am not turning back now. I know what to tell them at the hospital.'

After I had tried to explain to Mr Ellis that I had this pain behind my knee, he said, 'I'll change the plaster for you. It's probably just nipping a bit.'

I was overcome with relief when I realized that the plaster could have been causing the trouble. But almost immediately the pain started again. Mr Ellis read my distress signals, rushed me down to the operating theatre, removed the plaster, held my leg up by the heel and rubbed his hand down the back of my leg. The expression on his face changed from plain concentration to worry and concern. I knew there was something wrong.

There was a bloodclot the size of a grapefruit behind my knee. Suddenly I was being filled with injections and before I knew where I was I was being being wheeled into the intensive-care unit, where I stayed for three days. I lost a lot of blood, but the swelling subsided. They kept me in hospital for over a month. I was out of racing for six months. My first winner after the accident was on the flat on Sonnenblick, who won a six-furlong two-year-old race at Hamilton in July.

During my six months off after Teesside and my thirteen months after Bangor, I was anxious to get out and about on the racecourse as soon as possible. I did not want to be forgotten and it does not take long for that to happen in racing. It was not so easy after Teesside because I was tied to the movements of the Richardses, with whom I was living. But I made a point in the New Year of 1981, as soon as the leg was improving, of showing the world that I was on the mend and went racing as often as I could without crutches. If owners, trainers, jockeys and various friends knew that I was looking forward to returning, they would at least bear me in mind. There was a period of two or three months when I should have been walking on crutches but did not because I used to drive to the racecourse and park in the jockeys' car park, where invariably there was a policeman on duty. I was frightened that if I got out of the car on crutches the policeman would pull me up and tell me that if I couldn't walk without them how could I drive without being a danger to the community.

Jean Richards died from a heart attack early in 1979. Although she would never admit it, her health was far worse than mine when she was nursing me through the aftermath of my broken leg. She fed me her heart pills when I couldn't sleep and yet her need was greater than mine. She drove me to the North Tees Hospital when her heart condition was more serious than my troublesome leg. But Jean refused to let her suffering interfere with those around her.

She was in terrible pain driving me to Cheltenham on Gold Cup day in 1974, and while I was at fault for not grasping the severity of the situation, she never once asked me to take over the wheel. As we passed Haydock on the M6 in Lancashire she complained of pains in her chest, but she continued, leaving me to doze peacefully in the passenger seat. However, near Tewkesbury in Gloucestershire she was so overcome by the pain that she drove the car off the M5 onto a minor road to a pub. I panicked when I saw how she was covered in sweat and could not walk. With help she reached a bench in the pub where she lay until an ambulance whisked her off to hospital in Cheltenham.

Even after that monumental warning Jean continued to lead life as she believed it should be led – with a capital 'L'. Her sparkling, outgoing personality endeared her to everyone who became involved in Gordon's business, from the lads and jockeys to the owners. Her help to Gordon was inestimable in the office, where her filing-cabinet brain stored much of the vital information.

Perhaps it was fitting that she died at a wedding with a champagne glass in her hand. Enjoying life.

*　　*　　*

The Cantabfella gave me my first serious fall at Cartmel in the Lake District in 1973 when I broke my right wrist, left collarbone and lost a handful of teeth. Only Money dumped me on my backside on the jarring Perth turf in 1976, fracturing my eleventh vertebra and putting me out of action for four months. Around Christmas time in 1976 I was skating and sliding on the ice on a pond at Johnby near Greystoke with Richard and Jason Hale, sons of Gordon Richards's blacksmith Roger Hale. Blow me, if I didn't spin upside down on the ice and break my collarbone. Cracking the collarbone was not too bad – it was having to face Gordon and tell him I had broken it playing with the kids.

When Hugh Barber was examining the X-ray of my collarbone he discovered a previous fracture of my right shoulderblade, but I have no idea when or where I did the damage. I suppose it must have been sore at the time but it sounds worse than it is. After all, in our profession the falls and bangs mean that you are always creaking to a degree and some injuries you don't notice as much as others. The day you are free from aches and pains is the day to treasure. I believe I have broken my right collarbone three times and my left one twice; they both stick out so awkwardly from the top of my chest that Louise and Gillian are not too keen on having cuddles. They keep banging their heads on these unfriendly protrusions and understandably are reluctant to hang on in there with their old man. It is a standing joke that when Sheila and I have fish and chips on the beach or in bed, she puts her salt in the great cavities caused by my misshapen collarbones! More seriously, wearing a car seat belt is most uncomfortable.

Galloping down the hill approaching the last hurdle at Cheltenham no quarter is given and if you are lucky enough to be in the fighting line your mount is at full throttle. Every move is made in a split second. One December afternoon in 1978, two weeks before Christmas, Within the Law veered to the left so sharply that he gave me no chance to correct his wild, unexpected deviation. He dived through the wing of the hurdle and I took the full impact straight on my chest before he crashed through the rails beyond. I thought my loud gasp must have been heard in the grandstand, as the last breath of wind was knocked out of my lungs. For seconds I could not breathe as I lay stranded on the ground. But once I'd recovered I noticed sharp pains in the side of my chest and this discomfort did not leave me. Three broken ribs feel like a red-hot blade cutting into your chest. Hugh Barber made me a protective corset so I could continue racing, though the ribs did not let me forget that they had come off second best against the Cheltenham woodwork.

Smashing my fist into the ground at Punchestown in Ireland in April 1980 after landing awkwardly – rather than belting the turf in a fit of temper – I broke my right hand. Luckily I was still able to ride at Haydock a week later where I won a novice chase on the 1984 Grand National hero Hallo Dandy, whose brilliant jumping got me round safely. I rode left-handed and called a cab with my right hand at every fence. Forty minutes later No Bombs literally carried his one-handed jockey to victory in Britain's most valuable handicap hurdle, the Royal Doulton.

The critics are for ever firing the accusation that my total disregard for danger has committed my mounts to more than they can take and sent their jockey to hospital beds on more occasions than he should have been. I cannot say whether I am oblivious of fear or simply cannot recognize danger when my blood is up out there among the flying hooves.

The devil takes over when I am sizing up situations in a race; I derive tremendous satisfaction from making a move on a rival and finally outwitting him. That is raceriding.

When the right gap opens up in front of me I cannot resist going for it. A motor switches on inside me when I am in the thick of the action and tells me I have got to go when two horses part in front of me or another hangs off the rails. I become so lit up I cannot stop myself and I accept this is a fault. I take chances I shouldn't and at times pay the penalty. But there are occasions when it pays off handsomely.

When it does you look brilliant. But when it doesn't the snipers are quick to put the boot in. The day I lose the kick that drives me through those gaps I shall pack up my saddle. If that fire burns itself out tomorrow, I shall retire there and then.

Physically, the Grand National has left me virtually unscathed – only a bruised back when Meridian II fell at the thirteenth fence in 1976. But the losing battle I have waged with the world's most challenging and exciting fences over the Aintree country has given my pride a real bashing. The National is the race we all dream of winning and yet it has become my *bête noire* – the one I want to forget.

On eight rides from 1973 to 1983 I have failed to get any farther than the Canal Turn second time round. It was in 1977 that Sir Garnet jumped the Canal Turn and was swinging left-handed to head for home when I was knocked clean out of the saddle by another horse. That's the National.

Rag Trade started favourite in 1978 but his legs could not stand up to the continual pounding which they had withstood so gallantly on his famous path of Grand National glory two years before. I had no choice but to pull him up at the fence before Becher's. Alverton's tragic death at the world-renowned brook second time round in 1979 was my most painful Aintree experience. I was convinced he would break my Grand National hoodoo, so smoothly was he galloping. But fate overtook him and left all those who loved him full of anguish. In 1980 Another Dolly fell at Becher's first time, and two years later Again the Same's lameness overtook him before we reached the eighth.

I wore the first colours of the late Mr Noel le Mare on

Glenkiln in my first National in 1973. The reason was simple. Of his two runners, Mr le Mare thought Glenkiln had a better chance, but we made a terrible mess of the biggest fence on the course, the Chair, in front of the stands. Mr le Mare's other runner, on whom Brian Fletcher wore the distinguishing yellow cap, was a horse called Red Rum. That was one time I wished I had been on the second string! Another was in the 1979 Schweppes Gold Trophy at Newbury when Peter Easterby's 25–1 outsider Within the Law, ridden by Alan Brown, beat me on the stable's more fancied Major Thompson.

In 1983 Red Rum's trainer, Ginger McCain, was determined that I should make up my mind six weeks before the National and agree to ride the horse he bought specially with Aintree in view – Beacon Time. Normally I would keep my options open as long as possible to secure the best mount available. But after I had finished seventh on Beacon Time at Southwell – and I did not give him a hard race once I realized he could not catch the winner Snowtown Boy – Ginger put a package together with Beacon Time's owner Stan Markland, who had very kindly lent his house in Jersey to Sheila and me for our honeymoon.

The package was more like a carrot, as I saw it. A £10,000 carrot. Ginger explained the deal. If I agreed to ride Beacon Time I would be on £10,000 plus the normal 10 per cent of the £52,000 first prize if he won. If we were placed my share was £4,000. Stan Markland, who had sold out from the steel tube business, had backed Beacon Time with Ladbrokes to win £10,000 to cover the riding fees.

It was an offer I could not refuse. But sadly my Grand National luck did not change and Beacon Time broke down and fell at the nineteenth fence. The National pay day that never was.

Realt Na Nona sadly was the Grand National ride that never

materialized. This magnificent mare came to the rescue and dragged me out of more dark corners than any other horse in my life, but we never had the opportunity to pit our wits against the peak of National Hunt racing that is Aintree: Becher's Brook, the Canal Turn, Valentine's and the mighty Chair fence. Realt Na Nona was such a character, a lady with a mind of her own, that when she decided to do something she put her act together like Vivien Leigh. She could get it right on the night, and I suspected that she just might take it into her head that Liverpool was her stage. When she did she would pop away at her fences all day long and there were no doubts about her back-tracking once the 494-yard run in was reached. Realt Na Nona could gallop on for ever. Staying was her forte and Peter Easterby, her trainer, Arthur McCluskey, her Glasgow-based owner, and I firmly believed that she was the big hope for the 1984 Grand National.

But at Newcastle on 3 December 1983, exactly two years and two days after our perfectly timed comeback win at Wetherby, Real Na Nona left us clutching at marvellous memories and pondering over what might have been. The Ladbroke Trophy, over three and three quarter miles, was part of the Aintree build-up and Realt Na Nona had put in one of her foot-perfect rounds until she jumped the seventeenth fence a bit big and landed almost vertically, crashing onto a hind leg which snapped under the sudden and unexpected twisting pressure. That day I should have been riding at Sandown, but after the meeting had been abandoned because of frost I made a late dash to Newcastle. I wish I hadn't.

Realt Na Nona is the Irish Gaelic for Star of the Evening. After winning her bumper race in Ireland she was bought as a four-year-old by Arthur McCluskey, who hails originally from Emo, County Laoise. Arthur sent Realt Na Nona to spend the summers of 1981, 1982 and 1983 lazing around in the fields at Ivy House, the farm which I had bought in 1980.

When she first arrived little did I realize what an integral part she would play in my climb back to the saddle. Not settling for her role backstage in the little lanes of Cumbria, Realt Na Nona had to be the star of the comeback show at Wetherby on 1 December 1981.

She was the first horse I rode along the local lanes which eventually led to the Wetherby winner's enclosure. Her broad back took the strain as I stood up, pressed down and crouched, all the time sounding out any weakness in the right leg. She became a friend, though on occasions she would try our friendship close to breaking point. On the mornings when a rush was on to finish various jobs you could stand in the field trying to catch Realt Na Nona for nearly an hour. She knew the game and so did we after three summers. She would canter towards you, pull up, walk right up to you, give you a nudge, and before you could catch her she would bound off with a buck and a kick as if laughing at you.

Other mornings she would try your patience by simply standing in the lane refusing to walk backwards or forwards. It was impossible to say whether she had spotted a rabbit in the hedgerow or a bird in the woods. She would stand for minutes while I overexercised my leg kicking her in the belly, but she would move only when she wanted to.

In the fields or on the lanes Realt Na Nona thought she was the Queen. She was, but most of all on the racecourse.

12

Ekbalco… and Gypsy Dave

There have been times when the very existence of Tawfik
Fakhouri has been questioned. He is a Jordanian businessman
who owned the controversial and ill-fated hurdler Ekbalco, but
never saw him run.

Roger Fisher, Ekbalco's Cumbria trainer, is adamant. 'Tawfik
Fakhouri exists all right. He used to pay the bills. I well remember
when I first met him on business in London and he used to visit the
Victoria Sporting Club to play the roulette tables. I said that if he
liked a gamble he ought to buy a decent horse. He told me to find
him one and I paid 10,000 guineas for Ekbalco as an unbroken
three-year-old at Doncaster Sales in 1979.

'Mr Fakhouri and his wife flew to Walney Island, near Barrow
in Furness, seven miles from my stables, to see Ekbalco. He was so
nervous about flying in a small plane that he hired two pilots in
case one of them was taken ill on the flight. He had lunch, signed
the necessary papers, organized his racing colours and that was
the first and last he saw of Ekbalco. But he did back him on
several occasions.'

T.R.

My reflection in the mirror doesn't mean much to me first
thing in the morning when I am having a shave or trying to
pull a comb through my crinkly hair, but on the Friday before
Hallo Dandy won the 1984 Grand National I nearly cracked
the mirror in our bathroom. My whole face was disfigured.
The swelling came from a cut over my left eye, caused by one
of Man Alive's flailing hooves in the Kaltenberg Pils
Handicap Chase the previous day. The odds against my being
passed fit to ride must have been astronomical; I could
scarcely pull on my crash helmet. I drove south resigning
myself to the fact that I would have to sit out the rest of the
Aintree Festival and so I was not too disappointed when my

worst fears were confirmed by Dr Michael Allen, the Jockey Club's medical officer.

But I had not bargained for a letter, which was waiting for me on the notice board at the entrance to the Aintree weighing room.

From memory it read something like this:

Dear Mr O'Neill,
I suppose you think you are very clever with your horses, particularly crying in front of the crowds over losing Ekbalco at Newcastle. But what about all the people who were killed in the recent Harrod's bombing? Who is going to take the blame for that atrocity?
If it wasn't for you and your f— IRA it would never have happened.

I did not bother to read who had sent the letter, I was so upset. My cut eyebrow and Dr Allen's sensible decision to ground me paled into insignificance when I absorbed the nonsense that had been addressed to me. I was so angry I threw the letter into the nearest rubbish bin.

To associate me with the IRA was ludicrous, but I suspect the author was trying to say that I should not be upset about losing a horse when people were dying at the hands of the Harrod's bombers. Of course, there is no comparison because there is no value that can be put on a human life. Even so, I am not ashamed that I cried openly as I carried Ekbalco's saddle back through the Newcastle crowds after Roger Fisher's magnificent hurdler had tragically broken his shoulder in the 1983 Fighting Fifth Hurdle. What some members of the public don't understand is that horses are looked upon with heartfelt devotion by the people who spend their lives with them, although I must stress that I would never try to compare a horse's life with that of a human. Quite simply, the two cannot be equated.

There are also the clever dicks who, all too often, tell us how cruel we are to be racing horses like Ekbalco and asking

them to jump hurdles. Of course, there is the annual outcry
that the Grand National should be abolished because it is too
dangerous for the horses taking part.

What absolute rubbish. There are fatalities by virtue of the
fact that there are dangers involved in the jumping business.
But it makes my blood boil when I hear misinformed critics
sounding off. The majority of racehorses live in five-star
hotels, better known as stables. They are highly tuned
athletes, living on the best feed that money can buy. Some
horses enjoy the luxury of having two or three rugs in winter,
plus an infra-red lamp in the box – the equivalent of our
central heating. Their beds are cleaner than a lot of human
sleeping quarters. They live in better conditions than some of
the lads who look after them. There can be no doubt that
racehorses are far healthier and better cared for than a
number of riding-school horses and ponies, particularly at
busy seaside resorts, where they are overworked and do not
always live in the best kept accommodation like their racing
counterparts. You only need look at some riding-school
ponies to realize their condition, although there are plenty of
schools where the horses are well looked after.

An admiring remark I made to the Ulverston trainer Roger
Fisher about Ekbalco after I had finished behind the horse
at Catterick in February 1980 led to Dave Goulding's
memorable and at times controversial partnership with
Ekbalco. Roger, who is chairman of Sovereign Chemicals in
Barrow in Furness, telephoned me to ask if I could ride
Ekbalco in the keenly contested Greenham Group Handicap
Hurdle at Newbury the following month. I was already
committed to Peter Easterby's Thumps, on whom I had won
at Newcastle the previous Saturday.

'Who can I get?' Roger asked. 'If I can't find a top jockey I
don't want to run Ekbalco.'

I suggested that he tried Dave Goulding. Roger contacted
Dave and that was the start of an association which

developed into a love–hate relationship between Ekbalco, Dave and the racing public. Dave went to Newbury armed with the knowledge, imparted by Roger Fisher, that Ekbalco would pull very hard and even run away with him if he did not anchor him early on. Sure enough, Dave trailed most of his twenty-one rivals into the straight after executing a perfect job of settling Ekbalco, and then proceeded to pick them off one by one and win by three lengths at 33–1. Thumps, who had been backed to 11–2 second favourite in the highly competitive field, failed to finish in the first nine.

After Dave had demonstrated to everyone how well he understood Ekbalco, he openly passed on his knowledge of and insight into the up and coming young hurdler. He always said that Ekbalco had one fault: he would try and do too much for you once he started to motor for home; he would go for his hurdles a stride too soon and would come down on top of the timber. He was not a horse you could ask to fiddle his jumps. Dave, sporting the earring which earned him the nickname 'Gypsy Dave', went to Sandown twice the following season on Ekbalco and won the Mecca Bookmakers' Handicap Hurdle and the William Hill Imperial Cup, on both occasions producing Ekbalco late and full of running so he could gallop up Sandown's famous hill in the style of a future champion. The Goulding patience – and he is endowed with far more than the average jockey – paid rich dividends. It is this patience that is Dave's greatest asset and I suspect it played a great part in the making of Ekbalco.

One morning at Gordon Richards's we all had our patience tried as we watched Dave's calm handling of a potentially brilliant horse called Pattern Maker, a half-brother to the dual champion hurdler Bula. Pattern Maker had the infuriating habit of bucking all the way to the gallops and all the way back, but Dave was not in the least perturbed by these antics. In fact, it seemed that he secretly cherished the challenge of keeping his partnership with Pattern Maker intact, but to do so he employed the patience of Job. The rest of the lads in the string marvelled as Dave sat quietly while Pattern Maker hurled his backend skywards. Each time Dave's bottom would point upwards in unison with Pattern Maker's. After a quarter of an hour of this my patience would have begun to run out and I would have said to myself, 'I know what Pattern Maker wants – a good crack round the backside.' But that was not the treatment he received from Dave, who, in complete contrast, sat up there whistling away, full of the joys of spring, dishing out the occasional pat on the neck and telling Pattern Maker what a good boy he was. Dave arrived at the gallops unruffled – certainly more relaxed than us spectators – gave Pattern Maker his required quota of work and then started the return walk to the stables being bucked every third or fourth stride and keeping in time with every movement, his backside just above the saddle. It taught me a lesson in patience, though I doubt if I would ever have remained as cool for as long as Dave did.

One can argue that Dave was too cool on some occasions on the racecourse when it appeared from the grandstand or the stewards' box that he had not made the necessary effort on a horse. But more often than not his judgement was correct, though his quiet style of riding would lead him into all sorts of trouble with the authorities.

Following some fifteen appearances before the stewards for ostensibly 'not riding out his mount' in the 1979–80 season, Dave received a letter from the Jockey Club's Licensing Committee asking him to visit their headquarters at Portman Square in London during the summer close season. Dave's interview lasted only five minutes but it was enough time for the authorities to explain that he had been called before the local stewards more often than any other jockey and that they were concerned because he was looked upon as one of the country's top riders, which of course he was. The Jockey Club was worried that younger, up and coming jockeys would start copying Dave's quiet style of riding and end up in the same trouble. He was asked to be more aggressive and look busier in his riding if he wanted to be granted a licence for the following season. Dave explained to them that it was his style of horsemanship and that he had won on many difficult horses who had got the better of other jockeys. He stressed that it was his way of riding them that had enabled them to win. I have talked long and hard with Dave, who was misunderstood so often but remained determined to stand by his own very individual, but brilliant, understanding of horses.

It is Dave's theory that many jockeys are liable to confuse the difference between a rogue and a one-paced horse, a trap I have fallen into, I am sure. If there has been a slow gallop and your horse is going well coming into the straight, then you ask him to quicken and there is nothing there, it is easy to explain away your mount's failure by saying he dropped the lot and did not want to know. But nine times out of ten the horse lacks the necessary pace to accelerate – he remains galloping at the pace set in the early stages of the race. Therefore if the early gallop is slow and you are on a one-paced horse you must keep him up with pace or, if necessary, make your own running. If it's too fast early on, drop him out at the pace that suits him; then he will come through, but not with a late run because he does not possess one. He will keep on at his own pace, while the leaders are coming back to him. The whole strategy of raceriding revolves round judgement of pace.

If Dave could not win he would be easy on his mount. He maintains that more often than not the second and third horses are subjected to a harder race than the winner. They are being punished to catch the winner or withstand his challenge. Dave invariably fell foul of the local stewards when they considered that he did not take enough trouble to ensure that his mount finished as close as it could. The stewards were thinking of the paying customers and punters at home who had backed horses each way or in forecast bets. But Dave always reasoned that if you don't knock a horse about unnecessarily he will go home, eat up, and come out and win next time if he is good enough. Too hard a race can result in a horse taking a long time to recover his sparkle, and if he is subjected to a series of exacting battles on the racecourse he can even turn sour. It was not often that you saw Dave Goulding brandishing the whip; instead he was asking his mount for a forward move by squeezing and pushing him after perhaps a crack down the shoulder or one behind the saddle. Dave's patience is such that there were numerous occasions when he turned into the straight in sixth or seventh place and going nowhere, particularly when the ground was heavy, and the leaders started to come back to him. It was not as though Dave was going any faster; the horses in front simply fell in a heap. Dave would win by three or four lengths by sitting still. It was very deceptive because his mount did not show any great acceleration, but simply plodded through exhausted horses, thanks to Dave's willingness to sit, sit and sit while his rivals made their moves and burned out their mounts.

But many is the time when Dave was on the mat for overexercising his patience. The day I signed for our first house, Deep Ghyll at Plumpton, and went on to Carlisle to win on John Dixon's The Last Light, Dave found himself frustrated beyond words; unfortunately he ended up by telling the stewards what he thought of them. It was 15 December 1977, and Dave was riding Catoctin Creek for Gordon Richards in a two-and-a-half-mile chase, the fifth race of the day. He was very upset after finishing third to Fair View and Sanskrit because, at the time, he felt he had caused Catoctin Creek to break down. As it transpired his mount had not broken down, but, nevertheless, was hopping lame immediately after the race. David believes he felt Catoctin Creek's leg go under him when he was lying second as the field galloped down the far side of the course, but he refused to pull him up for fear of being accused of stopping a horse who, from the distant stands, appeared to be going well. He persevered with Catoctin Creek and was eventually beaten by twenty-five lengths, but all the way up the straight he knew his mount was not happy and was trying to hang with him. He dismounted and led him into the unsaddling enclosure distraught and angry that he had allowed his fear of the stewards to step between him and the wellbeing of his horse. He admits that he was confused after a series of brushes with the local authorities and not certain whether or not he should try at the expense of his mount.

Half an hour later Dave rode the second favourite Palace Royal, a newcomer trained by Gordon Richards, in the second division of the Caldbeck Novices Hurdle. This was a classic example of Dave being misunderstood and of the festering rift between him and the stewards. Climbing up the stiff home straight, Palace Royal was not transmitting to Dave the feeling of confidence he would have liked at that stage. Conscious of the disaster of the previous race, Dave was content to hold Palace Royal together and let him come home in his own time in sixth place, thirty-five lengths behind the winner Beau Brigg. He hung on to his head, and did not move a muscle on the run to the line and the stewards rightly inquired into his riding. They believed he did not try. Dave told them that if he had not held Palace Royal together he would not have climbed over the last flight. Palace Royal was so tired he was out on his legs. The stewards accepted the explanation, but Dave could not contain himself any more and in an outburst told the assembled officials, 'If it wasn't for you, Catoctin Creek would not be as lame as he is. I would have pulled him up, but then I thought I would have been hauled in here for another grilling.'

Arguably the most controversial of Dave's brushes with the stewards was at Newcastle during the autumn of 1981 when the central character was Ekbalco, who showed his colours as a Jekyll and Hyde. In fact, his contrasting performances, just seventeen days apart, set tongues wagging, with many misinformed people pointing accusing fingers at Ekbalco, Dave Goulding and Roger Fisher. On 28 October, in his first appearance of the season, Ekbalco finished fifth, beaten by nineteen lengths by Freight Forwarder in the Long Town Hurdle at Newcastle. On 14 November he contested the far more competitive Fighting Fifth Hurdle on the same course and improved by a matter of stones, not pounds, with an explosive performance to beat Pollardstown, Gaye Chance, Bird's Nest and Sea Pigeon, who admittedly was over the hill by then. Two such deeply contrasting races resulted in the local Newcastle stewards referring the matter to the stewards of the Jockey Club in London.

Roger Fisher, his vet Meredith Jones, Dave Goulding and Jenny Moffatt, the wife of Roger Fisher's assistant Dudley Moffatt, appeared at the Jockey Club's headquarters in Portman Square and, after all four parties had given their evidence, their explanation was accepted.

Roger and Dudley were away at the Newmarket Sales when Ekbalco ran in the Long Town Hurdle, and it was left to the dedicated Jenny to travel her hero from Ulverston on the coast of the Lake District in Cumbria across country to Newcastle. Jenny had Ekbalco boxed up and ready to leave at seven in the morning, with Billy Johnson, Roger Fisher's relief driver, at the wheel. As soon as Ekbalco was enclosed in the horsebox he started to sweat, became nervous and very gee-ed up. The narrow winding roads were choked with traffic and after only about five miles, at a village called Greenodd, Billy did well to avoid a collision with an oncoming car on a narrow humpback bridge. The approaching vehicle was in the middle of the road, causing Billy to slam on the brakes and give his prize cargo an unsettling jolt. In order to miss the car Billy had to pull over towards the stone parapet, which he scraped with the wing of the lorry, making such a fearful high-pitched tearing noise that even the most relaxed racehorse would have taken fright. Ekbalco was a bad traveller on the smoothest of journeys, but after this minor accident he was badly distressed. Jenny tried to calm and comfort him, but her sweet talking did not work and some four hours later when they arrived at Newcastle racecourse stables she had to wash him down because he was soaked in sweat. He looked as if he had just run a race.

Jenny went to the weighing room to declare Ekbalco for his race and returned to the stables to find him awash again. Dave reported that he was uncharacteristically lifeless during the race and seemed extremely distressed after his exertions. He fretted and sweated on the return journey and once home Jenny stayed with him in his box for two hours before finally deciding to telephone the vet, Meredith Jones, as his condition was not improving. Ekbalco was dehydrated after so much sweating and the vet gave him an injection to help him settle back to normal in his customary surroundings.

With Dudley Moffatt back from Newmarket and Ekbalco fully recovered, they set off for the Fighting Fifth Hurdle the day before the race, and the overnight stay in the stables gave Ekbalco time to unwind and familiarize himself with the place before having to think about racing. However, this vital factor in his dramatic improvement in form was not widely appreciated at the time. To the media and racing public Ekbalco had produced an exhibition worthy of a champion hurdler seventeen days after he had run like a donkey. So the cries of 'We was robbed!' were understandable, although the circumstances underline just what a complex character Ekbalco was.

He was a highly strung three-year-old when he arrived at Roger Fisher's Great Head House Stables in 1979 for Jenny Moffatt to break. 'Balco', as he became affectionately known, was first ridden out by Dudley, but he tried to wrench the arms out of any man who rode him. However, when they discovered that he would not pull and fight against Jenny, all seven stone of her, in the same way, the petite brown-haired mother of two was appointed his regular partner at home. Ekbalco was happy when Jenny took him on his excursions across the thousand-acre Birkrigg, a vast expanse of common land alongside the coast road at Bardsea a mile from the stables. Jenny used to hack him along the tracks and even pop him over the gorse bushes which are a feature of this area of grassland. Sometimes you would see Jenny and Ekbalco standing beside a gorse bush, acting as a wing, while the young horses jumped the bush. Ekbalco would refuse to go home until Jenny had let him skip over the bush. They became a vital part of each other's daily life and Jenny always gauged Balco's wellbeing by the amount of squealing he did during exercise. If Ekbalco went silent on her she knew something was wrong and would report the disconcerting news to Roger. As Jenny groomed and dressed him in his box, Ekbalco would playfully rear up, and when she bent down to attend to his legs his intelligent head would find its way across her back and he would wrap his neck round her tiny waist.

'Balco used to squeeze me as if he was giving me a hug,' Jenny recalls with pride and emotion. 'He made my life.'

Dave Goulding fanned the flames of controversy with his waiting tactics on Ekbalco when they were beaten by a head by Donegal Prince and John Francome in the 1982 Schweppes Gold Trophy, a race which has thrived on sensations and dramas ever since Ryan Price won it with Rosyth, whose second victory in 1964 cost him his trainer's licence, and then in 1967 with Hill House, who manufactured his own dope. Dave was in his customary place near the back of the field swinging into the home straight with twenty-four rivals to weave through. He touched down fractionally ahead of Donegal Prince at the last flight but was outslogged on the run to the line. I doubt if anyone else could have finished any closer on Ekbalco, who, under 11 st 7 lb, had done no harm to his Champion Hurdle prospects. But on the big day at Cheltenham he lacked the acceleration from the last and finished third to For Auction and Broadsword.

Depression and anger would set in with Dave when he received criticism from the media, although by and large he managed to ride it. But he had to find some relief and often used to take it out on fellow jockeys with practical jokes. Indeed, we all need to release the tension in some form and invariably jump jockeys resort to light-hearted pranks.

One morning I was sitting in a Penrith shoe shop waiting to try on a new pair of riding boots when the door swung open and in marched Dave, who turned everyone's head with the threatening remark directed at me: 'There you are. I've been looking for you.'

I was at a loss to know what he was going to do next as he strode across the shop towards me and announced, 'Now I've got you!'

With that he jumped on top of me, knocked me off my seat and rolled about on the carpeted floor keeping a tight grip on me so that I could not scramble to my feet and run to safety. We knocked over two chairs and a pile of shoeboxes. As the struggle became more intense I seriously began to wonder if Dave had gone mad. 'Dave,' I shouted at him, 'pull yourself together and stop this fooling around. We're going to make a real mess of the shop.'

Dave simply growled and snorted, kicking his legs and propelled me along the floor towards the end of the shop where the staff had gathered. A female assistant said that she was in the process of ringing for the police as there was a lunatic in the shop. Then Dave pretended to hit me and the women in the shop let out shrieks of horror; in fact Dave had not followed through with his dummy punches so I knew he was only joking. All of a sudden a small man appeared from the back of the shop wielding a pole used for taking shoeboxes down from high shelves. He threatened Dave with the big stick and ordered him out onto the street. Dave realized he was being challenged by the manager and started to pull himself to his feet, by which time I could not contain myself any longer and burst out laughing.

The horrified onlookers realized it was an enormous hoax. The female assistant quickly gathered her composure and rang to cancel her 999 call to the police, while Dave apologized to the manager and drew a final laugh from him by saying that he had been trying to get me arrested. As we scampered out onto the pavement I remembered that I had not bought my new riding boots, but I couldn't go back and face the assembled assistants.

The morning Gordon Richards lost his voice Dave and I behaved like a couple of little schoolboys, laughing and giggling behind his back. Even now as supposedly mature men we still permit ourselves a little chuckle when we remind each other of how we were guilty of messing up one of his gallops. Normally Gordon would send us to the bottom of the gallop and we would do a short stretch of fast work on the way back, pulling up at the double gates. But on this particular morning Gordon rode across to the double gates and opened them. When Dave and I reached the bottom of the gallops we looked at each other and asked what we were meant to be doing. I thought Dave knew the orders and Dave thought I had been given the instructions. Should we pull up at the double gates or gallop through them and go on to the top, which was more like a mile than a sharp four furlongs?

We reached the double gates and Gordon, sitting astride that high-class chaser Tamalin, was shouting and bawling at us.

'What's he saying?' I called across to Dave.

'We've got to go to the top,' Dave shouted back.

After pulling up we walked back through the woods to find Gordon and Tamalin hurtling towards us. Gordon's hat had blown off and his coat, wide open, was flapping in the slipstream.

'Watch it, we're in for it now,' Dave muttered.

Gordon was screaming at us even before he pulled up, and as he stood alongside us he continued at the top of his voice, shouting, ranting and raving, wondering what the devil we had been doing asking our mounts to do double the exercise he had intended for them. He had lost his temper, and justifiably so because the misdemeanour was entirely our fault. It took us between five and ten minutes to rejoin the rest of the string and during that time the air was blue with Gordon's remonstrations. He went on to such an extent that he became hoarse.

Later that day Gordon went to Doncaster Sales. By then he had cooled off, but he could not resist repeating the morning's tale of woe to other fellow trainers round the sale ring. Apparently he was unable to complete the story because he could not make himself heard. He had actually lost his voice chastizing us!

Another of Dave's favourite tricks was to swap our clothes round in the jockeys' room while we were riding in the last race. Then, when we came in wanting to dash off home, we would find a brown sock and a green sock in one place and trousers with the legs tied in knots hanging on the peg. Underneath my seat would be a black shoe and a grey one. Some people would describe such deeds as silly schoolboy humour, but Dave helped to produce an air of weighing-room camaraderie which went a long way to disguising the danger that confronted us each time we ventured out in our colours and breeches.

Dave's friendship was underlined when I crashed through the wing on Night Affair at Teesside in January 1975, smashing my right leg. Dave, on Persian Way, had a clear view of the accident and recalls, 'Night Affair side-stepped and shot Jonjo against the wing – it was like throwing a cat against a wall. As soon as he hit the wing and slipped down into a heap on the ground I knew there was something seriously wrong with him. My immediate reaction was to pull up and go across and help him, but I thought the stewards would want to know why I had pulled up, and coming to the aid of a fellow jockey in distress is hardly a good enough reason for opting out during a race. So rather than risk a fine I reluctantly continued, only to finish last.'

Dave, who maintains contact with the gypsy world at the annual summer Appleby Fair, which takes place alongside the A66 between Scotch Corner and Penrith, announced his retirement in 1984, after a series of bangs on the head had taken their toll. Happily, he no longer suffers from headaches. He has built his own bungalow in Brigham, Cumbria, where he has a milk round. The curtain has come down on a career which at times looked like blossoming brilliantly only to splutter suddenly into controversy and decline before taking off again. Dave was a much maligned rider, who was dished out worse than his due in racing. At times he infuriated me. At times he infuriated everyone. But behind the big square jaw and large grey eyes is a character, a little complex perhaps, of the kind that racing loves.

The day before my thirtieth birthday, I took over from Dave on Ekbalco in the 1982 Welsh Champion Hurdle at Chepstow. Roger Fisher had been generally disappointed with the season. He felt that although Ekbalco had to be held up he needed to be more in contention – ten lengths off the pace rather than twenty-five lengths behind – and he had found it difficult to impress this on Dave enough for him to change his tactics, if only slightly. In other words, Roger felt Ekbalco would benefit from a change of jockey, although I began to doubt this from the moment Jenny Moffatt gave me a leg-up in the parade ring. Ekbalco, with all his intelligence, threw his back up and started to buck, as if to say, 'Who's this? It's certainly not the man I know, Dave Goulding!'

I hurriedly took my feet out of the stirrup irons and walked Ekbalco round the paddock, patting his neck and talking to him. By the time we reached the start he accepted the stranger on his back. I employed waiting tactics, held him up and produced him after the last flight to pass Pollardstown in the final hundred yards. We won by a length, with Broadsword a further three lengths back in third place. Only the previous month Broadsword had finished a length and a half in front of Ekbalco when they were second and third behind For Auction in the Champion Hurdle.

We started the 1982–83 season in sharp contrast to the previous one, with a ten-length victory in Newcastle's Long Town Hurdle, the race which had had such dramatic consequences twelve months earlier and has since been re-named in his honour the Ekbalco Hurdle, which was won in 1984 most appropriately by Roger Fisher's Ballydurrow. Our next race, the Fighting Fifth Hurdle, was packed with the sort of drama I would prefer to forget. Ekbalco, unleashing his glorious late flourish, stretched for the final hurdle a stride too soon, landed on top of it, skidded along the ground and threw me underneath the rails. He had just passed his old rival Donegal Prince and should have won in breathtaking style. Happily, we both lived to fight another day, which was at Cheltenham before Christmas in the Tia Maria Bula Hurdle. Ekbalco served notice that this was to be his year for the hurdling crown by beating Ireland's reigning champion For Auction with an emphatic show of speed up the Cheltenham hill. Broadsword finished third and I must confess we all started to breathe excitement whenever the Champion Hurdle was mentioned. This looked like Ekbalco's year. He scrambled home by a head from Broadsword in the Ladbroke Christmas Hurdle at Kempton on Boxing Day, and even though he only beat Sula Bula by half a length in

January in Haydock's Champion Hurdle Trial, his last race before the big one, I still had faith in him.

He was entitled to be joint favourite with For Auction, but the betting market was the only part of the day he dominated. Form students can argue that in finishing fifth, only a head and a neck behind For Auction and Broadsword, he had finished much closer to them than in the previous year's Champion Hurdle. But, in all honesty, he struggled round and lacked the fire for which he had become famous. He never held out any hope of getting to grips with Gaye Brief and Boreen Prince, who finished first and second.

Roger Fisher, as the trainer, shouldered the blame after such a bitterly disappointing run. He recalls, 'Ekbalco's only two engagements after his Haydock race were supposed to have been in the Schweppes and at Wolverhampton, but they were abandoned because of bad weather. This left him without a preliminary outing before the Champion so I galloped him on Carlisle racecourse and gave him plenty of work at home. He was a big horse who required a lot of preparation for a race. I blame myself for not having entered him for Nottingham's City Trial Hurdle, the race won by Gaye Brief immediately before he took the championship. If Ekbalco had run there it might have been a different story.'

For some reason Ekbalco was never quite 100 per cent on Champion Hurdle day, but I have little doubt that he was one of the best horses never to win the Cheltenham championship. In some respects, he was similar to Sea Pigeon – exciting and very powerful, invariably with that explosive speed from the last which so often spared blushes when all the riders in the stands thought you had left your challenge too late. The famous final burst would carry you to the line in the nick of time. Again in the Sea Pigeon mould, Ekbalco needed switching off early on, and once you pressed the button you knew you were on course for something special. The times when he flew over those last two flights of hurdles are precious moments in my life that no one can take away. Money could never buy such a lasting experience. The sense of power at being able to dominate the finish of a race with so much galloping authority underneath me used to fill me with an excitement unlikely to be repeated in my lifetime. On Sea Pigeon and Ekbalco I knew I would get there.

It always astounded me that Ekbalco's owner, Tawfik Fakhouri, a Jordanian with business interests in Saudi Arabia, saw his horse only once, when Ekbalco was an unbroken three-year-old. Roger met Mr Fakhouri through his chemical business and Ekbalco was named after Mr Fakhouri's telex number: EKBALCO.

We won our second Welsh Champion Hurdle at Chepstow in 1983, where Ekbalco had seven lengths to spare over Royal Vulcan, who took his revenge by a head eleven days later in the Scottish Champion Hurdle. Ekbalco was later disqualified for failing the post-race dope test after the Welsh Champion Hurdle. Penicillin cream containing Procain, a prohibited substance under Jockey Club Rules, had been applied to a saddle sore a week before the race and, unbeknown to Roger Fisher and his vet, the ointment found its way into Ekbalco's bloodstream.

Barging through the Newcastle crowds with poor Ekbalco's saddle after the 1983 Fighting Fifth Hurdle, I was propelled by bitter sorrow and heartache. I could barely see where I was going through the tears in my eyes, but I knew I just wanted the solitude of my place in the jockeys' room. Cynics who suggested they were tears for publicity are hardly worth answering. Having a highly intelligent, active part of one's life snatched away has a devastating effect. I felt it that November afternoon at Newcastle but not half as much as poor Jenny Moffatt, who stuck to her job of leading Humyak House round the pre-parade ring before the last race with her head buried in her handkerchief. We were overtaken by the emotion of the whole tragic affair.

Ekbalco was cantering alongside Gaye Brief and his pacemaker Migrator at the second last hurdle when he took off a stride too soon – as he had done the previous year – only this time his shoulder took the full impact as his half-ton frame hit the turf with a deadly thud. I knew it was the end. I quickly beckoned the vet who could not have completed his unpleasant task with more speedy efficiency. In less than a minute Ekbalco was mercifully released from his suffering.

We had scaled the heights together, plumbed the depths together. It is never easy waving the final goodbye to a friend. If only one had the strength to live up to the words of Rudyard Kipling:

> If you can meet with Triumph and Disaster
> And treat those two imposters just the same ...

13

1984 – John Francome and All That

John Francome was champion jockey for the sixth time in the 1983–84 season with 131 winners. But, in my view, Jonjo reached an even greater pinnacle with his total of 103.

Francome had first call on his services from the powerful Fred Winter stable, for whom he rode fifty-four winners, but he also enjoyed the luxury of a second retainer from John Jenkins, who provided him with another thirty-three winners. In contrast, Jonjo, as a freelance, had to dig most of his success out of the *Racing Calendar* with the help of the formbook, tedious telephoning and his own hard work and judgement.

His chapter of frustrating injuries from the New Year onwards resulted in only thirty-one winners during the last five months of the season. 'Jonjo's having a bad winter' became the absurd, ill-informed cry. At which the man himself smiled, 'What will happen when I have a good one?'

Francome recalls, 'After Jonjo's tearaway start I said that, barring accidents, he was an absolute certainty to become champion again. Then he had one injury after another, but always came back with that big smile, never losing his sense of fun. Then right at the end again he had a bloody good run, which just shows what he is made of.'

Francome, the master jockey, respects Jonjo professionally more than any rider he has competed against. He says, 'After he broke his leg the second time there was a strong lobby of opinion that Jonjo would not get going again. But they hadn't bargained for his single-minded dedication. He eats and sleeps the job. It's his life.

'At that stage he could have said, "Blow it. I've had enough. What's the point of struggling?" But that isn't Jonjo O'Neill.'

Though it very nearly was after his mount Man Alive had kicked him in the face on the opening day of the 1984 Grand National meeting.

T.R.

The dishevelled hair and tie askew gave the doctor the air of a man who had been ruffled by the continuous activity in the casualty ward of Liverpool's Walton Hospital, which is only a mile or so from Aintree racecourse. His white coat countered the false impression by covering him with an air of authority, which was endorsed when he spoke calmly indicating a placid person within. But even the friendly tones were quickly forgotten when his words sank into my dazed brain. He said, 'The plastic surgeon will come and see you as soon as he has finished in the operating theatre.'

That chilling announcement set my alarm bells ringing. I had spent the previous threequarters of an hour staring blankly at the clinically white ceiling above my bed. Time dragged while I lay there wondering what the medics would do to me this time. The mention of plastic surgery put the wind up me and made me think that the two-inch cut above my left eye was worse than I had been led to believe.

Suddenly all my resistance caved in. My mind started to race. This was the time to pack in the whole business and retire. Of that I was certain. Since Christmas my body had been bludgeoned by a series of niggling rather than serious injuries. Bruised elbows, arms, fingers, battered ribs, chest, back, legs and a broken cheekbone. It had been enough to interrupt what had become a stuttering uphill climb to the winner's enclosure after a start to the season which had been even more flushed with winners than my record-breaking winter of 1977–78. My bones and muscles were starting to tell me that enough is enough. I had become frustrated and depressed by the chapter of falls, but after returning to the Cheltenham Festival to win the Champion Hurdle on Dawn Run and complete a quick first-day double on Mossy Moore I was back in top form. Seconds on Little Bay, Donegal Prince and Path of Peace secured the Ritz Trophy as the leading jockey at the most important meeting of the season. I was flying, awash with confidence. The horses I was riding were running out of their skins and I had been looking forward to teaming up with Afzal, Little Bay, Dawn Run and Jennie Pat at Liverpool.

Then this. It was more than I could stomach. The first fence on the first day of the Grand National meeting. Crash. I was down and out again and, without putting too fine a point on it, with the arse torn out of me. The expression describes precisely the way I was feeling.

I honestly believed racing wanted to get rid of me. I thought someone up there was trying to tell me something. 'It's time to quit, to get out while you are still in one piece ...'

My dazed thoughts were interrupted by a new face, this time black, standing over me and inspecting the cut in my eyebrow and forehead. With a reassurance and charm common to so many doctors he explained that he was from plastic surgery and would be able to stitch my wound in a way that would leave me with as small a scar as possible. I was far too vain to allow any thoughts of retirement to interrupt the doctor, who was clearly trying to preserve my good looks! Some people might say that he had to find them first! After a quick operation I was fit enough to drive home to Skelton Wood End.

The flashing grey Man Alive, trained in Cheshire by Ray Peacock, was the last horse you would expect to take his fences so irresponsibly that you had no chance of keeping the partnership intact. Ron Barry won the 1979 Mackeson Gold Cup on him at Cheltenham when he was trained by Gordon Richards and a year before our Aintree debacle Neale Doughty rode him in the Kaltenberg Pils Handicap Chase when he ran out while still galloping strongly in the lead at the third last fence. Perhaps he remembered that as we cantered to the start of the 1984 Kaltenberg as he did not feel right underneath me; when I showed him the first fence on our way down he did not seem his normal self. He gave me the impression of being a worried horse, but I thought that, once his blood became stirred up at the start, the dubious memories of the previous year would disappear and he would gallop into action. But he did not want to jump off; I missed the break on him when the tape went up. As we went to the first fence I left him with his years of experience to measure and meet the obstacle in his own time. But he did not take off; instead he ran smack into the fence, kicking spruce in all directions. I thought that if he was not enjoying himself he would have been wily and refused; instead, after hitting the fence, he turned over in the most dramatic style. Unbelievably I got a soft fall, or at least I thought I did until his metal shoe caught me just above the eye. Blood was pouring everywhere and I thought my nose had been broken. A stout St John Ambulance girl came over to me immediately, patched me up and held me together until the ambulance came to take me straight to Walton Hospital.

Grand National day was the blackest of the season for me. On the Friday I had missed winning the Liverpool Hurdle on Afzal for Reg Hollinshead. As I sat at home on the sofa in front of the television trying to savour the Aintree big-race atmosphere through the BBC's marvellous coverage, I felt groggy and sick from my cut on the head. With time on my hands, depression crept in, bringing with it a heavy cloud of gloom.

John Francome deputized on my first-race mount, Little Bay, in the Captain Morgan's Aintree Handicap Chase, which they won impressively. They looked so good together – Little Bay, the infuriating enigma that he is, was transformed from temperamental bad boy to brilliant two-miler. Watching him win from the comfort of the sofa was like taking a punch in the solar plexus. I consoled myself by trying to explain to Sheila that Little Bay was such a character that he was probably more effective with a change of jockey each time he ran. Having tried to explain Little Bay's waywardness I felt better, although Sheila was clearly not convinced by my theory. I had to get it all off my chest – the inner frustration and fury of not being part of such a stylish winning show in front of the expectant Grand National crowd and millions of television viewers.

Little Bay is exasperating. If he hits the front too soon he downs tools and waits for his rival to come back at him. Then on another occasion you feel he would enjoy himself more bowling along in front, which is a complete contradiction of the first theory. His complex mind and attitude to racing make him totally unpredictable.

The first time I rode Little Bay was at Aintree in 1982, in the Tim Brookshaw Memorial Chase, run in memory of the brave 1958–59 champion jockey who was paralysed in a Liverpool fall and, along with Paddy Parrell, who also broke his back there, was the first beneficiary of the Injured Jockeys' Fund. I took my feet out of the irons after jumping the last fence and flapped about on Little Bay like an inexperienced, incompetent rider. He was so shocked to find me bouncing about completely out of rhythm with his stride that he forgot himself and started to sprint for the line, only just failing to catch the winner, Polar's Laddie. Forty-eight hours later we turned out again for the first race on Grand National day, the competitive Sunratings Chase, which included Michael Dickinson's current and future champion two-mile chasers Rathgorman and Badsworth Boy.

Even now, the graphic description in *Timeform*'s *Chasers and Hurdlers 1981–82* brings the drama back as if it were yesterday:

> The race turned out to be one of the most eventful of the season. The amateur-ridden clear leader Spinning Saint took the wrong course after four fences, galloped between two mechanical diggers preparing the Melling Road crossing and dislodged his rider when half-jumping the first fence on the Grand National course. At the first fence in the final straight four from home, the smoothly-travelling favourite Rathgorman was a faller, bringing down Run With Pride, and then at the last Rathgorman's stable companion Badsworth Boy, looking sure to take a lot of beating, completely

misjudged his jump and took a heavy fall. Little Bay had been going very well all the way and was a close third to Badsworth Boy and Western Rose at the last. After being almost brought down by the fallen Badsworth Boy, Little Bay was rousted along in pursuit of Western Rose and, ridden most forcefully, collared him in the last hundred yards to win going away by two and a half lengths.

As we watched the Sandeman Aintree Hurdle, I knew I had lost the ride on my Champion Hurdle winner Dawn Run. She and Tony Mullins, the son of Paddy Mullins, Dawn Run's trainer, passed the post ten lengths clear of Very Promising. A haunting hush fell over Ivy House while we tried to swallow another bitter pill. I was close to tears. I knew the ride on Dawn Run really belonged to Tony, who had won on her before I was approached to take over during the Champion Hurdle campaign. But at quarter to three on Saturday, 31 March 1984, I was in no fit state to see reason. As far as I was concerned Dawn Run had galloped out of my life. It was the parting of the ways. The end of a glorious, if brief, association.

As a freelance you rely heavily on having at least one good horse in your bag of ammunition and throughout my career I have always been lucky enough to enjoy the backing of a top-class hurdler or chaser. In some respects it takes the place of a retainer from a stable and provides the heartening prospect of winning some of the big races. I firmly believed I had the security of Ekbalco for the 1983–84 season, but then he tragically crashed and died. Next, like a fairy godmother, up popped Dawn Run to fill the vacuum. Six days after the horrors of the Fighting Fifth Hurdle Dawn Run gallantly stepped out on the golden path to Cheltenham in the spring by carrying me to a last-gasp success at Ascot. Earlier, Ekbalco had replaced Sea Pigeon, who had been the standard bearer in my career for so long. On the chasing front Alverton had been followed by the great Night Nurse. The gap left by one top-class horse had always been filled by another prospective champion. For the first time I became conscious of the void left by a big-race ally, I was far from certain that it would be filled.

An air of emptiness joined my gloom and depression, a bad atmosphere through which the highly professional television presentation of David Coleman, Julian Wilson, Richard Pitman, John Hanmer and Tony Gubba had to fight its way from Aintree.

Hallo Dandy and Neale Doughty's famous Grand National victory helped to remove some of the misery. It was Little Bay's trainer Gordon Richards, who had brought Hallo Dandy to his peak seven miles down the road at Greystoke. Richards had also won the National with Lucius six years earlier.

I had been with Hallo Dandy's original owner, the West Yorkshire businessman Jack Thompson, when he bought Hallo Dandy as a three-year-old at Ballsbridge Sales in Ireland. Mr Thompson sent him to be trained by Ginger McCain at Southport. I rode Hallo Dandy in most of his races when he was with Ginger. Jack Thompson, who later sold him to London insurance broker Richard Shaw, sent him to me at Skelton Wood End for a change and some road work in the summer before the 1981–82 season, by which time he had been moved to Greystoke. I used to ride him along the tiny Cumbria lanes and up the springy turf of the fells. He won his first race at Carlisle in October and, although he had been back with Gordon for several weeks, Gordon smiled afterwards, 'I don't know who should take the credit for training him.' Watching Hallo Dandy's greatest moment gave me a kick for, although I had nothing to do with his success, it was nice to have been partly involved with him.

Jack Thompson won the last race on Hallo Dandy's Grand National day with Jennie Pat, my other intended mount and the last leg of my treble that never was. Denis Coakley, a promising Irish lad attached to Gordon's stable, took over on the mare.

That night John Francome threw me a lifeline. While time was already beginning to heal the mortifying memories of my three missed Grand National-day winners, John provided me with a tremendous tonic by picking up the telephone and dialling my number as soon as he walked through the door of his Lambourn home after three tough days at Aintree and an arduous drive south. The warm, friendly Wiltshire drawl gave me the contact with racing and one of its centre-stage characters I needed after I had been restricted to the confines of the drawing room, instead of being able to compete against the man on the other end of the phone.

'How are you? I know exactly how you feel,' said John sympathetically. 'It's cruel enough missing any winner, but three on National Day at Liverpool – that's rotten luck, mate. How's your head after Thursday's bang?'

John did not have a great deal more to add to our conversation – just a few passing observations about the day's racing – but the fact that he had given me a thought before putting his feet up lifted me out of the doldrums.

Despite our rivalry on the track, John and I are good friends and we often console each other on the telephone after a fall. During John's lightning start to the 1984–85 season I phoned him in August when he had ridden about twenty winners in less than a month to ask what the hell was up with him.

'Who's on your tail?' I asked. 'For Christ's sake, steady up because it's not me. But then, on second thoughts you'd better kick on before I get into full swing.'

In all seriousness though, we never discuss the championship; individual winners perhaps – but not who's going to get the title. John has been champion six times, once sharing the title with Peter Scudamore, and is the ideal man for the job as he is a gifted after-dinner speaker. He actually entertains us at those Champion Jockey dinners and there are not many jockeys who can boast such a gift. His speech at the Derby Awards Lunch at the Royal Garden Hotel in Kensington in 1983, when he received his Derby award from the racing press as National Hunt Jockey of the Year, received more coverage in the media than any other speech made by a jockey. John referred to the stewards, with whom he had been having repeated contretemps over his riding throughout the season, as Cabbage Patch Dolls.

The Francome stables and house, which he built himself, lie within easy reach of the Lambourn gallops and consist of twenty boxes and an indoor school on about 6 acres of land. John is preparing to set up there as a flat trainer. He and his lovely wife Miriam, who is a model, are extremely hospitable whenever I stay with them for southern meetings, though Miriam reckons she is only just beginning to understand my Irish accent!

As a trainer John makes no secret of his developing involvement with the flat rather than jumping. He says, 'One encounters so many more injury and training problems with jumpers. I have seen the guv'nor [Fred Winter] patiently prepare one for a race and just before it is due to run it gets a leg. It must be so disheartening. We have been breaking a number of flat horses and I find them most interesting. Paul Cole's good two-year-old Prince Georgetown was with us and Jeremy Tree's champion sprinter Sharpo lodged here as well.'

Francome would be the top of any class for dedication alone, but to measure his singlemindedness one only has to follow his progress as a tennis player. He started playing with his friend Alan Argeband, who is a regular racegoer in the West Country where he owns several market stalls. Now, after hundreds and hundreds of hours' practice, John hits the ball hard and true and can enjoy a close game with that colourful character Charles Benson, who, despite his roly-poly figure, is a tennis player of some standing. Charles, the Scout for the *Daily Express*, trained with Vitas Gerulaitis, one of the great crowd-pullers at Wimbledon. He also plays in the Pro-Am at Queen's Club on the middle Sunday of Wimbledon and, with his Australian partner, John Alexander, has reached the semi-finals.

John admits, 'If I have the choice of a couple of rides somewhere or a game of tennis I'd probably go for the tennis. It is great relaxation and I don't mind how much I get beaten so long as I am playing well. But when I am playing badly I throw my racket out of court and kick the balls all over the place. It's not that I'm a bad loser; I just get annoyed with myself.'

As if John's determined drive to improve his tennis isn't demanding enough, he has taken it upon himself to write his own book. By the summer of 1984 he had written 24,000 words, all in longhand. He now keeps a daily diary and says that whenever he is sidelined by injury he can swap his saddle for his pen and compose a tale or two for 'The Life and Times of J. Francome'. There are not many champion jockeys who can boast John's talent for tennis or the ability to sit down and write his own autobiography.

It was perhaps my shortsighted decision not to take a week's holiday in the New Year of 1984 that cost me the jockeys' championship. Deciding against grabbing an opportunity to recharge the batteries was the greatest mistake I made all season.

I desperately needed to be freshened up after my hectic flying start to the season. I had ridden seventy-two winners by the end of December, just four less than in my record-breaking season six years earlier, and the O'Neill operation was at full revs again. But the interminable quest to secure winning rides in as many races as possible began to take its toll. The demanding job of freelancing – poring over the formbook and the *Racing Calendar*, assessing which horses were most likely to win; hours and hours each week on the telephone deciding where I should be riding and for which trainers – meant that I was in great danger of burning myself out before I had even steered my mount out onto the winter turf of the track and started to compete as a jockey. Probably I would not have had so many falls after Christmas if I had enjoyed a week away from it all. As the spills and injuries piled up, the winter run became a crawl and the season turned sour, dragging me under the wave on which I had been riding high and forcing me to hold my breath until I could surface again.

The more I am written off the more determined I become to succeed. So you can imagine my reaction to the cries – 'He's finished', 'Retire' and 'Quit before you kill yourself' – that went up from those anonymous riders in the stands. Drifts of such idle chatter kept reaching me long after I broke my leg at Bangor in 1980 and I formed the impression that a number of onlookers, some professional, were of the opinion that I would never ride as well as I did before the accident. Talk is cheap in racing but when the rumours start to gather momentum there is no stopping them and when you are the hub of the talk it is not funny. I have never been able to put my finger on the source. But such ill-informed comments acted as a transfusion of determination. The challenge had been thrown down and once I realized I had the rub of the baize with the winners rolling in, the scent of a third championship grew stronger in my nostrils with each day.

I wanted my title back. Not simply as a feather in my helmet, but, more important, so I could raise two fingers very firmly at all those doubting Thomases.

Twenty-eight winners by the end of September was thirteen ahead of my record-breaking schedule in 1977; I hit the half century at Cheltenham on 11 November – a day more than Josh Gifford's fastest fifty in 1966 – when I won on

Onapromise and Sea Merchant with exactly three weeks and three days to spare over 1977. The press were inching forward to the edge of their seats as they repeatedly reminded me that I was on target to beat the magic total of 149. But I wasn't even thinking about it. The championship, yes; I had set my heart on becoming top jockey again. But I could not see the point in totting up winners, trying to break records; they just happen. I took it day by day.

The twists and quirks of the game favoured me. But for smashing his thigh on the opening day of the season at Market Rasen, Chris Grant would have ridden Onapromise. Ridley Lamb, recovering from a seriously infected hip, was Sea Merchant's regular jockey. So that sunny November afternoon when the Cheltenham executive celebrated my fifty landmark by presenting me with champagne – which the other lads drank in the weighing room – was typical of how the wheels of racing can turn in your favour at the expense of your friends. Ten of those fifty winners were for Chris Grant's number-one stable of Denys Smith at Bishop Auckland in County Durham.

I wish the howling December winds at Cheltenham had blown me away after my irresponsible actions on Lawnswood Miss had caused pandemonium amongst the punters. I was saved by a rapidly diminishing whisker from being lynched by a posse of racegoers who had backed Lawnswood Miss. The strong gusts blasted into my face and whistled fiercely around my ears and into my helmet, deafening me against the warning sounds of cracking whips and pounding hooves. Lawnswood Miss led over the last three flights of hurdles and, unable to hear how close the pursuers were, I glanced over my shoulder to see a bunch of challengers breathing down my neck. We shook them off after the last and as Lawnswood Miss galloped away from them up the famous Cheltenham hill I relaxed in the belief that we could not be caught. About a hundred yards from the line I dropped my hands on her neck and allowed her to ease up and stroll past the post. I had not heard the determined efforts of Sam Morshead, who was quick to seize on my overconfidence and galvanize Papa's Buskins into a rallying run. Sam caught me with all my defences down and I didn't even have time to give Lawnswood Miss a despairing push before the winning post. Even though I hardly dare watch the video I could see how it looked in the eyes of the rest of the racing world – that I had thrown the race.

On the long walk back to the unsaddling enclosure, I might have been going to the gallows. Each time a racegoer approached I became edgy, expecting to be pelted with eggs and tomatoes. I was convinced Sam had caught me napping and the punters who had backed Lawnswood Miss would want their pound of flesh.

Lawnswood Miss's Staffordshire trainer Reg Hollinshead, who probably runs more horses and travels more miles than any other trainer in the country, was quietly amused by the whole embarrassing episode. He had left the stand convinced that Lawnswood Miss had won as she was so far clear with a hundred yards to run. He strode across to the unsaddling enclosure with Papa's Buskins's trainer Mercy Rimell, who also was in no doubt that her horse had been well and truly beaten into second place. Suddenly the lad who looked after Papa's Buskins raced up to Mercy and said he had watched the race on television and he thought they had just got up. Reg was amazed to hear that there had been a photo finish and could not understand what had gone wrong, though it did not take him long to find out from the general racecourse feeling that I should be lynched. When I dismounted and started to explain the clanger I had dropped we still did not know the result and I was mighty relieved to see that Reg's usual calm, warm exterior was not in the least bit ruffled.

The weight of the world was released from my shoulders when I heard the announcement that Lawnswood Miss had hung on by a short head. It was exactly the same error that I had made on Sea Pigeon in the Tote Ebor Handicap at York in 1979.

Reg, for whom I rode nine of my 103 winners last season, never has a cross word and, however drastic the situation, the temperature of his warm exterior never changes. He sends his horses wherever he considers they have a hope of winning. Whenever possible he saddles them himself and I have known him drive from Rugeley in the Midlands to Scotland's Hamilton Park and back in a day and then repeat the journey twenty-four hours later. He always gives me the opportunity to ride for him and our working relationship has blossomed into one of real understanding. He appreciates the trials and tribulations of freelancing. The dilemma of trying to please everyone all the time; he even understands when I find myself being offered a better mount than the one he has already booked me for in the same race.

I agreed to ride Adjusted for him in a novice hurdle at Bangor in November, but the night before the race I received a late phone call from Ginger McCain pleading with me to switch to his horse Champ Chicken. Ginger dangled the irresistible carrot: 'We think he will win.'

'For heaven's sake, why did you not contact me before?' I asked. 'I am committed to Reg Hollinshead's horse and I don't think I can change at this late stage.'

'It was only after looking at the overnight declarations that we decided Champ Chicken could win and I've had to talk to the owners,' Ginger explained.

I had ridden Champ Chicken in his first race at Uttoxeter a couple of weeks earlier and he had finished an encouraging fifth behind Michael Dickinson's odds-on State Case, who had won by twenty-five lengths. I had dismounted that day fully aware that there was a race or two to be won with him, although I thought he needed a little more time to reach his peak. Ginger was convinced this would be his race at Bangor.

I told him to sleep on it and offered to speak to Reg in the morning. Having accepted Reg's firm booking to ride Adjusted I had formed a contract; if it was broken it could only be done with the blessing of Reg and the horse's owner. After discussing it with the owner, Reg released me, and naturally I was delighted to have been allowed the opportunity to switch to a better prospect at the eleventh hour – indeed a winning prospect, according to Ginger. His judgement was vindicated by Champ Chicken's four-length victory at 7–1 over Mercy Rimell's odds-on Sandwalker, with the early leader Adjusted finishing well beaten.

Ginger, never short of a tale to tell, related to me a week or two later how Champ Chicken's owners Alan Orritt and John Singleton, who run a string of High-street poultry shops throughout the Northwest, deployed their shop managers with military precision. They instructed them to leave their shops at 3.15, half an hour before the race, go straight to their local betting offices and back Champ Chicken. Ginger says figures in the region of £130,000 were mentioned when the winnings were being collected. They had engineered an ingenious coup and I had been hauled in at the last minute unwittingly to help them execute it. Courtesy of the ever obliging Reg Hollinshead.

A tall, broad figure, topped with a flash of flaming orange hair, greying at the temples – that is Ginger McCain, who became an overnight hero when in 1973 he sent out Red Rum to win his first Grand National from his stables behind his second-hand-car salesroom on Upper Aughton Road in Southport. Red Rum, the most celebrated of all Grand National winners, triumphed again the following year and then became a unique part of history in 1977 as the first triple winner of the National. Ginger, his gallops those endless acres of Southport's staring sands, and always able to rely on his solid back-up of extra horsepower from his car business, had arrived. He possesses that wonderful gift of successfully transmitting the fun he derives from racing to all those around him, including his jockeys. I firmly believe I am a 10-lb better jockey for Ginger simply because he makes sure I extract maximum enjoyment from the job.

Off duty, the McCain mix is much the same, but on the town Ginger can be positively lethal! After the 1972–73 season Ginger had won his first National with Red Rum, Ron Barry was champion jockey for the first time with a record of 125 winners, and I was champion junior rider with thirty-eight. The three of us went to the end-of-season party thrown by the Sportsman Club in London. Let Ginger tell the story he takes so much delight in repeating.

'In the Sportsman Club they have these Bunny Girls and I said to Ron, "It's time this young man had a drink".

'Ron says, "Jees, you're right boss."

'So we both gave this fine, big girl a fiver and, pointing out Jonjo to her, said, "Whenever this young man has an orange, make sure there is a large vodka in it."

'After Jonjo had drunk three he kept saying how funny the orange tasted and we convinced him it was London orange, which is always a bit different. By this time he was getting quietly pickled. We moved on to a club belonging to an owner Ron used to ride for, and after a few more drinks I said to Ron, "It's time Jonjo had himself a woman.'

'So we approached one of the girls and asked her how much she charged for her services. She said £40, and Ron and I went halves, chipping in twenty quid each. At the end of the evening we were getting up to go when Jonjo started to come with us.

'I said, "Jonjo, you're all right, you're organized. So stay put."

'He said, "Jesus, no. I'm coming with you."

'I turned to the girl and said, "You keep your side of the deal. We've paid you."

'The girl replied, "Yes, but Jonjo has given me £40 to leave him alone."

'At the hotel next morning I have never seen a person look more like a sheepdog at heel than Jonjo did as he followed Ron into the dining room. Hung over, head bowed, he walked in like a small boy behind the headmaster on his way to be caned.'

Ron and I were riding at Sedgefield the next day so we caught the train north with me feeling ghastly. Apparently, I consumed five large vodkas the night before. Anyway, the Northern Jockeys' Dinner was being held at the Scotch Corner Hotel after racing at Sedgefield. I can't say I felt exactly in the mood for another party, but I joined the lads for a few hours before retiring to bed in the hotel.

I fell sound asleep, only to be woken by a lady climbing into bed with me. I was still coming round from my slumbers when she grabbed me and said, 'Jonjo, I love you. I've always loved you.'

'Will you f— off,' I said. 'Leave me alone. I don't know who you are and I don't care because I feel as if I'm going to die. And so would you if you'd had a night like I had in London last night.'

With those words there was a crash in the darkness followed by roars of laughter. Pat Buckley, who won the Grand National on Ayala in 1963, had fallen out of the wardrobe and Dave Goulding appeared from under the bed. They had set the girl up.

It is one of Ginger's party pieces telling the assembled company how I love the night life.

January 10th at Wetherby was where the rot started in the New Year with a fall on the flat when Swop Shop, who was running very nervously, clipped the heels of a horse in front of her and came down on the bend before the short straight of the old course. She kicked me in the ribs and left me on the ground gasping for breath.

It was the start of a series of niggling, depressing and frustrating injuries which tempered my tearaway season. The floodgates had effectively been slammed in my face and from 10 January to the end of the season – just under four months – I managed to claw my way onto the backs of only twenty-eight winners.

January 13th – Black Friday – at Ascot, Torreon broke his back and I felt I had been thrown out of the top window of a block of flats, landing on my backside and having every breath of wind jolted out of me by the Ascot turf. I was coming back in the ambulance when all of a sudden I felt desperate and wanted to be sick. I was taken straight to the local hospital, but was discharged that night, then flew back to Manchester and drove home from there.

January 31st at Leicester, Fearless Seal put his foot in a hole in the very soft ground and tripped up on the flat, bringing down Peter Scudamore on Sir Gordon. I was kicked on my left elbow, which was agony; the pain took weeks to ease. I did not have time to have it X-rayed but I must have chipped my funny bone.

February 11th was Schweppes Gold Trophy day and after winning the first for Reg Hollinshead on Afzal I thought I was going to be trampled to death in the big race, which is always a cavalry charge. My mount, Path of Peace, was bursting with health and bouncing underneath me, but he caught the top of the third flight of hurdles and paid the penalty. We had been lying about sixth with some twenty runners behind us and I felt as though I was being passed from Bobby Charlton to Kevin Keegan to Bryan Robson and back again. I got away lightly with only a bruised body. Sheila had a piping hot bath ready for me at home and I soaked in a special mixture, which stinks and stings but brings out the bruising. I seemed to be spending most of my spare time snoozing in the bath at that painful stage of the winter.

February 14th was Valentine's Day, best remembered, I'm afraid, for my visit to the North Tees Hospital with a suspected broken elbow – yes, the same pain-wracked left one again – after Flittermere had buried me in a fall on the far side of the course at Sedgefield in County Durham. This time I was sure I had broken it, but the X-rays dispelled my worst fears. The funnybone must have been banged in exactly the same place as it was at Leicester because I could hardly move it. I had won the second race on Graham Lockerbie's Goosey Gander, who is part owned by Pat Muldoon though he does not carry the Sea Pigeon colours. To make matters worse I heard on the car radio on the way home that my last race mount, Cue World, had won with Andrew Stringer deputizing.

February 21st at Huntingdon, I broke my left cheekbone after a clash of heads with Afzal. Approaching a hurdle down the far side of the course he went for a gap, which suddenly closed and prevented him from seeing the jump. Afzal galloped straight through it, but his head disappeared towards the ground and he catapulted me skywards. As he brought his head up I was coming down vertically and my head banged into his before I crashed in a heap on the ground. I was badly dazed and it was a welcome sight in the ambulance room to see the smiling face beneath the curly locks of John Francome as he brought me a cup of tea. I was driven to Peterborough Hospital where the broken cheek was confirmed, but before I could hit the road back north I had to avoid a posse of press photographers who had wasted no time in pursuing me to the hospital. They must have wanted my picture for the chamber of horrors as my face was badly swollen and distorted. The next day I had an operation in Carlisle Hospital to lift the cheekbone. I nursed myself back to win the Champion Hurdle on Dawn Run on 13 March, my first winner since our victory in the Wessel Cable Champion Hurdle at Leopardstown on 18 February. When Mossy Moore completed a quick double for me on that sunny Cheltenham afternoon, I knew I was back – until I clambered aboard Man Alive at Aintree.

14

Dawn Run

The battling bay mare, heralded as the 'Queen' of all Ireland, enjoyed a record-breaking campaign in 1983–84. Dawn Run won eight of her nine races and amassed £149,000, more first-prize money than any other horse has won in a single jumping season. She also became the first winner of the Champion Hurdle to complete the double and win the French Champion Hurdle in the same year. But she was in grave danger of being robbed of her Cheltenham title only minutes after the race.

T.R.

Cheltenham racecourse would be well advised to tighten their security and certainly vet every person who passes in and out of the vast new unsaddling enclosure. Then there would be no chance of a jockey having a race literally pinched off him as I so nearly did after winning the 1984 Waterford Crystal Champion Hurdle on Dawn Run. It is not an experience I wish to repeat.

There was not one familiar face among the massing herd, but I was reassured to discover that they were friends rather than irate punters with a score to settle. 'Ecstatic fans' would be a more apt description, I decided, as about twenty of them surrounded me and cut me off from the main, noisy, admiring crowd which numbered thousands on the steep steps overlooking Cheltenham's vast amphitheatre, which has become the new unsaddling enclosure and parade ring at Prestbury Park.

Panic nearly set in as I fought against a sea of people pressing me from all sides. My number cloth slid from under my saddle and my breastgirth was being tugged from my arm, which was laden with tack. Without these vital pieces of equipment I would fail to pass the eagle-eyed clerk of the scales, George Gregory, at the weigh-in and he would object to the stewards, who, in turn, would have no option but to do the unthinkable and disqualify Dawn Run.

Only minutes earlier the mare, hailed by the horse-loving Irish as their queen, had crowned a season when triumph was followed by triumph with the ultimate prize, the Champion Hurdle. Was our moment of glory turning sour as I struggled with my saddle towards the weighing room, desperately trying to prevent Dawn Run's courageous victory from being snatched from under my nose?

I searched for someone I knew, but there was still a ring of total strangers around me. A chilling feeling of loneliness swamped me – I was on my own at the heart of an overexcited mob. The walk from the number-one spot to the steps in front of the weighing room is about forty yards, but on this sunny day at Cheltenham it had ceased to be a walk simply because my feet were not touching the ground. The jostling bunch of punters who were exerting pressure on me from the front, from behind, from the left and the right, unwittingly had lifted me above the ground so that I had no control over my course from the chaotic unsaddling enclosure to the entrance to the weighing-room block. I was out of my depth in the midst of a swirling mass of people, my route steered by the erratic sway of the evertightening bunch.

I was frightened that I would not win this unexpected struggle; the heat and perspiration under the dark red woolen colours of Dawn Run's owner, Mrs Charmian Hill, were becoming unbearable. I noticed that my knuckles were white with tension from pulling at the number cloth, which I was desperately trying to keep in my possession. It was being wrenched from me by a souvenir hunter who was partially hidden behind a large, red-faced Irishman whose bulky black coat was all but suffocating me. A hand had appeared round the side of the big Irishman and grasped the corner of my number cloth and now I pleaded with the obscured owner of the hand to let go. In response to my plea, the Irishman immediately grabbed the number cloth and pulled towards me, causing the plundering hand to release its vicelike grip.

No sooner had that battle been won than I realized someone else was tugging at my breastgirth. There seemed to be hundreds of souvenir hunters clamouring for Dawn Run's Champion Hurdle mementos. By now my feet were on the ground, and I called on all my reserves of strength for one last wrench and the second 'invisible man' gave up just as tamely as the first.

I did not need to be a Sherlock Holmes to establish that most of my pursuers were Irish. I could distinguish the cries of the racecourse officials trying to sort out the chaos in the unsaddling enclosure and clear a way up the steps into the comparative tranquillity of the weighing room.

The emotional reception Dawn Run received as I steered her towards the far end of the parade ring will ring in my ears for ever more. The admiring thousands stood shoulder to shoulder above us and, as I raised my arm with a wave of appreciation before I dismounted, the response was instantaneous. The bellowing Irish throats roared their approval, acclaiming their 'Queen', and the crescendo of voices must surely have reached far beyond the rolling Cotswolds and even across the Irish Sea to the Emerald Isle itself.

But the mob rule which ensued and so nearly took over with disastrous results must never be allowed to happen again. Imagine the consequences if Dawn Run had been disqualified because I had failed to weigh in. Rapturous joy would have turned to fury and those idolizing people would have torn down the weighing room brick by brick.

I love to hear the cheers of acknowledgement after one of my wins. A few pats on the back make me feel good. I don't mind being jostled by wellwishers but I am worried by the prospect of what could happen. The situation will only deteriorate if no action is taken.

If stricter security is not thrown round the enormous unsaddling enclosure there will be a disaster. The resiting and combining of the parade ring with the unsaddling enclosure has enabled more racegoers to enjoy a better view of the horses before and after each race. It has also meant freer movement for the massive crowds at the Festival meeting in March. But the birth of this exciting new project in the early eighties has brought with it a giant security headache. The enclosure must be made safe against unwanted invaders scrambling over, under or round the perimeter rails.

The Queen Mother has done more than any single person to promote National Hunt racing over the last thirty years, not only as an owner, but also by presenting trophies and showing as much interest in the stable lads as she does in the owners and trainers. Her undeniable warmth, even on the coldest afternoons, has generated the ever increasing enthusiasm. This has come about by the way in which the Queen Mother acknowledges Mr Average Punter as she rubs shoulders with him on the various parts of the racecourse. It would be tragic if a minority were allowed to run riot and end up barging and buffeting her.

She must be able to continue to join in our celebrations. Racing needs her. But it does not need the irresponsible few that threaten her safety and even the results of races. High fencing round the parade ring and unsaddling enclosure is the sort of bitter pill the authorities might find difficult to swallow. Barricading the crowds from the sacred turf is an unheard-of suggestion, particularly at the greatest jump meeting in the country, but it is perhaps the only answer in situations as dangerous as this.

The watching world, through its television sets and from the special spectators' steps, saw Dawn Run's sixty-five-year-old owner Mrs Charmian Hill being thrown skywards some dozen times by another section of the Dawn Run fan club – all in the best party spirits.

Mrs Hill said afterwards, 'I have had so much fun from Dawn Run I like to see others get some enjoyment from her. I recognized the men around me in the winner's spot from the races in Ireland and they asked if I would mind being given some celebration bumps. I was more than happy to join in. But I did start to worry afterwards because there was such a crowd around Dawn Run and she tends to kick out and someone could easily have been seriously hurt. Positive action must be taken by the Cheltenham executive before it is too late. It does not make sense that there is overcrowding in the winner's enclosure when the viewing facilities from outside are first rate.'

The watching world did not see my struggle to hang on to vital parts of my tack en route for the weigh-in. Perhaps Cheltenham should follow the example of Aintree, where two burly policemen escort the winning jockey of the Grand National and plonk him on the scales. For me the most worrying part of the 1984 Champion Hurdle was trying to reach the weighing room.

The threatening sight of John Francome, Tommy Carmody, Frank Berry, Jimmy Duggan, Sam Morshead and Peter Scudamore sitting waiting to pounce on Dawn Run's tail as I glanced over my shoulder at the top of the hill was the biggest worry I had during the race. To a man, they were coiled above the saddle, ready to unleash their mounts. The obvious untapped power beneath them was enough to make us run for our lives. So I asked Dawn Run to stretch down the hill to take the sting out of our lively pursuers and her answer was emphatic. She hurled herself at the third last hurdle, flew over it and transformed the rest of the field from a bunch bristling with dangers to a string of stragglers. The harder you throw the mare at her hurdles the greater her steely response. She loves a fight and transmits an exhilaration as the going gets tougher. The bigger the challenge the more she gives you.

Unfortunately, Tommy Carmody on another Irish challenger, Buck House, did not jump the second last flight fluently, for if he had stayed with me at that critical stage of the race he would have helped carry Dawn Run to the last hurdle and she would have won by four or five lengths. Instead, Dawn Run, who had been in front or disputing the lead throughout the two miles, went to the last hurdle ahead of Cima and Peter Scudamore, who were closing quickly.

Not only were we alerted to the danger from behind but suddenly ahead of us was a wall of noise, a deafening din which became like an echo chamber as the roar from the packed stands reverberated round the big bowl-like arena, where at that prized moment Dawn Run was holding centre stage. Straightening up for home was like galloping into a tunnel designed for testing decibels rather than racehorses and Dawn Run quite naturally pricked up her ears, wondering what on earth she was running into. For one dreadful moment I thought she might dig her toes in and stop, for her concentration was broken, taken up by this mind-splitting furore, from which she must have thought quite rightly that there was no escape. As she bore down on the final flight with each determined stride so the cheers rang louder and louder until I feared they would discourage her rather than lift her up the hill to the finish. I did not ask her for a big one at the last lest we risk disaster; I allowed her to pop over it and, sure enough, her lack of concentration resulted in an untidy jump as she caught her hind legs in the hurdle.

It can be lonely out there on your own at the head of the field; and there is always the risk that your mount will become bored, lose interest, forget he or she is meant to be racing and begin to idle. Dawn Run has proved almost unbeatable when forcing tactics are employed on her, but having to face the new experience of this unique noise single-handed rather than with the comfort of other horses around her threw her out of her stride. Suddenly all this vociferous support as well as the tough hill stood between us and the hurdling crown.

I squeezed, I shoved, and in response Dawn Run communicated a grim determination through my legs which was enough to tell me that her mind and limbs were charged in readiness for this last struggle. She ground her teeth as if to growl from the corner of her mouth, 'Come on then, try and pass me if you can. Come on ... come on.'

Her right ear shot back as she listened out for any snorts or pants from the advancing Cima or for any sharp cracks from the whip of his indefatigable jockey Peter Scudamore. Her left ear remained forward; she had one eye on where she was going and the other keeping a check on any challengers. I never had any doubt that Dawn Run would not let Cima pass her up the hill, but she started to hang towards her rival so I hit her three cracks down the shoulder to straighten her up and give her the necessary encouragement. At the line we had threequarters of a length in hand from Cima.

I always believed that Dawn Run would win. Her path to glory had been set firmly in my mind some time before Champion Hurdle day, and yet so many acknowledged racereaders and critics were disappointed that she was not more impressive. I believe that she was a stone better than her Cheltenham rivals on that March Tuesday but she is inclined not to exert herself more than necessary. She did enough to win the title in her own way, without the panache and flamboyance of a Sea Pigeon, who was the complete opposite of Dawn Run with his pulverizing late dashes to the line. Her guts and courage hoisted her onto a pedestal above all other hurdlers in 1984, particularly when she was racing over two miles, which is not far enough to bring her limitless stamina into play. She is happiest when she has a fight on her hands and in that respect is similar to Night Nurse, who also had to be ridden up with the pace and had the heart of a lion.

The 1983 champion Gaye Brief had to miss his eagerly awaited Cheltenham clash with Dawn Run because of a training setback involving torn ligaments in his back some ten days before the Festival. It was a wretched blow for his owner Sheikh Ali Abu Khamsin, trainer Mercy Rimell and jockey Richard Linley, and we shall never know if he would have taken his revenge on Dawn Run, who had beaten him by a neck at Kempton on Boxing Day.

Dawn Run's relaxed, easygoing style of racing and her couldn't-care-less attitude to life take very little out of her. If you like, it is self-preservation which has enabled her to last so long as a top-class race mare. All being well, if she takes to steeplechasing she will be a natural; perhaps even the first novice to win the Cheltenham Gold Cup since Mont Tremblant in 1952, and that would break all National Hunt records for no champion hurdler has ever gone on to glory in the Gold Cup.

Dawn Run crossed to France in the summer of 1984 to beat all sorts of odds and, ridden by Tony Mullins, win the French Champion Hurdle at Auteuil in Paris. After such a successful campaign in three countries – Ireland, England and France – one can understand the comment of her amazing owner Mrs Charmian Hill when the curtain finally came down on Dawn Run's extended season: 'I wonder how long this can last. It is remarkable how Dawn Run manages to steer clear of injury and keeps on winning.'

If Mrs Hill herself is any yardstick, then life is only just beginning for her prized mare. It would almost seem that Dawn Run has picked up much of her own enthusiasm and iron characteristics from her owner, who, despite advancing years, rode her horse once a week on Paddy Mullins's gallops in Gorsebridge, Kilkenny, during the big season of 1983–84. Mrs Hill, being no ordinary patron of the Mullins set-up, thought nothing of driving the thirty-six miles from her home just outside Waterford City to join in stable routine on her mare, whose hard pulling tactics would put a young man to the test, never mind the frail frame of a sixty-five-year-old lady, who is a grandmother nine times over. But I suspect Dawn Run enjoys her mornings with her most ardent fan, for, within reason, she does her own thing and doubtless finds refreshing this slightly different approach to exercise. Mrs Hill admits that Dawn Run takes a strong hold with her and she has difficulty keeping her behind the string, but they both thrive on their canters together and the occasional bit of fast work up the all-weather gallop.

In November 1981 Mrs Hill marked off about six possible purchases in the Ballsbridge Sales catalogue including Dawn Run, though she did not believe the mare to be worth looking at on the grounds of expense. Mrs Hill recalls, 'I only had 6000 Irish punts to spend and I was certain that there would be keen competition from the English to buy Dawn Run. I inspected the other horses I had ticked in the catalogue and left Dawn Run until the last. But the moment I saw her I thought, What an athlete. You only needed to see her move to realize she was something special and that convinced me she would be out of my price range. So you can imagine my disbelief when I bought her for 5800 Irish punts.'

Among Mrs Hill's cherished early memories were the days when she used to educate Dawn Run, hacking her newly acquired three-year-old filly round the Waterford lanes and across the 30 green acres owned by her husband, Dr Eddie Hill, who is a general practitioner. After three months at home Dawn Run was sent to Paddy Mullins's stables, where many of the Hills' horses have met with noticeable success over the years.

Tralee races in 1982 brought out Mrs Hill's fighting spirit with a vengeance and the affinity between the galloping granny and her horse is easily discernible; their gritty resolve and never-say-die outlook on life complement each other. The morning of 23 June started under a black cloud when

Mrs Hill opened a letter from the Irish racing authorities informing her that she would not be licensed to ride in any more races. At sixty-three and, in her opinion, riding as well as ever, Mrs Hill was shattered by the decision.

'I went to Tralee more determined than ever,' she recalled. 'In fact, I felt I would have died in the attempt to win on Dawn Run.'

Dawn Run carried her new owner home in triumph, bringing down the curtain on a fairytale riding career which started when Mrs Hill was forty-one and encompassed seventeen point-to-point winners and nine under Rules. As one chapter in Mrs Hill's eventful life closed another opened. Dawn Run, tasting success for the first time, found the recipe to her liking and won her next two races, though watched with mixed feelings by Mrs Hill. 'I nearly killed myself when I was not part of those victories, but at least I have the happy memory of riding her to her first win.'

Tony Mullins, then an amateur, took over and forged a golden partnership with Dawn Run. Their runaway win at Down Royal on 5 November 1983 made Paddy's phone call to me a few days later all the more surprising. In fact, it came like a bolt out of the blue when he asked me to ride Dawn Run at Ascot only thirteen days after Tony's Down Royal success. Naturally, I jumped at the opportunity, particularly as Paddy was talking in terms of a campaign leading up to the Champion Hurdle. I learned later that Mrs Hill wanted a more experienced jockey if Dawn Run was to go to Cheltenham; she was keen to keep it an all-Irish association and suggested to Paddy that he contact me. I was delighted.

The Champion Hurdle seemed an eternity from Ascot that November afternoon. Dawn Run started at 3–1 on and only just scrambled home by a short head from Amarach. While recognizing that she hated the firm ground, I was convinced that Ascot's two and a half miles was more her handwriting than two miles at Cheltenham in March. Frankly, I was disappointed and I expressed my sentiments to Paddy Mullins, telling him that I could not visualize her as a championship prospect. That was my first experience of Dawn Run, and Paddy clearly knew better.

At Naas before Christmas I had my hopes raised after Dawn Run had again galloped her heart out and beaten all but Boreen Deas, to whom she conceded 22 lb. She blazed her own trail out in front until making a hash of the last flight, where Boreen Deas grabbed the advantage and went on to beat her by three lengths. The tempo towards Cheltenham had quickened since our Ascot inauguration.

Even so, if I am honest, I could not see her putting the Champion Hurdler Gaye Brief in his place in the Ladbroke Christmas Hurdle at Kempton on Boxing Day. The fast ground and right-hand track would conspire against us, I thought. But Dawn Run had different ideas and nothing was going to deny her that day, not even Gaye Brief, who hurdled with the fluency of a true champion. But Dawn Run jumped the last three flights as if she were jet-propelled and trying to tell the world something at the same time. Like an extrovert, she wanted to make her point in front of the millions captivated by the Boxing Day racing on television. And how! Hurdling with the authority of a horse going places, she held off Gaye Brief by a brave neck.

It transpired that Gaye Brief had gone to post on an interrupted preparation after suffering a hairline fracture of the cannon bone. Mercy Rimell, a very smart lady and one of the most professional members of the National Hunt scene, had produced Gaye Brief to run the race of his life against all odds. However, the stark facts of the race were that he could not pass us after looming threateningly galloping into the last. Even on the run in Gaye Brief still appeared to have a full tank and looked like taking us at will. But he did not and the day belonged to Dawn Run.

At long last she was transmitting the message to her new

rider that she was improving with every race and that the Cheltenham crown was no longer a forlorn hope. Quietly, I began to fancy our chances of toppling Gaye Brief again at the Festival.

I returned home to a hot line across the Irish Sea with friends asking why Gaye Brief had been given more credit than Dawn Run in the big-race postmortem by ITV commentators John Oaksey and Graham Goode. Apparently in Ireland they could hardly contain themselves with joy after watching Dawn Run's nailbiting victory on television. An enormous cheer went up at Leopardstown races and betting-shop punters punched the air as the commentary reached its climax. I must admit that both John and Graham seemed more taken with Gaye Brief's narrow defeat than Dawn Run's triumph. Quite rightly, Irish friends, relatives and colleagues asked what on earth an Irish horse must achieve in England before he or she receives full credit and recognition? After viewing the video of the Boxing Day racing I was upset that Dawn Run was not awarded the accolades she deserved after those brilliant winning jumps over the last three flights. For some reason the English press gave her a raw deal.

Our runaway win on home ground in the Wessel Cable Champion Hurdle at Leopardstown in February simply served to confirm the Irish conviction that Dawn Run would beat Gaye Brief at Cheltenham. By then I knew that Gaye Brief would have an extremely tough fight on his hands up the final hill if he was going to expose any chinks in Dawn Run's exceptionally resilient armour. I began to ask myself: Why *should* Gaye Brief avenge his Kempton defeat? Sadly, the rematch never materialized.

The O'Neill record on Dawn Run reads: four wins and a second, from five races. And I was bitterly disappointed to be robbed by injury of riding her to victory in the Sandeman Aintree Hurdle on Grand National day, less than two weeks after we had won the Champion Hurdle together. Tony

Mullins took over again and they produced an impressive ten-length victory over Very Promising, emphasizing how much the Aintree trip of two miles five furlongs suited the mare.

I fully appreciate that Tony has played a leading role in the early education and the moulding of Dawn Run into a champion. But that doesn't stop me from wishing I could partner her again. The races we had together are heady memories, which I shall always look upon as one of the big bonuses of my life.

To familiarize herself and Tony Mullins with French hurdles, which are similar to a smaller version of the English fence, only easier to gallop through, Dawn Run was sent to Auteuil for the Prix la Barka over two and a half miles. She won this prep race for the French Champion Hurdle, throwing down a serious challenge for the title, which was due to take place during Royal Ascot week in June.

So vastly superior was Ireland's 'Queen' to the French-trained runners that she turned an improbable rumour into a ludicrous joke. During the big-race build-up on the afternoon a rumour gathered momentum that there was a plot to carve up Dawn Run during the race at a spot on the far bend out of sight of the stands and, apparently, the only place where the stewards did not have an eagle-eyed scout in the country.

As 'off' time approached, pressure was building up on the Mullinses, and Brough Scott and John Oaksey, the two racing journalists and ITV commentators who were covering the race for their papers, took it upon themselves to go and see the stewards to alert them to this dubious ploy. The stewards assured Brough and John that they had people stationed on every conceivable turn of the track for the very purpose of ensuring there was no foul play.

The whole idea became laughable the moment the field jumped off for Dawn Run went into a five-length lead and by the time she passed the stands on the first circuit had scorched nearly twenty lengths clear. The horse and rider who were allegedly going to do the dirty deed were about two hundred yards behind.

Scott turned to Oaksey in the stands and said, 'They will have to cut across the middle of the course and do Dawn Run at the bottom bend, or stop, lay down and trip her as she comes up the home straight.'

Even if the French had wanted to unsettle Dawn Run without resorting to foul play they would have found it impossible. The whole idea of beating Dawn Run by fair or foul means was a farce.

Her eagerly awaited debut over fences at Navan in November filled the new 1984–85 season with expectation. After her foot-perfect fencing and fluent victory the bookmakers were quoting her for the Cheltenham Gold Cup, but Paddy Mullins's immediate reaction was one of caution and to restrict Dawn Run to novice chases. Whether or not Paddy is tempted by the Gold Cup in 1985, Dawn Run's immensely exciting future as a chaser is likely to fire enthusiasm with the thrilling prospect of something they have never witnessed – a champion hurdler winning the Gold Cup, even if they have to wait until 1986.

15

Spin-Offs, the Farm and the Future

As I tried to force 10p into a temperamental telephone in a dank Carlisle kiosk, its glass windows vandalized, I did not realize I was at the head of the queue for the services of Jonjo O'Neill. And I am not sure Jonjo did either. It was Monday, 20 October 1980, forty-eight hours after he had broken his leg at Bangor, and I had just left his hospital bed after asking him to join the *Daily Mirror* with a weekly ghosted racing column. Doped up to the eyeballs, Jonjo agreed he could not even write his name at that moment but he was sufficiently au fait with the situation to insist that I contact his accountant and agent, John Lowthian, before any deal was done. I eventually spoke to Lowthian, reverse charge courtesy of British Telecom because its phone would not accept the 10p. O'Neill Enterprises paid for the call, but, as it turned out, they made a sound investment. For the 'Jumping with Jonjo' column now spans five years.

Out of racing but certainly not out of action, Jonjo, on his recently purchased Cumbria farm, could be seen carrying two straw bales at a time on crutches and climbing perilously steep ladders with his right leg still in plaster.

Meanwhile, the ever active Lowthian ensured there were more spin-offs to follow the *Daily Mirror* assignment, and perhaps none more unusual for a jockey than the making of an advertisement for milk.

T.R.

The instructions were crystal clear but they were so ludicrous that I felt like jumping from the broad back of my fourteen-year-old steed and dashing across the green acres of Newbury racecourse to catch the train, which was slowing down as it approached the distant station on its way to London. I was convinced that this producer fellow did not know what he was talking about. Or was he taking the mickey? What had I let myself in for? I wondered. But before I could arrive at an answer, I tried to work out how I could escape from the surrounding insanity. I gave up and concentrated on trying to follow my incredible orders.

Newbury racecourse was slumbering under the November clouds of 1981 – the tranquillity of the slim poplars, their bright autumnal golden yellows and orange browns projecting them as tall beacons high above us, the empty enclosures lonely in the shadows of the old grandstand distanced by the vast lush carpet of grass in the middle of the track.

The open ditch on the far side of the course from the stands was the scene of many history-making leaps from Arkle, Mill House and Mandarin, Red Rum, Bregawn and Brown Chamberlin. It stood peacefully awaiting the thunder of more hooves at the next meeting, only to be rudely awakened by the most bizarre carry-on I can recall on any racecourse anywhere. Camera crews with their whirring machinery and bright lights and a dozen horses of all shapes and sizes together with their riders were about to launch this perfectly ordinary open ditch into the sitting rooms of millions of unsuspecting television viewers.

I was fulfilling my role in the production of a television commercial for the Milk Marketing Board. Snooker stars Hurricane Higgins and Steve Davis, and big John Lowe the darts player had also agreed to appear, though not I hasten to add, at Newbury's open ditch, which by now was beginning to take on the bustle and pandemonium more familiar at Piccadilly Circus in the rush hour.

I asked the producer a second time, 'Do you really mean that I must jump the fence in time to the music and with someone singing "Lotta Bottle" and then turn to the camera on landing and shout "Lotta Bottle"?'

He nodded and quickly reassured me, 'You should be all right once you get into the rhythm of the tune. I think it will work nicely.'

I am glad he did. For I had not left the ground on a horse during the twelve months since I smashed my leg at Bangor. Not jumped a plain fence or even a hurdle, and here I was confronted with a forbidding open ditch. First I had to summon enough confidence to put full pressure on my right leg at take off and on landing. Happily, my mount was slow, steady, surefooted and quite capable of looking after himself, and with luck he would protect my untried limbs during our foolhardy expedition. We jumped the fence solo and with as many as eight other horses and there was no problem until the music, piped to me through an earpiece, was switched on.

I had to concentrate all my resources on riding and jumping in time with the tune. Of course I couldn't do it, and found myself in the most terrible muddle. At least the producer kept his cool and retained his patience. I was ready to throw in the towel and go home; after all, it was the most absurd situation in which I have ever found myself. I must have jumped the fence between twenty and thirty times, and only once or twice was it to the satisfaction of the producer, who had been keen to show the jump on film as more forbidding than any ordinary fence, which is why he chose the open ditch. It did not show up on the film, though the finished advertisement turned out to be a highly polished professional job. I just hope everyone is drinking more milk as a result of those mad hours spent at Newbury. I don't think Hurricane Higgins, Steve Davis or John Lowe, for that matter, were confronted with the same problems round their snooker tables and dart board!

I am the sort of person who cannot sit still for long; even with a leg in plaster my life of perpetual motion slowed only to a limp when it could so easily have ground to a complete halt, thanks largely to the industrious and forceful personality of John Lowthian, who from his accountant's office in Carlisle, succeeded in keeping me in the public eye by providing plenty of occupational therapy. His meticulous organizing ability secured contracts with the ITV racing commentary team one week and the BBC the next, in addition to making milk commercials. John negotiated my ghosted column in the *Daily Mirror* and I was also invited to open betting shops in various parts of the country. It was vital during those thirteen tedious months that I keep my face and name in front of the fickle racing world. Had I been content to sit quietly at home it would not have taken long for people to start asking, 'Jonjo who?' or 'Who's Jonjo?' Instead, when I resumed raceriding I felt as though I had hardly been away.

Assisting Julian Wilson and the BBC commentators during the 1981 Cheltenham Festival proved a sweet and sour experience. The work was stimulating and meant I retained an involvement in racing, and having to mug up on form kept my finger on the pulse. But watching my two big rides, Sea Pigeon winning his second Champion Hurdle and Night Nurse bravely chasing Little Owl to the line in the Gold Cup, served as harsh reminders that I was only in the second-best place. One Saturday I would find myself sitting alongside John Oaksey in the ITV paddock commentary box at Sandown, the next I would be rubbing shoulders with Brough Scott while he hosted the show at Newcastle. On occasions I would drive to my television appointment, with John Lowthian in the passenger seat reading out the form of the relevant races. Another day he would be behind the wheel, leaving me to peruse the papers and the formbook. I was learning all the time.

My 'journalistic' career started in the late seventies with the *Daily Star*, in which I had my first ghosted column. The *Daily Mirror*'s 'Jumping with Jonjo' is the longest-running ghosted column on the racing pages of a national daily. At the start of the 1984–5 season I embarked on my fifth winter with the *Mirror*. It has fallen to Tim Richards, and in his absence Charles Fawcus, to produce the words on my behalf. Tim invariably wakes me with a 6.30 a.m. telephone call on

Thursday mornings in the winter for half an hour's chat about the article for Friday's *Mirror* before I go out with the horses.

On the day of my comeback, 1 December 1981, the *Mirror* carried a picture of me breaking my crutches with my 'suspect' right leg before returning to raceriding. At worst I thought it was gimmicky and, quite frankly, perfectly innocuous, so you can imagine my surprise when letters from angry readers rolled in, taking me to task and pointing out that I had wasted a crutch at a critical time of Government cuts in hospital spending and medical supplies. Through the columns of the *Daily Mirror* I have come to understand how impossible it is to please everyone all the time.

John Lowthian always maintains that his first love is not racing, but fell foxhunting on foot with the Blencathra, the pack John Peel hunted on the fells where I exercise the horses. In the mid-seventies John moved his office and renamed it Arkle House after a mountain in the northwest of Scotland – as he tells his non-racing clients. He particularly enjoys his National Hunt racing and holidaying each winter in the Caribbean where he plays golf with flat racing's jet-setting Robert Sangster, his trainers Barry Hills, Jeremy Hindley and Bill Watts as well as Geoff Lewis. He cannot resist the thought of a day at the races and carried the mantle of the Good Samaritan on the occasions when he offers his services as chauffeur.

Watching his dapper figure, protected from the elements by an immaculate cavalry coat, pace up and down at the Knutsford services on the M6 in Cheshire on Boxing Day 1979, I never dreamed he would be making the Kempton headlines on the racing pages of the national press the next day. Ron Barry and I were comfortably ensconced in the warmth of John's BMW while we waited to meet Tommy Carmody, who was riding Silver Buck against me on Jack of Trumps and Ron on Border Incident in the day's top race, the

King George VI Chase at Kempton. After half an hour, John telephoned Sheila, who phoned Tommy's wife Tina to be told that Tommy had left his Harrogate home in good time for the arranged meeting. Another half-hour elapsed and we were becoming agitated because I was riding in the second race, the 1.15. We were about to ring Tina Carmody and tell her we must leave without Tommy when Ron had a brainwave.

'I'll pop over to the northbound side in case Tommy is waiting there by mistake,' he announced, jogging towards the stairs and bridge over the motorway. We couldn't believe our eyes when Ron reappeared with Tommy running at his shoulder, saddles under one arm and bag in the other hand.

'I arrived early, over an hour ago, and went into the café on top of the bridge for a cup of coffee, came out and, with both sides looking identical, unwittingly turned and went down the wrong side,' explained Tommy, who sat alongside John in the front.

Every time the Polos were passed round on the journey and Tommy was about to take one out of the tube, I leaned forward and said 'No, that's the wrong end, Tommy!' My joke began to wear a bit thin after the third round of Polos and Tommy, clearly becoming annoyed, said curtly, 'Don't worry, I'll have the last laugh.'

Sure enough he did, with Silver Buck beating Jack of Trumps by one and a half lengths. Ron made sure the entire carload finished in the money by chasing us home a respectful twenty lengths third. Naturally, during the post-race euphoria and presentations John could not resist relating how Tommy nearly missed out on the big winner because he was waiting on the wrong side of the motorway. Predictably, the assembled hacks lapped up the story.

While John was responsible for delivering us safely and with alacrity that Boxing Day, more than fourteen months earlier he had held up the ambulance taking me to hospital on account of a call of nature. It was the day I broke my right

arm at Kelso and John had arrived at the races with a terrible
thirst on him. To quench this he had been knocking back
bottle after bottle of beer. He saw my spill, dashed to the
ambulance room and accompanied me to hospital so that he
could, if necessary, organize a lift home for me. Every corner
and bump accentuated the pain in my arm and I could not
grasp what was happening when John thumped the window
through to the driver's cab and asked him to stop. He quickly
opened the back doors, threw down the steps and scampered
out. There followed a moment's silence. Then the sound of
running water diverted my mind from its preoccupation of
trying to steel itself against the pain racing up my arm and
into my shoulder. The running water stopped, John jumped
aboard, closed the double doors and said with an air of relief,
'That's better. I couldn't wait any longer. I was bursting.'

A rare sight indeed, the occupant of an ambulance
answering the call of nature by the back wheel, illuminated at
the side of the road by the flashing blue emergency light.
When I realized the cause of the hold-up I laughed. 'It's a
good job I'm not dying.'

Before catching an early-morning train from Carlisle to
London Euston in March 1981, I presented Sheila with a long
list of jobs and instructions for the builders who were busy
altering and rebuilding Ivy House, which we had bought the
previous year. I asked her to drive the eight miles from Deep
Ghyll at Plumpton to Skelton Wood End to be certain that
they understood exactly what was required. I caught the train
totally unsuspecting that Sheila would be aboard a London-
bound train only an hour behind me. And if I had known the
yarn she spun to the builders over the phone the moment I
walked out of the house I think I would have been asking
some leading questions! Little wonder the builders found
plenty to gossip about.

Sheila telephoned, explained my instructions, then signed

off by saying, 'I'm going away for a couple of days, but Jonjo doesn't know. If he rings don't tell him I have not been over to deliver his list personally and don't say anything about my being away.'

Sheila recalls that she could almost hear the builder's imagination working overtime down the phone and was fully aware of the extent to which she had set tongues wagging. She had told me that she would be staying with her mother Audrey, at Ivegill, three miles from Ivy House. But she did not say that the phone would be taken off the hook to prevent me ringing up. John Lowthian had organized two radio interviews for me in London that Monday, 23 March 1981. The following day I was to attend an ITV pre-Grand National dinner. I met up with Colin Turner, racing correspondent of LBC, and he duly extracted the necessary news and views from me on the subjects of my injury and the build-up to the Grand National. Later in the day I explored the London shops, taking periodic breaks to try to ring Sheila at her mother's to check on the builders' progress. I could not understand why the number was continually engaged. I still had not dialled through by the evening and was beginning to spit and curse into the mouthpiece each time I lifted a telephone. I arrived at the Thames Television Studios early on Tuesday evening and only seconds after I had put a boiled sweet in my mouth Eamonn Andrews appeared from nowhere to announce, 'This is your life,' and lead me into the studios and onto the stage, where, of course, I met Sheila and little Louise, to say nothing of my family from Ireland and many friends in racing.

Thanks to Sheila's and her family's discreet handling of the build-up to the programme I was taken by complete surprise. It was a moving experience, particularly when two-year-old Louise walked through the sliding doors onto the stage after we had been watching film of her on her pony Sparky at Becher's Brook and in the winner's enclosure at Aintree. I felt

honoured that I should have been considered a suitable
subject for a programme with such a wide audience. But when
I came down to earth I began to wonder if, at twenty-nine,
they hadn't missed rather a large chunk of my life.

The builders and workmen at Ivy House thought it was the
funniest television programme they had seen after the
instructions they had received from Sheila!

Sheila insists to this day that I would have retired from riding
and we would be living a very different lifestyle now if we
hadn't taken the plunge and bought Ivy House on 17 June
1980 – the first day of Royal Ascot. The next day we set off on
holiday to Ireland with very mixed feelings. Thrilled at the
prospect of owning our own farmhouse, outbuildings and 45
acres, but concerned as to exactly how we were going to pay
for the privilege of being landowners. Four months later,
after Bangor, our concern deepened when I was faced with
the prospect of months without my regular earning power.
But the worry was short-lived with John Lowthian
negotiating for various jobs and promotions.

My frustrations at being sidelined and having to watch the
rest of the racing world gallop on while I tried to sit still were
absorbed by my involvement in the planning and rebuilding
of Ivy House and its stable yard. Subconsciously, my daily
trips between Deep Ghyll and Ivy House became increasingly
therapeutic. Sheila maintains that without Ivy House and all
its exciting prospects I would have wanted to retire.

I had been receiving more and more inquiries about taking
horses in during the summer and at Deep Ghyll, where we
had only half an acre, there were simply not the facilities.
When Ivy House came on the market I walked round the 45
acres of fields more than twenty times to satisfy myself that
the land was suitable. The tiny farmhouse was in a
tumbledown state and almost an eyesore, but the potential
was there. We renovated and extended the house and have

built seventeen looseboxes. My knowledge of farming was nonexistent and, to be perfectly honest, one of the attractions of the situation of Ivy House at Skelton Wood End is that it stands only three miles from Sheila's father, Stan, who manages the 300 acres at Braithwaite Hall, Ivegill. Only when I bought the farm did it dawn on me that I had no stock and I had to go to the bank and borrow more money to buy some sheep and cattle.

Sheila had to do most of the physical moving-in thirteen months after we bought the place and only a month or so after I had returned from having my leg replated by Professor Allgower in Basle in May 1981.

Bourbon Street, an Irish chaser who won two races for Peter Easterby and one for Ginger McCain, was the first horse to take up residence, but the build-up started steadily with me gingerly trying out my leg along the Cumbria lanes on that wonderful mare Realt Na Nona. Hallo Dandy, hero of the 1984 Grand National, joined us for his summer rest. High Debate, who was beaten by only half a length by Trojan Fen at Newmarket in 1984, arrived here as a foal after being bought at the Newmarket Sales for 4800 guineas. He was resold as a yearling at a loss for 3600 guineas and went into training at Malton with Gordon Richards's former travelling head lad Malcolm Jefferson. After the owners had turned down an offer of £1,000,000 from an oil sheikh, they moved High Debate to be trained by Henry Cecil at Newmarket.

The insight into dealing with owners, bloodstock agents, trainers, vets, blacksmiths, and the paperwork, which I detest, is sound experience of the practical side of training racehorses. I employ a staff of four, including myself. The day starts at half past six when I feed the horses, and then we all muck out. If necessary I box up one or two and drive them five miles to the fells, where they can enjoy a wide variety of routes on the wonderful spongy turf. On returning, the yearlings have to be exercised, then it is surgery time with injections and attention to any cuts and bruises. At breakfast, around nine o'clock, I usually perch in my office, a cup of tea in one hand, toast and jam in the other and the phone balanced in my neck. The problems start when the second phone rings! Back out to the yard to check the horses before driving to the races and with luck a winner or two. Evenings are spent inspecting the horses again before working on the formbook and the *Racing Calendar* so I can sort out my rides over the next few days. A heavy workload. But it is bound to be while I am still riding and trying to prepare myself for the switch to training. That will come when I see the red light.

So many people question the wisdom of embarking on a training career, which, they continue to tell me, will be full of hassle and worries. Quite simply, I hate being away from horses. Even if I worked in a shop I would have to own a hunter. It is common sense to make your living in a trade you enjoy, and I love horses.

Sheila and I have looked at numerous properties in the Midlands and the North, particularly in Yorkshire, with a view to buying a suitable training establishment. But after each excursion we have returned home feeling that Ivy House and the farm are far more suitable than anywhere we have seen to date. Building an indoor school and all-weather gallop are the top priorities and one day I would like to purchase more land where I can work the horses.

'Move South' has been the advice freely offered. In fact, Peter Easterby and the former Yorkshire trainer Jack Ormston have both urged me to find a place around Newmarket or one of the big training centres, which, they reason, are ready-made attractions for the wealthy owners, so vital to any successful stable. But racing has been over-generous to me here and, furthermore, I have already trained two winners at Ivy House.

It was 13 March 1982, the Saturday before Cheltenham

and I was recovering from a heavy bout of flu and hoping to be fit in time for the Festival three days later. However, the bright spring afternoon acted as encouragement to wrap up and go to the Cumberland Farmers' point-to-point at Dalston, about ten miles away, near Carlisle.

Ousky, on whom I had won a novice chase at Haydock in 1979, exactly half an hour before the epic race between Silver Buck and Night Nurse in the Embassy Chase Premier Final, was the Ivy House representative. I felt lousy as I walked onto Dalston's natural grandstand, the hill alongside the course. Les Hudson, associated with John Dixon – who sadly had died after a long illness – and now working for his son John Jr, made most of the running on Ousky and stayed on too strongly for Broad View, a horse I used to ride for Peter Easterby. I could not tell you what happened as the race reached its climax over the last three fences. I was jumping and shouting so much.

For a moment little Dalston with its enthusiastic farming supporters looked more like Cheltenham to one member of the crowd. I suddenly felt much better.

Perhaps Ousky was the tonic I needed before going to Cheltenham, where against all odds I won the Ritz Trophy as top jockey. Ousky won again at the Eglinton point-to-point at Bogside in Scotland a fortnight later.

I wonder if he was signposting the future.

I waved goodbye to 1984 with a broken left arm, a great sigh of relief and that flicker of determination burning in my belly, ignited by the haunting question: 'Are you going to retire?'

A dislocated hip in October, followed by a broken left arm in November, made for an abortive start to the 1984–85 season and I began to wonder if the doomsday predictions of George Orwell's celebrated book *1984* had come true so far as I was concerned. Perhaps 1984 was meant to be the end of my raceriding world. After all my biffs and bangs I look back and can see only two shining lights beaming out of the year – our new baby Tom and Dawn Run.

Hugh Barber says the best thing that happened to me in 1984 was being kicked by a horse after I had fallen from Afzal at Chepstow and dislocated my hip. I hit the turf knees first with such a bone-shaking thud that the green of the grass was imprinted through my breeches, through my tights and firmly onto my kneecaps. Apparently, the most common cause of hip dislocation is when you crash your knee against the dashboard of the car in an accident. I managed it at thirty miles an hour but was lucky enough to have a horse following me to kick the hip straight back into its socket. Hugh explained that if the hip had not been booted back immediately I would have been out of action for months rather than weeks. Even worse, if I had chipped a piece of bone off the lip of the socket, a common occurrence with such an injury, I would have been sidelined for the whole season right through until June.

As it was I missed only a fortnight, but then, just ten days after resuming, I had one of those innocuous soft falls from Goosey Gander at Wetherby, although I was all right until another horse stamped on my arm as it galloped past. Even as I scrambled to my feet on the landing side of the final flight of hurdles in front of the stands I believed I had escaped unscathed. Then suddenly the pain knifed ferociously through my arm and, as I cradled it with my right hand trying to comfort myself, I knew the worst. The whiffs of painkilling gas I inhaled with great relief in the ambulance on the way to Harrogate's District Hospital acted like an intoxicating drink, making me oblivious of the waves of agony which had overcome me.

Dave Goulding's brother John, who had been riding at Wetherby, drove me home with my arm in a splint in readiness for the Hugh Barber treatment. With all his thoroughness Hugh had sent to Welwyn Garden City for a plate from the manufacturers of the titanium alloy plate that Professor Allgower had inserted in my leg in Switzerland in 1981.

A dispatch rider sped up the M1 and M6 in the worst possible autumn weather, torrential rain and galeforce winds, to deliver the latest part of what has become popularly known as my bionic body to Carlisle's Cumberland Infirmary.

Hugh was not prepared to take the risk of my system rejecting any ordinary stainless-steel plate as it had done in the past. The four-inch strip of alloy and its six screws repaired the break and at the same time allowed movement of the elbow, wrist and fingers, ensuring that my muscles were in full use ready for the earliest possible return to the saddle.

As Hugh put it so succinctly, 'You will be able to shovel horse shit next week if you want to.' I smiled, knowing that would be the first of many tasks which would lead to complete fitness in the saddle.

Only hours after my Wetherby spill the phone was full of inquiries about my future. Had I thought about retiring? When? What would I do?

As always, these questions from the media infuriated me and crept right under my skin. Why the hell should I let them try to write me off just because I was flat on my back? They made me want to prove a point again.

Epilogue

John Francome's snap decision to retire on 9 April 1985 after a colourful, controversial and unequalled career encompassing 1,137 winners launched another seemingly endless question my way: 'Will you take over from John as number one jockey to the John Jenkings stable at Epsom?' The Jenkins operation is rapidly becoming a winner factory and after churning out 76 winners during the 1984/5 season his offer came as a most attractive bait.

Was this the impetus I needed to regain the championship, I asked myself. The prospect of sitting astride some forty or fifty ready-made winners laid on by John Jenkins had a golden appeal I knew I was going to find difficult to resist.

As I pulled up in racecourse car parks, carried my bags through the turnstiles and walked into the jockeys' rooms those words were continually aimed at me: 'Are you taking the Jenkins job?'

Yes, a handsome retainer had been bandied about, but no firm offer made. At first it appeared to be a proposition decorated with so much glitter and excitement that it would be impossible to decline. An automatic forty or fifty winners would hoist me halfway to my third jockey's title, I thought. What a way to bow out of the saddle; at the top.

Then I realized I was in danger of letting my dreams gallop away with me. I began to have second thoughts and became aware that teaming up full-time with the Jenkins horses would not be as simple as that. Epsom, the Jenkins home-base, is approximately three hundred and twenty miles from our Cumbria farm. Most of John's runners are on the tracks in the deep South, even further from Skelton Wood End than Epsom. The basic geography of the whole situation threw up enormous hurdles that would have to be crossed.

Sheila and I are very conscious of the thousands of hours, hard work and cash we have sunk into our forty-five-acre farm and naturally we felt very reluctant to pass it all up for a season on the southern circuit. In addition to my family two other men deserved very careful consideration. They are Reg Hollinshead and Peter Easterby. Reg, always so under-standing when I find my freelancing is pulling me in three different directions at once – perhaps to Newbury, Newcastle and Uttoxeter all on the same day – was planning to expand his successful training operation in Staffordshire. How could I desert Reg when he had kept Jonjo O'Neill so high on his list of priorities? Peter, at the helm of Britain's best drilled mixed stable of jumpers and flat horses, hoisted me on to so many highs during the great years and still produces some of the most talented riding material for me.

Sheila and I talked and thought long and hard and decided to have a look at various properties, farms and studs further south in the Midlands, across in Yorkshire, and we even explored two possibilities in the Newmarket area. But after each visit we returned home only to realize how lucky we are to have Ivy House, the stables and indoor school we have built there, plus the added variety of the local Fells, such a vital exercise area for the horses.

As the days ticked by we decided to remain, at least for the time being, where we had put down so many roots in Cumbria. John Jenkins agreed to see how his new riding arrangements worked and offered to share mounts between Steve Smith Eccles, Simon Sherwood and myself.

Career Record

Career Record

JONJO'S JUMPING RECORD
IN ENGLAND

1972/73	38 winners
1973/74	51 winners
1974/75	27 winners
1975/76	64 winners
1976/77	65 winners
1977/78	149 winners
1978/79	62 winners
1979/80	117 winners
1980/81	17 winners
1981/82	34 winners
1982/83	74 winners
1983/84	103 winners
1985/86	46 winners

At the start of the 1985/86 season Jonjo had ridden 847 jumping winners in Britain. He had also ridden 15 jumping winners in Ireland and 1 in Belgium. At the start of the 1985/86 season his total of jumping winners worldwide was 863. On the flat, at the end of 1985, Jonjo had ridden 15 winners: 13 in England, 1 in Ireland and 1 in Belgium.

Total number of winners ridden on 3.8.85: 878.

Jonjo rode over 100 winners in a season on three occasions:

1977/78

30.7	*Border River*	(11/4)	W. C. Watts	Market Rasen	1
30.7	*Night Adventure*	(15/2)	D. McCain	Market Rasen	2
1.8	*Captain Midnight*	(7/2)	H. P. Rohan	Market Rasen	3
6.8	*Night Adventure*	(3/1)	D. McCain	Worcester	4
20.8	*Chukka*	(85/40f)	D. McCain	Bangor	5
20.8	*Night Adventure*	(4/1)	D. McCain	Bangor	6
22.8	*Aorist*	(3/1)	P. Green	Worcester	7
22.8	*Border River*	(9/4f)	W. C. Watts	Worcester	8
29.8	*Rantzesther*	(1/1f)	D. McCain	Cartmel	9
29.8	*Chukka*	(4/6f)	D. McCain	Cartmel	10

10.9	Kings Oak	(20/1)	S. Norton	Sedgefield	11
13.9	Wanlockhead	(7/4)	D. Sasse	Hereford	12
17.9	Kings Oak	(11/10f)	S. Norton	Carlisle	13
27.9	Charlie Battle	(2/1f)	S. Norton	Sedgefield	14
29.9	Chukka	(5/2)	D. McCain	Perth	15
1.10	Some Hazard	(16/1)	R. Allan	Kelso	16
10.10	Red Earl	(6/1)	J. Berry	Ayr	17
10.10	Pewter Spear	(3/1)	D. McCain	Ayr	18
12.10	Simmering	(16/1)	D. McCain	Wetherby	19
15.10	Pewter Spear	(8/13f)	D. McCain	Bangor	20
19.10	Newgate	(4/5f)	A. Scott	Hexham	21
29.10	King Weasel	(11/8f)	M. H. Easterby	Catterick	22
29.10	Kolligan Kangaroo	(5/2)	D. Ringer	Catterick	2
2.11	The Last Light	(8/1)	J. Dixon	Carlisle	2
2.11	Holly Twist	(4/1f)	J. Dixon	Carlisle	2
2.11	Arctic Mist	(7/1)	M. H. Easterby	Carlisle	2
4.11	Hidden Value	(2/1f)	S. Norton	Doncaster	2
4.11	Young Thomas	(10/1)	J. A. Turner	Doncaster	2
5.11	Colonel Taj	(8/1)	H. Blackshaw	Cheltenham	2
7.11	Birdland	(1/1f)	M. H. Easterby	Wolverhampton	3
8.11	Newgate	(4/5f)	A. Scott	Hexham	3
8.11	Golden Express	(5/1)	J. Dodds	Hexham	3
9.11	Crofton Hall	(2/5f)	J. Dixon	Kelso	3
9.11	Newfoundland	(5/4f)	Mrs I. Hamilton	Kelso	3
10.11	Eborneezersdouble	(11/8f)	E. Carter	Southwell	3
11.11	King Weasel	(8/11f)	M. H. Easterby	Wetherby	3
11.11	Father Delaney	(11/4f)	M. H. Easterby	Wetherby	3
11.11	The Last Light	(13/8)	J. Dixon	Wetherby	3
12.11	Eborneezersdouble	(9/2)	E. Carter	Wetherby	3
12.11	Within The Law	(12/1)	M. H. Easterby	Wetherby	4
14.11	Stag Party	(14/1)	B. Wilkinson	Carlisle	4
14.11	Iwanawin	(5/4f)	M. H. Easterby	Carlisle	4
15.11	Hidden Value	(4/5f)	S. Norton	Teesside	4
15.11	Katmandu	(2/1f)	E. Carter	Teesside	4
16.11	Blabbermouth	(5/2)	T. Gillam	Sedgefield	4
18.11	Good Job	(8/13f)	J. W. Watts	Newcastle	4
18.11	King Weasel	(8/13f)	M. H. Easterby	Newcastle	4
1.12	Within The Law	(7/4f)	M. H. Easterby	Haydock	4
2.12	Good Job	(4/7f)	J. W. Watts	Market Rasen	4
5.12	David Tudor	(11/4)	D. Ringer	Southwell	5
5.12	Harry's Fizzale	(9/4f)	B. Richmond	Southwell	5
5.12	Nellie's Lad	(1/1f)	J. Skilling	Southwell	5
7.12	China God	(7/4)	B. Cambidge	Ayr	5
7.12	Holly Twist	(4/6f)	J. Dixon	Ayr	5
7.12	Leirum	(1/5f)	J. B. Lusk	Ayr	5
10.12	Netherton	(8/11f)	M. H. Easterby	Newcastle	5
12.12	Grecian Fighter	(6/1)	B. Richmond	Teesside	5

13.12	*Nice And Friendly*	(2/1f)	H. P. Rohan	Teesside	58
13.12	*Eborneezersdouble*	(4/9f)	E. Carter	Teesside	59
13.12	*Urser*	(5/1)	M. W. Easterby	Teesside	60
14.12	*Yentala*	(6/4)	J. Harris	Southwell	61
15.12	*The Last Light*	(11/4)	J. Dixon	Carlisle	62
17.12	*Harry's Fizzale*	(10/11f)	B. Richmond	Nottingham	63
17.12	*King Weasel*	(6/4)	M. H. Easterby	Nottingham	64
17.12	*Son and Heir*	(7/2f)	J. Edwards	Nottingham	65
21.12	*Skiddaw View*	(3/1)	J. Dixon	Catterick	66
21.12	*Four Pals*	(14/1)	D. McCain	Catterick	67
26.12	*Netherton*	(1/2f)	M. H. Easterby	Wetherby	68
26.12	*Crofton Hall*	(6/5f)	J. Dixon	Wetherby	69
26.12	*Nunstar*	(12/1)	M. H. Easterby	Wetherby	70
27.12	*The Alickadoo*	(4/1)	M. H. Easterby	Wetherby	71
29.12	*Rambling Jack*	(6/4)	K. Oliver	Newcastle	72
29.12	*Newgate*	(6/5f)	A. Scott	Newcastle	73
31.12	*Young Thomas*	(5/2f)	J. A. Turner	Catterick	74
31.12	*Bountiful Charles*	(5/1)	Sir G. Cunard	Catterick	75.
31.12	*Nunstar*	(1/1f)	M. H. Easterby	Catterick	76
2.1	*March Morning*	(1/2f)	D. Ringer	Leicester	77
2.1	*Within The Law*	(7/4)	M. H. Easterby	Leicester	78
3.1	*Skiddaw View*	(13/8f)	J. Dixon	Ayr	79
7.1	*Wayland Prince*	(4/7f)	M. H. Easterby	Market Rasen	80
7.1	*Ireland's Owen*	(9/4)	J. Edwards	Market Rasen	81
9.1	*Netherton*	(8/11f)	M. H. Easterby	Leicester	82
10.1	*Royal Legend*	(6/1)	M. H. Easterby	Teesside	83
14.1	*Alverton*	(11/8)	M. H. Easterby	Newcastle	84
14.1	*Netherton*	(8/11f)	M. H. Easterby	Newcastle	85
14.1	*Rambling Jack*	(3/1f)	K. Oliver	Newcastle	86
17.1	*Tudor Jig*	(6/4)	M. W. Easterby	Wetherby	87
17.1	*Rambling Artist*	(9/4f)	T. Gillam	Wetherby	88
17.1	*Royal Legend*	(8/11f)	M. H. Easterby	Wetherby	89
21.1	*Another Captain*	(2/1f)	A. Scott	Haydock	90
21.1	*Tregarron*	(9/4f)	K. Oliver	Haydock	91
23.1	*Blessed Boy*	(5/1)	D. McCain	Teesside	92
23.1	*Alverton*	—	M. H. Easterby	Teesside	93
24.1	*Jason*	(3/1)	M. H. Easterby	Sedgefield	94
28.1	*Night Nurse*	(13/8f)	M. H. Easterby	Doncaster	95
4.2	*Sea Pigeon*	(2/1)	M. H. Easterby	Sandown	96
7.2	*Golden Express*	(12/1)	J. Dodds	Sedgefield	97
7.2	*Ingham*	(1/1f)	S. Nesbitt	Sedgefield	98
7.2	*Jason*	(11/10f)	M. H. Easterby	Sedgefield	99
8.2	*Sweet Millie*	(7/2)	C. Dingwall	Haydock	100
8.2	*Tregarron*	(2/1f)	K. Oliver	Haydock	101
25.2	*Ingham*	(5/6f)	S. Nesbitt	Teesside	102
25.2	*Rag Trade*	(6/1)	G. Fairbairn	Teesside	103
25.2	*Major Thompson*	(4/7f)	M. H. Easterby	Teesside	104

1.3	*Spare A Dime*	(9/4)	M. H. Easterby	Wetherby	105
1.3	*Little Owl*	(6/1)	M. H. Easterby	Wetherby	106
3.3	*Mayhem*	(1/2f)	M. Camacho	Haydock	107
3.3	*The Alickadoo*	(5/4f)	M. H. Easterby	Haydock	108
4.3	*Rambling Artist*	(3/1)	T. Gillam	Haydock	109
4.3	*Qualuz*	(5/2f)	M. H. Easterby	Haydock	110
10.3	*Tudor Jig*	(4/7f)	M. W. Easterby	Teesside	111
13.3	*Pewter Spear*	(4/1)	D. McCain	Ayr	112
27.3	*Blessed Boy*	(9/4f)	D. McCain	Wetherby	113
27.3	*Little Owl*	(1/1f)	M. H. Easterby	Wetherby	114
30.3	*Prousto*	(4/1)	A. Jarvis	Liverpool	115
5.4	*Prousto*	(2/1f)	A. Jarvis	Ascot	116
7.4	*Meldrette*	(12/1)	L. Griffiths	Sedgefield	117
8.4	*Father Delaney*	(1/1f)	M. H. Easterby	Hexham	118
8.4	*Eborneezersdouble*	(1/1f)	E. Carter	Hexham	119
11.4	*Princely Chief*	(8/1)	D. Ringer	Hereford	120
15.4	*King Weasel*	(1/2f)	M. H. Easterby	Ayr	121
15.4	*Major Thompson*	(1/2f)	M. H. Easterby	Ayr	122
15.4	*Sea Pigeon*	(7/4f)	M. H. Easterby	Ayr	123
18.4	*Father Delaney*	(2/5f)	M. H. Easterby	Perth	124
19.4	*Besciamella*	(7/2)	W. Crawford	Perth	125
19.4	*Majetta Crescent*	(13/8f)	M. H. Easterby	Perth	126
19.4	*Crofton Hall*	(7/2)	J. Dixon	Perth	127
19.4	*Father Delaney*	(4/5f)	M. H. Easterby	Perth	128
19.4	*Tiger Feet*	(7/1)	W. Atkinson	Perth	129
20.4	*Pewter Spear*	(10/1)	D. McCain	Ludlow	130
22.4	*The Alickadoo*	(5/2f)	M. H. Easterby	Uttoxeter	131
24.4	*Cromwell Road*	(7/4f)	K. Oliver	Hexham	132
24.4	*Coleraine*	(2/1f)	S. Nesbitt	Hexham	133
29.4	*Tully Town*	(10/1)	M. Naughton	Newcastle	134
1.5	*The Alickadoo*	(2/1f)	M. H. Easterby	Haydock	135
1.5	*Cancello*	(5/2f)	N. Crump	Haydock	136
3.5	*Little Owl*	(4/11f)	M. H. Easterby	Wetherby	137
3.5	*General Moselle*	(2/1f)	M. Camacho	Wetherby	138
9.5	*Hidden Value*	(4/1f)	S. Norton	Kelso	139
10.5	*Bosphorous Queen*	(20/1)	M. Naughton	Hexham	140
12.5	*Prousto*	(4/9f)	A. Jarvis	Taunton	141
17.5	*Wealth Tax*	(4/6f)	J. Leadbetter	Perth	142
18.5	*Hidden Value*	(6/4f)	S. Norton	Uttoxeter	143
18.5	*Wayland Prince*	(2/1f)	M. H. Easterby	Uttoxeter	144
20.5	*Sea Minstrel*	(5/1)	D. McCain	Market Rasen	145
20.5	*Father Delaney*	(1/1f)	M. H. Easterby	Market Rasen	146
27.5	*Three Musketeers*	(6/1)	W. Wharton	Southwell	147
29.5	*Toughie*	(11/10f)	M. Naughton	Hexham	148
3.6	*Lothian Brig*	(5/4f)	J. Alder	Stratford	149

Jonjo's 149 winners were for 42 different stables:

M. H. Easterby	45	T. Gillam	3
D. McCain	16	A. Jarvis	3
J. Dixon	10	M. Naughton	3
S. Norton	7	S. Nesbitt	3
E. Carter	5	B. Richmond	3
K. Oliver	5	M. Camacho	2
D. Ringer	4	J. Dodds	2
A. Scott	4	J. Edwards	2
M. W. Easterby	3	H. P. Rohan	2
J. A. Turner	2	C. Dingwall	1
J. W. Watts	2	G. Fairbairn	1
W. C. Watts	2	P. Green	1
J. Alder	1	L. Griffiths	1
R. Allan	1	Mrs I. Hamilton	1
W. Atkinson	1	J. Harris	1
J. Berry	1	J. Leadbetter	1
H. Blackshaw	1	J. B. Lusk	1
B. Cambidge	1	D. Sasse	1
W. Crawford	1	J. Skilling	1
N. Crump	1	W. Wharton	1
Sir G. Cunard	1	B. Wilkinson	1

1979/80

11.8	*Wayland Prince*	(3/1f)	M. H. Easterby	Southwell	1
18.8	*Twopenny Blue*	(10/11f)	T. Gillam	Market Rasen	2
25.8	*Mr Solo*	(6/1)	H. Wharton	Market Rasen	3
25.8	*Rahaj*	(7/4f)	H. P. Rohan	Market Rasen	4
25.8	*Landfall*	(7/1)	O. Brennan	Market Rasen	5
25.8	*Father Delaney*	(5/4f)	M. H. Easterby	Market Rasen	6
27.8	*The Fencer*	(1/2f)	W.A. Stephenson	Cartmel	7
22.9	*Barrettstown Boy*	(85/40f)	R. Fisher	Bangor	8
22.9	*Miss Plumes*	(10/1)	D. McCain	Bangor	9
27.9	*Twopenny Blue*	(2/1f)	T. Gillam	Perth	10
29.9	*Alick*	(9/4)	M. H. Easterby	Carlisle	11
29.9	*Our Sovereign*	(3/1)	J. Berry	Carlisle	12
4.10	*Sovereigns Escort*	(3/1f)	D. McCain	Ludlow	13
6.10	*Landfall*	(5/2)	O. Brennan	Kelso	14
11.10	*Bobjob*	(11/10f)	J. Brockbank	Perth	15
15.10	*Eminence*	(5/1)	M. H. Easterby	Ayr	16
15.10	*Gleason*	(4/11f)	M. H. Easterby	Ayr	17
17.10	*Alick*	(11/4f)	M. H. Easterby	Wetherby	18
17.10	*Father Delaney*	(7/4f)	M. H. Easterby	Wetherby	19
19.10	*Major Thompson*	(1/2f)	M. H. Easterby	Market Rasen	20

Date	Horse	Odds	Jockey/Trainer	Course	No.
20.10	*Bobjob*	(7/4f)	J. Brockbank	Kelso	21
23.10	*Wayland Prince*	(7/2)	M. H. Easterby	Sedgefield	22
24.10	*Bargellos Lady*	(6/5f)	R. Johnson	Hexham	23
27.10	*Gleason*	(1/1f)	M. H. Easterby	Newbury	24
31.10	*Brave Fellow*	(7/4f)	J. Fitzgerald	Newcastle	25
3.11	*Sea Pigeon*	—	M. H. Easterby	Sandown	26
6.11	*Tribal Warlord*	(16/1)	M. Naughton	Sedgefield	27
9.11	*Red Cleric*	(4/5f)	M. Naughton	Hexham	28
9.11	*Bobjob*	(1/1f)	J. Brockbank	Hexham	29
10.11	*Greenways*	(14/1)	A. Jarvis	Cheltenham	30
12.11	*Gleason*	(1/6f)	M. H. Easterby	Nottingham	31
14.11	*Sovereigns Escort*	(100/30)	D. McCain	Ludlow	32
17.11	*Norton Cavalier*	(9/4)	M. H. Easterby	Newcastle	33
19.11	*Stay Quiet*	(7/1)	G. W. Richards	Ayr	34
19.11	*Captain John*	(4/7f)	M. H. Easterby	Ayr	35
20.11	*Father Delaney*	(9/2)	M. H. Easterby	Ayr	36
20.11	*Silver Shadow*	(9/4)	M. H. Easterby	Ayr	37
28.11	*Netherton*	(5/6f)	M. H. Easterby	Haydock	38
28.11	*Gleason*	(1/2f)	M. H. Easterby	Haydock	39
1.12	*Colway Boy*	(6/1)	R. Akehurst	Sandown	40
5.12	*Crofton Hall*	(9/4)	J. Dixon	Ayr	41
8.12	*Netherton*	(11/8f)	M. H. Easterby	Newcastle	42
8.12	*Selby*	(2/1)	M. H. Easterby	Newcastle	43
8.12	*Norton Cavalier*	(13/8f)	M. H. Easterby	Newcastle	44
11.12	*Vascar*	(7/4f)	M. H. Easterby	Teesside	45
11.12	*Falkelly*	(9/4f)	M. H. Easterby	Teesside	46
12.12	*Pizza*	(16/1)	C. Vernon Miller	Worcester	47
13.12	*Jesters Night*	(5/2f)	R. Peacock	Uttoxeter	48
17.12	*Three To One*	(4/1)	K. Oliver	Kelso	49
27.12	*Vascar*	(1/3f)	M. H. Easterby	Wetherby	50
27.12	*Pennine Derek*	(9/4)	W. Wharton	Wetherby	51
29.12	*Caxton Hall*	(7/2f)	J. Fitzgerald	Newcastle	52
29.12	*Three To One*	(9/4)	K. Oliver	Newcastle	53
29.12	*Clayside*	(7/1)	M. H. Easterby	Newcastle	54
5.1	*Irish Gantlet*	(12/1)	E. Carter	Haydock	55
5.1	*Big Ginger*	(9/2)	T. Fairhurst	Haydock	56
8.1	*Jean Marjorie*	(2/1f)	D. Yeoman	Teesside	57
9.1	*Skiddaw View*	(11/10)	J. Dixon	Carlisle	58
9.1	*Big Ginger*	(2/5f)	T. Fairhurst	Carlisle	59
11.1	*Little Owl*	(9/4f)	M. H. Easterby	Newcastle	60
12.1	*Clayside*	(4/6f)	M. H. Easterby	Newcastle	61
12.1	*King Weasel*	(1/1f)	M. H. Easterby	Newcastle	62
18.1	*Bertie Me Boy*	(2/1f)	M. H. Easterby	Catterick	63
19.1	*Michelham Lad*	(11/2)	D. Weeden	Kempton	64
19.1	*Starfen*	(4/5f)	M. H. Easterby	Kempton	65
21.1	*Bamp*	(1/4f)	M. H. Easterby	Teesside	66

21.1	*Rambling Jack*	(8/13f)	K. Oliver	Teesside	67
22.1	*Henry Hotfoot*	(7/2)	E. Carter	Sedgefield	68
22.1	*Carnival Day*	(100/30)	T. Fairhurst	Sedgefield	69
22.1	*Schumann*	(11/4f)	M. H. Easterby	Sedgefield	70
25.1	*Mountain Hays*	(11/10f)	M. H. Easterby	Ayr	71
25.1	*Little Owl*	(8/11f)	M. H. Easterby	Ayr	72
26.1	*Silver Shadow*	(7/4f)	M. H. Easterby	Doncaster	73
6.2	*Big Ginger*	(9/4)	T. Fairhurst	Haydock	74
6.2	*Schumann*	(4/1)	M. H. Easterby	Haydock	75
9.2	*Bamp*	(11/10f)	M. H. Easterby	Newbury	76
12.2	*Crofton Hall*	(6/4f)	J. Dixon	Carlisle	77
12.2	*Grecian Fighter*	(2/1f)	B. Richmond	Carlisle	78
12.2	*Black Market*	(3/1)	T. D. Barron	Carlisle	79
12.2	*Cool Down*	(6/4f)	C. Thornton	Carlisle	80
13.2	*Little Owl*	(11/10f)	M. H. Easterby	Ascot	81
14.2	*Be Free*	(10/1)	M. Camacho	Southwell	82
18.2	*Silver Shadow*	(4/11f)	M. H. Easterby	Nottingham	83
20.2	*Song Of Life*	(11/8f)	D. Morley	Catterick	84
25.2	*Norton Cavalier*	(9/2)	M. H. Easterby	Doncaster	85
26.2	*Milbil*	(11/2)	D. Chapman	Huntingdon	86
27.2	*Falkelly*	(4/9f)	M. H. Easterby	Wetherby	87
27.2	*Thumps*	(8/13f)	M. H. Easterby	Wetherby	88
1.3	*Irish Gantlet*	(11/2)	E. Carter	Haydock	89
1.3	*Even Melody*	(5/4f)	N. Crump	Haydock	90
1.3	*Alick*	(6/5f)	M. H. Easterby	Haydock	91
4.3	*Green Dancer*	(10/11f)	R. Johnson	Kelso	92
7.3	*Dibbinsdale Lad*	(11/10f)	M. H. Easterby	Teesside	93
7.3	*Castle Arch*	(3/1)	M. Camacho	Teesside	94
8.3	*Alick*	(6/4f)	M. H. Easterby	Ayr	95
10.3	*Malboro*	(4/1)	J. Leadbetter	Ayr	96
11.3	*Sea Pigeon*	(13/2)	M. H. Easterby	Cheltenham	97
13.3	*King Weasel*	(5/2)	M. H. Easterby	Cheltenham	98
15.3	*Thumps*	(8/15f)	M. H. Easterby	Newcastle	99
15.3	*Scrunch*	(8/11f)	R. Brewis	Newcastle	100
28.3	*Starfen*	(3/1)	M. H. Easterby	Liverpool	101
7.4	*Sea Pigeon*	(4/6f)	M. H. Easterby	Chepstow	102
7.4	*Bridge Ash*	(9/4f)	J. Johnson	Chepstow	103
18.4	*Oisin*	(4/1)	R. Fisher	Ayr	104
29.4	*Gleen*	(5/2)	H. Bell	Kelso	105
5.5	*Hallo Dandy*	(11/4f)	D. McCain	Haydock	106
5.5	*No Bombs*	(7/1)	M. H. Easterby	Haydock	107
6.5	*Enchanted Evening*	(4/1)	C. Thornton	Nottingham	108
6.5	*Barrettstown Boy*	(11/10f)	R. Fisher	Nottingham	109
7.5	*Indian Brave*	(5/2f)	C. Thornton	Wetherby	110
8.5	*Jailer*	(9/2)	T. D. Barron	Hexham	111
20.5	*Lauso Pick*	(6/4f)	J. Berry	Bangor	112
23.5	*Merchant Prince*	(5/2)	B. Richmond	Sedgefield	113

24.5	*Barrettstown Boy*	(4/7f)	R. Fisher	Cartmel	114
24.5	*Oisin*	(7/4f)	R. Fisher	Cartmel	115
26.5	*Fair Person*	(7/4)	J. Leadbetter	Wetherby	116
27.5	*Relevance*	(7/2)	P. Ransom	Uttoxeter	117

Jonjo's 117 winners were for 37 different stables:

M. H. Easterby	51	R. Akehurst	1
R. Fisher	5	H. Bell	1
T. Fairhurst	4	R. Brewis	1
D. McCain	4	D. Chapman	1
J. Brockbank	3	N. Crump	1
E. Carter	3	A. Jarvis	1
J. Dixon	3	J. Johnson	1
K. Oliver	3	D. Morley	1
C. Thornton	3	R. Peacock	1
T. D. Barron	2	P. Ransom	1
J. Berry	2	G. W. Richards	1
O. Brennan	2	H. P. Rohan	1
M. Camacho	2	W. A. Stephenson	1
J. Fitzgerald	2	C. Vernon Miller	1
T. Gillam	2	D. Weeden	1
R. Johnson	2	H. Wharton	1
J. Leadbetter	2	W. Wharton	1
M. Naughton	2	D. Yeoman	1
B. Richmond	2		

1983/84

30.7	*Pretty Lass*	(2/1f)	R. Woodhouse	Market Rasen	1
1.8	*Lochlinnhe*	(2/5f)	Miss S. Hall	Market Rasen	2
6.8	*Farolito*	(2/1f)	R. Hollinshead	Worcester	3
13.8	*Laser Line*	(9/4)	R. Fisher	Bangor	4
20.8	*Foggy Buoy*	(4/5f)	P. Calver	Hereford	5
2.9	*Ballydurrow*	(9/2)	R. Fisher	Perth	6
2.9	*Strike Again*	(9/2)	F. Watson	Perth	7
2.9	*Pitpan's Glory*	(1/1f)	R. Fisher	Perth	8
3.9	*Father Delaney*	(10/11f)	D. Smith	Perth	9
3.9	*Concert Pitch*	(1/3f)	Miss S. Hall	Perth	10
6.9	*Pitpan's Glory*	(4/11f)	R. Fisher	Sedgefield	11
10.9	*Pounentes*	(5/1)	W. McGhie	Cartmel	12
13.9	*On The Warpath*	(4/5f)	C. Thornton	Carlisle	13
13.9	*Man Alive*	(4/7f)	R. Peacock	Carlisle	14
13.9	*Casal Royale*	(11/8f)	D. McCain	Carlisle	15
14.9	*Father Delaney*	(7/4f)	D. Smith	Wetherby	16
17.9	*Another Cygnet*	(12/1)	Mrs S. Davenport	Bangor	17

20.9	Bean Boy	(6/5f)	D. Smith	Sedgefield	18
21.9	Concert Pitch	(1/5f)	Miss S. Hall	Perth	19
21.9	Strike Again	(7/4)	F. Watson	Perth	20
21.9	Halyard	(5/2)	D. Smith	Perth	21
22.9	Father Delaney	(10/11f)	D. Smith	Perth	22
24.9	Oration	(2/1f)	C. Thornton	Carlisle	23
24.9	Selborne Rambler	(4/1)	H. Bell	Carlisle	24
26.9	Pounentes	(1/1f)	W. McGhie	Carlisle	25
26.9	Aruptagum	(5/1)	W. Raw	Carlisle	26
29.9	Alfie Dickens	(9/2)	R. Hollinshead	Ludlow	27
30.9	Bean Boy	(4/5f)	D. Smith	Sedgefield	28
1.10	Jetharts Here	(3/1f)	G. Renilson	Kelso	29
1.10	Chickham Lad	(11/1)	N. Chamberlain	Kelso	30
6.10	Pounentes	(11/2)	W. McGhie	Cheltenham	31
10.10	Kumon Sunshine	(2/1f)	D. Yeoman	Ayr	32
18.10	Carpenter's Silk	(5/4f)	D. Smith	Sedgefield	33
19.10	Troilena	(6/4f)	R. Fisher	Wetherby	34
20.10	Sea Merchant	(13/8f)	W.A. Stephenson	Uttoxeter	35
26.10	Beamwam	(13/8)	H. Bell	Newcastle	36
27.10	The Surveyor	(5/1)	R. Hollinshead	Southwell	37
28.10	Onapromise	(2/1)	D. Smith	Wetherby	38
28.10	Troilena	(6/4f)	R. Fisher	Wetherby	39
29.10	Sea Merchant	(8/11f)	W.A. Stephenson	Wetherby	40
31.10	Allerlea	(100/30)	H. Bell	Ayr	41
1.11	Albertat	(2/1)	D. Smith	Sedgefield	42
2.11	Sunny Time	(11/1)	M. Eckley	Wolverhampton	43
3.11	Casal Royale	(3/1f)	D. McCain	Uttoxeter	44
3.11	Sauna Time	(5/4f)	B. McMahon	Uttoxeter	45
4.11	Skateboard	(4/1)	D. Wilson	Sandown	46
8.11	Champ Chicken	(7/1)	D. McCain	Bangor	47
9.11	Norton Cross	(4/11f)	M. H. Easterby	Sedgefield	48
11.11	Onapromise	(9/4f)	D. Smith	Cheltenham	49
11.11	Sea Merchant	(5/6f)	W.A. Stephenson	Cheltenham	50
12.11	Spritebrand	(8/11f)	M. H. Easterby	Newcastle	51
14.11	Man Alive	(7/2)	R. Peacock	Carlisle	52
18.11	Dawn Run	(1/3f)	P. Mullins	Ascot	53
19.11	Spritebrand	(4/7f)	M. H. Easterby	Wetherby	54
19.11	Little Bay	(4/1)	G. W. Richards	Wetherby	55
22.11	Ballyice	(1/4f)	H. Wharton	Southwell	56
22.11	Riboden	(1/2f)	B. McMahon	Southwell	57
25.11	Belle Vue	(8/1)	R. Hollinshead	Leicester	58
26.11	Blackfeet	(13/8f)	J. S. Wilson	Catterick	59
26.11	Trocadero	(11/8f)	D. Yeoman	Catterick	60
2.12	Trocadero	(2/1f)	D. Yeoman	Sedgefield	61
8.12	Final Argument	(4/7f)	G. W. Richards	Carlisle	62
9.12	Lawnswood Miss	(7/1)	R. Hollinshead	Cheltenham	63
14.12	Clayside	(5/4)	M. H. Easterby	Haydock	64

15.12	*Comedy Fair*	(6/5f)	M. H. Easterby	Haydock	65
17.12	*Havenwood*	(17/2)	K. Stone	Doncaster	66
17.12	*Lawnswood Miss*	(9/4f)	R. Hollinshead	Doncaster	67
26.12	*Dawn Run*	(9/4)	P. Mullins	Kempton	68
27.12	*Torreon*	(2/1f)	M. H. Easterby	Wetherby	69
30.12	*Fearless Seal*	(5/4f)	R. Hollinshead	Leicester	70
31.12	*Outlaw*	(2/1f)	W. Clay	Catterick	71
31.12	*Ballydurrow*	(3/1)	R. Fisher	Catterick	72
6.1	*Comedy Fair*	(10/11f)	M. H. Easterby	Haydock	73
6.1	*Ballydurrow*	(3/1)	R. Fisher	Haydock	74
9.1	*Fearless Seal*	(4/11f)	R. Hollinshead	Nottingham	75
10.1	*No Bombs*	(7/4f)	M. H. Easterby	Wetherby	76
12.1	*Maid of Milan*	(11/4f)	M. H. Easterby	Southwell	77
6.2	*Donegal Prince*	(1/1f)	P. Kelleway	Wolverhampton	78
6.2	*Northern Trial*	(4/7f)	P. Kelleway	Wolverhampton	79
8.2	*Cybrandian*	(6/4f)	M. H. Easterby	Ascot	80
9.2	*Mend It*	(16/1)	N. Bycroft	Huntingdon	81
11.2	*Afzal*	(20/1)	R. Hollinshead	Newbury	82
14.2	*Goosey Gander*	(5/2f)	G. Lockerbie	Sedgefield	83
16.2	*Jukebox Katie*	(7/2)	W. Clay	Southwell	84
13.3	*Dawn Run*	(4/5f)	P. Mullins	Cheltenham	85
13.3	*Mossy Moore*	(11/2)	B. Chinn	Cheltenham	86
19.3	*Pause For Thought*	(4/1)	D. Smith	Newcastle	87
21.3	*Ballyice*	(12/1)	H. Wharton	Kelso	88
17.4	*Midsummer Special*	(6/1)	C. Mackenzie	Sedgefield	89
18.4	*Mr McCann*	(3/1)	R. Fisher	Perth	90
18.4	*Mister Moonshine*	(4/1)	R. Fisher	Perth	91
19.4	*Pounentes*	(4/1)	W. McGhie	Perth	92
19.4	*Galatch*	(7/2)	W. Wells	Perth	93
27.4	*The Engineer*	(11/2)	Lord Kilmany	Hexham	94
2.5	*Foggy Buoy*	(2/1f)	P. Calver	Kelso	95
12.5	*Louviers*	(9/4f)	G. W. Richards	Hexham	96
14.5	*Ellen Greaves*	(7/4)	R. Fisher	Hexham	97
24.5	*Ragabury*	(4/6f)	R. Fisher	Perth	98
25.5	*Indian Call*	(11/2)	H. Jones	Sedgefield	99
26.5	*Optimum*	(8/11f)	R. Fisher	Cartmel	100
28.5	*Indian Call*	(1/5f)	H. Jones	Hexham	101
28.5	*Islander*	(2/1)	Lord Kilmany	Hexham	102
29.5	*Easterly Gael*	(1/2f)	J. Jenkins	Uttoxeter	103

Jonjo's 103 winners were for 37 different stables:

R. Fisher	13	C. Thornton	2
D. Smith	11	F. Watson	2
M. H. Easterby	10	H. Wharton	2
R. Hollinshead	9	N. Bycroft	1
W. McGhie	4	N. Chamberlain	1

H. Bell	3	B. Chinn	1
Sally Hall	3	Mrs S. Davenport	1
D. McCain	3	M. Eckley	1
P. Mullins	3	J. Jenkins	1
G. W. Richards	3	G. Lockerbie	1
W. A. Stephenson	3	C. Mackenzie	1
D. Yeoman	3	W. Raw	1
P. Calver	2	G. Renilson	1
W. Clay	2	K. Stone	1
H. Jones	2	W. Wells	1
P. Kelleway	2	D. Wilson	1
Lord Kilmany	2	J. S. Wilson	1
B. McMahon	2	R. Woodhouse	1
R. Peacock	2		

JONJO'S RECORD ON SEA PIGEON

Jumping

23.10.75	7th	William Hill Hdle	Newbury	
5.11.75	Won (1/2f)	Bangor Hdle	Newbury	£1079
6.12.75	Won (5/1)	Trial Hurdle	Cheltenham	£2206
1.1.76	2nd	New Year's Day Hdle	Windsor	
7.2.76	Won (2/1)	Oteley Hdle	Sandown	£2924
9.10.76	Won (4/5f)	Culzean Hdle	Ayr	£1221
16.10.76	2nd	A Day At The Races Hdle	Kempton	
16.3.77	4th	Champion Hdle	Cheltenham	
31.3.77	Won (3/1)	Allied Manufacturing H'cap Hdle	Liverpool	£4155
16.4.77	Won (4/9f)	Scottish Champion Hdle	Ayr	£3667
26.11.77	fell	Colonial Cup	Camden, U.S.A.	
1.2.78	Won (2/1)	Oteley Hdle	Sandown	£3930
15.4.78	Won (7/4f)	Scottish Champion Hdle	Ayr	£5605
6.5.78	8th	Royal Doulton Hdle	Haydock	
3.79	2nd	Embassy Hdle	Haydock	
14.3.79	2nd	Waterford Crystal Champion Hdle	Cheltenham	
30.3.79	4th	Colt Sigma Hdle	Liverpool	
1.4.79	2nd	Scottish Champion Hdle	Ayr	
6.10.79	fell	William Hill Hdle	Newbury	
.11.79	Won	Holsten Pils Hdle	Sandown	£6846
17.11.79	2nd	Bellway Fighting Fifth Hdle	Newcastle	
1.3.80	Won (13/2)	Waterford Crystal Champion Hdle	Cheltenham	£24,972
5.4.80	Won (4/6f)	Welsh Champion Hdle	Chepstow	£7200
19.4.80	3rd	Scottish Champion Hdle	Ayr	

Flat

22.8.79	Won (18/1)	Tote-Ebor H'cap	York	£17,27
13.10.79	Won (100/30)	Sam Hall Memorial Trophy	York	£3876
28.6.80	4th	Coral Northumberland Plate	Newcastle	
21.7.80	3rd	Tennent Trophy	Ayr	
9.8.80	Won (9/2)	Vaux Gold Tankard	Redcar	£11,84
4.9.80	2nd	Harrison Drape Stakes	York	
17.9.80	Won (5/1)	Doonside Cup	Ayr	£9615

Jonjo rode Sea Pigeon in 7 flat races, winning 4 times, Jonjo rode Sea Pigeon in 24 jump races, winning 11 times. Sea Pigeon won 16 of his 45 flat races and 21 of his 40 races over jumps, including the 1981 Waterford Crystal Champion Hurdle, in which the injured O'Neill was replaced by John Francome.

JONJO'S RECORD ON ALVERTON

19.11.77	2nd	Black and White Whisky H'cap Hdle	Ascot	
3.12.77	2nd	Mecca Bookmakers H'cap Hdle	Sandown	
14.1.78	Won (11/8)	Widgeon Novices Chase	Newcastle	£1270
23.1.78	Won —	Faceby Novices Chase	Teesside	£771
25.11.78	2nd	Embassy Premier Chase Qualifier	Wetherby	
9.12.78	b/d	Massey Ferguson Gold Cup	Cheltenham	
26.12.78	2nd	Castleford H'cap Chase	Wetherby	
2.2.79	2nd	Leisure Caravan Parks H'cap Chase	Sandown	
3.3.79	Won (2/1f)	Greenall Whitley H'cap Chase	Haydock	£8488
15.3.79	Won (5/1f)	Piper Champagne Cheltenham Gold Cup	Cheltenham	£30,2
31.3.79	fell	Colt Car Grand National	Liverpool	

Jonjo rode Alverton in 2 hurdles, finishing second in both races. Jonjo rode Alverton in 9 steeplechases, winning 4 times. Alverton won 11 of his 26 races over jumps. He also won 11 races on the flat.

JONJO'S RECORD ON NIGHT NURSE

28.1.78	Won (13/8f)	William Hill Yorkshire H'dle	Doncaster	£2233
1.4.78	2nd	Templegate Hdle	Liverpool	
13.5.78	7th	I.C.I. Petrol Hdle	Newcastle	
30.9.78	u/r	Mablethorpe Novices Chase	Market Rasen	
30.3.79	Won (1/1f)	Sean Graham Trophy Chase	Liverpool	£431

21.4.79	Won (5/6f)	London and Northern Group Future Champions Novices Chase	Ayr	£4344
27.10.79	2nd	Hermitage H'cap Chase	Newbury	
10.11.79	7th	Mackeson Gold Cup	Cheltenham	
28.11.79	2nd	Edward Hanmer H'cap Chase	Haydock	
2.1.82	Won (11/2)	Bradstone Mandarin H'cap Chase	Newbury	£6037
23.1.82	2nd	Peter Marsh Chase	Haydock	
6.2.82	3rd	Freshfields Holidays H'cap Chase	Kempton	
27.2.82	Won (4/9f)	Pennine Chase	Doncaster	£3877
18.3.82	p/u	Tote Cheltenham Gold Cup	Cheltenham	
30.10.82	2nd	Worcester Evening News Chase	Worcester	
15.11.82	Won (1/2f)	Staveley Chase	Wolverhampton	£2924
27.11.82	p/u	Hennessy Cognac Gold Cup	Newbury	
27.12.82	5th	King George VI Chase	Kempton	

Jonjo rode Night Nurse in 3 hurdle races, winning once. Jonjo rode Night Nurse in 15 chases, winning five times. Night Nurse won 32 of his 64 races over jumps, including the 1976 and 1977 Champion Hurdles, in which he was ridden by Paddy Broderick. He also finished second to Little Owl in the 1981 Tote Cheltenham Gold Cup, in which he was ridden by Alan Brown.

JONJO'S RECORD ON EKBALCO

12.4.82	Won (2/1)	Welsh Champion Hurdle	Chepstow	£10,096
27.10.82	Won (4/7)	Long Town Hdle	Newcastle	£1253
13.11.82	fell	Fighting Fifth Hdle	Newcastle	
11.12.82	Won (2/1f)	Tia Maria Bula Hdle	Cheltenham	£8254
27.12.82	Won (1/2f)	Ladbroke Christmas Hdle	Kempton	£10,235
22.1.83	Won (8/13f)	Champion Hdle Trial	Haydock	£5969
15.3.83	5th	Waterford Crystal Champion Hdle	Cheltenham	
4.4.83	*Won (8/11f)	Welsh Champion Hdle	Chepstow	£8090
15.4.83	2nd	Scottish Champion Hdle	Ayr	
12.11.83	fell	Fighting Fifth Hdle	Newcastle	

*Subsequently disqualified for failing post race dope test.

Jonjo rode Ekbalco in 10 hurdles, winning 5 times. Ekbalco won 10 of his 31 races over hurdles.

Career Record

JONJO'S RECORD ON DAWN RUN

18.11.83	Won (1/3f)	V.A.T. Watkins Hdle	Ascot	£10,5
7.12.83	2nd	Racehorse Trainers Association Hdle	Naas	
26.12.83	Won (9/4)	Ladbroke Christmas Hdle	Kempton	£15,7
18.2.84	Won (4/5f)	Wessel Cable Champion Hdle	Leopardstown	£21,7
13.3.84	Won (4/5f)	Waterford Crystal Champion Hdle	Cheltenham	£36,6

Jonjo rode Dawn Run in 5 hurdles, winning 4 times. At the start of the 1984/85 season Dawn Run had won 12 of her 16 races over hurdles, including the French Champion Hurdle, in which she was ridden by Tony Mullins.

Index

Index